Diaspora 12

Remembering the Past, Inventing the Future: Italian American Artists and Writers between Nostalgia and Dream

Edited by
Francesca D'Alfonso

CASA LAGO PRESS
NEW FAIRFIELD, CT

Diaspora
Volume 12

As "diaspora" is the dispersion or spread of people from their original homeland, this book series takes its name in the intellectual spirit of willful dispersion of subject matter and thought. It is dedicated to publishing those studies that in various and sundry ways either speak to or offer new methods of analysis of the Italian diaspora.

COVER PHOTO: Letters from immigrnats

ISBN 978-1-955995-19-1
Library of Congress Control Number: Available upon request

Printed in the United States of America

CASA LAGO PRESS
New Fairfield, CT

TABLE OF CONTENTS

Preface

Francesca D'Alfonso

This book originates from the international conference organized by the Centro Universitario di Studi Italoamericani e Canadesi (CUSIAC) at the University of Molise held on June 6-7, 2024. Conceived as one of the Center's most significant initiatives, the conference gathered scholars from Italy and North America, fostering exchanges across disciplines and perspectives. What began as an encounter of voices has here taken shape in a collection of essays that not only seeks to preserve that dialogic energy but also to expand it into a broader scholarly conversation. The volume reflects this spirit of exchange even in its linguistic form: some contributions are in Italian, others in English. This deliberate choice foregrounds the bilingual – indeed, *italoamericano* – character of the field. Such coexistence of idioms mirrors the very condition of diaspora, where memory and imagination are perpetually mediated across linguistic thresholds.

The title of both the conference and the present volume – *Remembering the Past, Inventing the Future: Italian American Artists and Writers between Nostalgia and Dream* – functions as more than just a title: it offers a key to interpretation and a lens through which the dynamics of memory and invention may be critically apprehended. To remember the past is not to crystallize history into commemoration; rather, it is to revisit memory in its fractures, silences, and contradictions. It means confronting what has been forgotten or suppressed, as exemplified in Pietro di Donato's *Christ in Concrete*, where the death of the protagonist's father becomes not simply the story of an individual, but the emblem of immigrant labor transfigured into sacrifice. Remembering, in this sense, is never passive: it interrogates, reclaims, and reshapes, granting continuity where rupture has occurred and voice where silence has long prevailed. To invent the future, by contrast, is to embrace transformation, to imagine identities and expressive forms that emerge precisely from displacement and loss. Pascal D'Angelo's *Son of Italy* epitomizes this reinvention, recounting the trajectory of a young

Abruzzese worker who chose to dream in English and whose verse – nourished by the cadences of Shelley and Keats – projected an immigrant self into the literary culture of America. Here, dreaming is not a flight of fantasy but a creative labor: the forging of new idioms, the effort of turning fracture into possibility.

Therefore, nostalgia and dream – key themes of this collection – are not radically opposed but complementary dimensions of a diasporic imagination. Nostalgia, far from mere sentimentality, preserves fragments of language, gesture and tradition that risk being lost, transforming them into resources of meaning – as in the neo-dialectal poetry at the center of Luigi Bonaffini's reflections and critical poetics. Dreaming, on the other hand, represents projection and reinvention: it emerges in Tony Vaccaro's photographs where devastation and beauty reframe the migrant gaze, and in Louisa Calio's performances, where feminine spirituality transforms memory into a vision of global openness. It eludes the confines of recollection; it reconfigures loss as the very ground of invention. Together, nostalgia and dream delineate a dynamic field in which Italian American writers and artists have moved for over a century – an unstable yet fertile space where the past is never simply the past, and the future is constantly being rewritten. From the lyrical cadences of D'Angelo to the ecological anxieties voiced by John Ciardi, from Scarpitta's "bandaged canvases" to the subtle post-stereotypical identities analyzed in contemporary television by Alessandra Serra, Italian American culture has continually balanced the tension between remembering and imagining, between what is inherited and what must still be created.

The essays collected here demonstrate how Italian American creativity has consistently inhabited this liminal dimension, sustaining memory even while developing new linguistic formulae of belonging. It is no coincidence that the opening contribution, by Anthony Julian Tamburri, interrogates the very vocabulary with which Italian American identity has been defined. By privileging the term "diaspora", Tamburri emphasizes fluidity and process, situating Italian Americans within a broader comparative frame. His analysis establishes the conceptual coordinates of the collection, reminding us that identity is never fixed but always negotiated. A comparable widening of perspective is offered by

Alberto Barausse, who reconstructs the history of Italian schools in Rio Grande do Sul, Brazil. By challenging the cliché of migrant indifference to education, his study shows how schooling functioned as a locus of cultural resilience and adaptation, making clear that Italian America must be understood hemispherically, as both North and South.

From this framework the volume turns to the literary canon. Francesca Caraceni revisits *Christ in Concrete*, emphasizing its spiritual dimension and its depiction of suffering as collective redemption. Pascal D'Angelo occupies an equally emblematic position: the contributions by Francesca D'Alfonso, Renzo D'Agnillo, Michela Marroni, and Francesca Crisante investigate his trajectory as a poet and autobiographer, charting the complexity of a voice suspended between languages and traditions. D'Alfonso reads *Son of Italy* as a *Bildungsroman* of migration; D'Agnillo emphasizes its lyrical poetics; Marroni foregrounds D'Angelo's choice of English as an act of disruption and reconfiguration; and Crisante situates him within the broader lineage of English Romanticism. Together, these works explore the ideas of an Italian by birth who nonetheless chose to imagine his poetic self in English – an emblematic figure of the dialectic of nostalgia and dream that animates Italian American literature. Language itself emerges as a theme in Joseph Perricone's reflections on translation, conceived as a bridge that renders dialect voices intelligible while preserving their singularity. Luigi Bonaffini, whose essay is placed at the heart of the collection, underscores the vitality of neo-dialectal poetry, which for him constitutes not a marginal survival but a privileged site of innovation, a counter-canon that both preserves and reinvents identity.

Visual culture provides another arena where diasporic imagination unfolds. It is examined by Piernicola Maria Di Iorio, showing how Tony Vaccaro's, notion of "twin nostalgia" informed a lifetime of photography from Normandy to the studios of Picasso and Loren. Lorenzo Canova examines Salvatore Scarpitta, whose iconic pictorial works and kinetic sculptures embody the interplay of memory and experiment, bridging Europe and America. Norberto Lombardi reconstructs the career of Frank Monaco, tracing a trajectory from Brooklyn to London and back to Molise, which culminated in the symbolic gesture of having his ashes returned to the river Biferno.

Finally, the contemporary scene is probed by essays that bring Italian American studies into new domains. Elisabetta Marino highlights the poetry and performance of Louisa Calio, where feminism, spirituality, and intercultural dialogue converge. Sabrina Vellucci, through an eco-critical lens, reconsiders John Ciardi's *Mystic River*, where polluted waters dramatize both nostalgia for place and ecological anxiety. Arianna Mazzola reflects on reportage as a hybrid genre that resonates with itinerancy and observation, echoing diasporic subjectivity. Alessandra Serra turns to television narratives, comparing *The Sopranos* and *The Bear* to trace the shift from stereotype to post-stereotypical identity. Her investigation shows how ethnicity once marked by excess – food, violence, Catholic ritual – has been recast through subtler linguistic and emotional registers, pointing to a new grammar of representation in contemporary media. Taken together, the essays in this collection form not a catalogue but a polyphonic narrative, in which literature, art, translation, photography, and media discourse converge. They demonstrate that Italian American culture cannot be reduced to a single canon or medium: it is interdisciplinary, transnational, and always poised between remembrance and reinvention. The trajectory of the volume encapsulates the double movement announced in its title: the necessity of remembering the past as the very condition for inventing the future. Thus, this book testifies to the vitality of Italian American studies, to the relevance of interdisciplinary approaches, and to the importance of institutions that sustain such dialogues, linking local heritage to global conversations.

I wish to conclude by acknowledging those whose support has been essential. My gratitude goes first to Giuseppe Peter Vanoli, now Rector of the University of Molise but, at the time of the conference, Pro-Rector with responsibility for the strategic initiatives of the University. His constant attention to the activities of CUSIAC, his sensitivity and generosity, and his farsighted support for international projects have been crucial to the realization of this book, and I am especially grateful to him. I would also like to thank Ruggiero Dipace, Director of the Department of Law and a dear friend, for his steady encouragement and his personal closeness throughout the preparation of the conference and this volume. I owe a profound debt of gratitude to my mentor Francesco Marroni, whose guidance and example have accompanied me throughout my career; and to Luigi Bonaffini, who first introduced me to the Italian American scholarly community in New York, opening a path of dialogue that has profoundly enriched my work. I am also sincerely grateful to Daniela Fabrizi, Amy Muschamp, and Barbara Quaranta of the University Language Center. Their constant presence, not only during the organization of the conference but also in the everyday life of the Center, has been invaluable. They are for me not only indispensable collaborators but also dear friends whose support I greatly value. Finally, I would like to express my heartfelt appreciation to Anthony Julian Tamburri, for welcoming this book into his distinguished series at Casa Lago Press, and to all colleagues, students, and friends whose dedication accompanied both the conference and the making of this volume. Without their commitment, the voices gathered in Campobasso in June 2024 would not have found their enduring form in these pages.

Osservazioni sulla diaspora italiana, ieri e oggi: ri-pensare lo scrittore con il trattino

Anthony Julian Tamburri
JOHN D. CALANDRA ITALIAN AMERICAN INSTITUTE

Abstract: Questo saggio analizza il concetto di diaspora italiana, soffermandosi sulla sua evoluzione storica, sulle questioni identitarie e sui processi di coesione della popolazione italoamericana e delle sue articolazioni contemporanee. Attraverso un confronto con altre diaspore (afroamericane, ebraiche, latine e greche), esploro come migrazione, senso di appartenenza e memoria collettiva abbiano influenzato la costruzione della comunità e delle sue narrazioni, evidenziando allo stesso tempo le difficoltà e le sfide legate alla trasmissione intergenerazionale del patrimonio culturale. Si sottolinea inoltre la necessità di un approccio più inclusivo e multidisciplinare per interpretare la diaspora in termini sia storici sia contemporanei, proponendo una riflessione sul ruolo delle reti sociali, delle produzioni culturali e della consapevolezza identitaria nel garantire la vitalità e il riconoscimento del gruppo nel contesto globale attuale.

Nel suo saggio innovativo, "Breaking the Silence: Strategic Imperatives for Italian American Culture" (1990), Robert Viscusi ha avanzato la tesi secondo cui la storia dovrebbe essere concepita come un'entità collettiva. Nonostante i considerevoli progressi raggiunti in questo ambito, numerose associazioni italiano/americane sembrano ancora perseverare in un'azione isolata, affrontando tematiche specifiche e, in alcuni casi, agendo senza il supporto di esperti di storia e cultura.[1] Tuttavia, un'azione concertata tra un maggior numero di gruppi italiano/americani, che richiede un'intensa collaborazione con la comunità degli studiosi, potrebbe produrre risultati significativi per la popolazione italiano/americana. Tale collaborazione permetterebbe di sviluppare una varietà di progetti che contribuirebbero a formulare un programma italiano/americano, con l'obiettivo di approfondire la storia degli italiani negli Stati Uniti.[2] Per conseguire tale obiettivo, è necessario che la collettività riveda i propri processi concettuali mentre valuta e sostiene il proprio "patrimonio e la propria cultura italiana", un tema che molte associazioni considerano come la propria principale iniziativa socioculturale.

---

[1] Per l'uso della barra ("/") al posto del trattino ("-"), si veda Tamburri 1991.

[2] Uso qui l'espressione "popolazione italiano/americana" in contrapposizione a "comunità italiano/americana" per la semplice ragione che non esiste un unico collettivo (leggi, comunità); piuttosto, ci sono diversi processi di pensiero che abbracciano la gamma del pensiero sociopolitico italiano/americano.

Si propone, pertanto, di avviare la presente discussione con una domanda: Qual è – o quale potrebbe e/o dovrebbe essere – il punto d'incontro attorno al quale gli americani italiani troverebbero un senso di comunanza? Effettivamente, sia gli americani africani che gli americani ebrei presentano, rispettivamente, una questione, per quanto tragica, che rende coerente il gruppo. Ciò che si intende per "schiavitù" è ovviamente la forma più estrema di sfruttamento lavorativo, mentre con "discriminazione" si allude alla disparità di trattamento che ha caratterizzato la storia delle popolazioni di colore. Per quanto riguarda la seconda parte, si fa riferimento ai due millenni di diaspora e al genocidio del ventesimo secolo.

Quali fattori possono essere identificati come elementi di coesione per la comunità degli americani italiani? Si può considerare, ad esempio, l'immigrazione, l'arco di tempo che va dal 1880 al 1924, quei quarantaquattro anni che sono ormai diventati un marcatore storico per gli americani italiani contemporanei? Si possono altresì considerare tragedie specifiche, come il linciaggio di New Orleans del 1891, per il quale sussiste la possibilità di essere stati vittime di uno dei più grandi linciaggi di gruppo documentato.[3] Si potrebbe altresì evidenziare la discriminazione storica, che risale al XIX secolo e che raggiunge il suo apice, ai giorni nostri, in produzioni quali *Everybody Loves Raymond* o *The Sopranos.*

Sebbene questi ultimi due esempi rappresentino spunti di discussione pertinenti, non si pongono come fattori unificanti per la popolazione italiano/americana, in modo comparabile a quanto accade per altri gruppi. Si potrebbe quindi interrogarsi su quale sia la questione onnicomprensiva che unisce, ad esempio, i Latinx. Oltre a un forte senso di cameratismo linguistico che possono condividere per quanto riguarda la loro cultura, l'esperienza migratoria, intesa come senso di non appartenenza al Paese ospitante, potrebbe rendere coerente il comportamento dei Latinx.[4] Non si può negare l'evidenza: le persone

[3] Dopo centoventotto anni, la città di New Orleans ha presentato scuse formali. Per i dettagli, si veda Ryan Prior. In effetti, si è dovuto aspettare una sindaca africano/americana per avere qualcuno in carica che potesse davvero immedesimarsi in questa tragedia storica.

[4] La complessità di Latinx è tale che dobbiamo sottolineare che alcuni Latinx vedono sé stessi come indigeni, dato che le loro radici possono essere tra i popoli come i nativi americani, i Maya, i Taino o i Quechua. Si veda López e Gonzalez-Barrera. Quanto, inoltre, alle nostre continue e più ampie discussioni sugli americani italiani e sulle nozioni di diaspora, dobbiamo essere più inclusivi del rapporto con altre etnie. Un altro gruppo che viene in mente è quello degli americani greci. La ricerca sulla loro esperienza è notevole e, in

provenienti da tutti i Paesi latinoamericani non hanno certamente lo stesso senso di fedeltà alla nozione di "vecchio Paese" e a tutto ciò che ne consegue. Non si intende suggerire che tutti gli individui di origine latino/americana abbiano un senso automatico di appartenenza a quel gruppo etnico, così come definito negli Stati Uniti. Tuttavia, non si può negare la percezione di un senso di appartenenza che ha origine nell'esperienza migratoria e/o linguistico-culturale, nella misura in cui gli individui si percepiscono come *outsider* e, in quanto tali, si aggrappano alla loro cultura di origine. La combinazione di differenza e specificità linguistica e culturale, in parte fondata sull'esperienza migratoria, emerge come un fattore determinante della coerenza del gruppo.

Si potrebbe pertanto formulare un'ipotesi secondo cui una formula analoga potrebbe rivelarsi valida anche per gli americani italiani. L'immigrazione, con la sua storia ultracentenaria, può potenzialmente fungere da agente coesivo, sebbene debole. La necessità di un forte senso di appartenenza è un requisito fondamentale per la coesione della popolazione e per il progresso, al fine di integrare lo studio della cultura italiano/americana nel panorama culturale mainstream, così come già avviene per altre comunità linguistiche degli Stati Uniti. Certamente, un ulteriore elemento di complessità deriva dal fatto che esiste una distanza maggiore tra gli americani italiani e la propria storia migratoria. Perciò, è necessario uno sforzo aggiuntivo per colmare questo divario di conoscenza e, in definitiva, per correggere alcune delle narrazioni che frequentemente sentiamo, tra cui quella riguardante la questione dell'immigrazione "illegale" odierna rispetto a quella "legale" storica italiana.[5] Nondimeno, oltre a considerare la questione in una prospettiva cronologica, si potrebbe anche riflettere sull'eredità più complessa di questo evento. Attraverso questa prospettiva, ci avventuriamo nella semiosfera di riconoscimento e rivalutazione della dispersione degli italiani al di là dei confini nazionali, con particolare riferimento agli Stati Uniti, e di come tale patrimonio di dispersione abbia generato nuove articolazioni contemporanee delle popolazioni di origine italiana e dei loro discendenti in tale regione e in altre parti del mondo. Il riconoscimento in esame,

---

alcuni casi, comparabile con quella degli americani italiani. Si vedano Yiorgos Anagnostou (2009); Theodora Patrona (2017); e Yiorgos Anagnostou, Yiorgos D. Kalogeras e Theodora Patrona (2022).

[5] Ho affrontato queste notevoli lacune conoscitive in due miei saggi (2021, 2022a).

unitamente alla rivalutazione ad esso concomitante, definisce il concetto di diaspora italiana inteso come studio storico di un gruppo etnico e dell'impatto che questo esercita sui propri membri e sul Paese che lo ospita.[6]

Avevo utilizzato il termine per la prima volta nel 2006 e successivamente nel 2007. In quel periodo, si riteneva che la ragione per cui si doveva impiegare questo termine fosse evidente, nonostante le opinioni di coloro che lo consideravano un uso storicamente più restrittivo.[7] È opportuno notare che, in ogni caso, Donna Gabaccia aveva già pubblicato il suo studio nel 2000. Nel 2017, il concetto di "diaspora italiana" è stato brevemente delineato come un termine che non si contrappone al più popolare binomio "italiano/americano", ma piuttosto come un modo per illustrare il concetto di necessità dell'atto migratorio storico, sia negli Stati Uniti che in altre parti del mondo. In effetti, il termine "diaspora" presenta diverse definizioni, di cui almeno due si applicano a ogni concezione di una "diaspora italiana". In tale accezione, può riferirsi a due significati principali: (1) "qualsiasi migrazione o fuga di gruppo da un Paese o da una regione" e, con maggiore pertinenza, (2) "qualsiasi gruppo che è stato disperso al di fuori della sua patria tradizionale, specialmente involontariamente" (Dictionary.com, s.v.). È stato inoltre affermato che i circa quattro milioni di italiani che emigrarono dall'Italia verso gli Stati Uniti durante il periodo storico dell'immigrazione (1880-1924) costituivano una "migrazione di gruppo". Inoltre, si affermava che questi stessi quattro milioni di immigrati costituivano un "gruppo... disperso" al di fuori della "sua patria tradizionale". Inoltre, il fatto che molti italiani siano rimasti nella loro "patria" avrebbe potuto facilmente condurli a uno status socioeconomico sottoproletario, se non addirittura alla fame vera e propria. Tuttavia, la frase "soprattutto involontariamente" si è rivelata ugualmente rilevante nella nostra spiegazione dell'uso dell'espressione "diaspora italiana" (Tamburri 2025, 6-7). Detto questo, e come punto di partenza, accogliamo quindi la definizione di diaspora data da John Armstrong nel 1976 come "qualsiasi collettività etnica che non ha una base territoriale all'interno di un determinato

---

[6] L'uso del termine "diaspora" con la "d" minuscola sta a segnalare un fenomeno generale di spostamento di un gruppo specifico da un Paese o da una regione a un'altra a causa di forze che di solito sfuggono al suo controllo, come si vedrà in seguito. L'aggettivo nazionale/etnico specificherà poi il gruppo, come si fa qui.

[7] Si veda Luconi sul perché non si debba usare "diaspora" negli studi sulla *dispersione* italiana.

sistema politico, ovvero è una minoranza relativamente piccola in tutte le parti del sistema politico" (393).

Seguendo le indicazioni di Robin Cohen, Gabaccia distingue tra "diaspore vittime" (africani ed ebrei) e "diaspore attive", ovvero coloro che hanno esercitato un'ampia libertà di scelta riguardo al momento e al luogo di partenza. Il loro raduno non è stato involontario o improvviso in un esilio senza fine" (6). Nel contesto di una discussione che utilizza una prospettiva comparativa, quando si analizzano le esperienze di popoli che hanno subito diaspore forzate che hanno anche compromesso la propria incolumità (come nel caso degli africani e degli ebrei), se questi ultimi (specificatamente gli ebrei, data la loro condizione di vittime di un allontanamento imposto dalla propria patria) fossero rimasti in tale territorio, l'uso da parte di Gabaccia della dicotomia tra "diaspore vittime" (africani ed ebrei) e "scelta" risulta coerente. Sarebbe opportuno sottolineare la differenza in questi casi. La mia adesione alla nozione di "particolarmente involontario" nel contesto specifico della diaspora italiana e di tutte le sue peculiarità non è necessariamente in contraddizione con il discorso multi-diasporico di Gabaccia. Le semiotiche adottate risultano significativamente diverse per tutti i soggetti coinvolti, sia per i soggetti che per gli investigatori. Cohen, a sua volta, esprime la seguente opinione riguardo alla diaspora ebraica: "Le esperienze diasporiche ebraiche sono risultate notevolmente più diversificate e complesse rispetto a quanto la tradizione catastrofista consenta e... come si evince dalle fonti consultate, tale interpretazione è stata imposta e interiorizzata, ma anche avanzata e contestata. Si citano due illustri studiosi di spicco per evidenziare le sfumature del discorso sulla "diaspora italiana", in particolare, e, più ampiamente, sulla "diaspora" come concetto generale.[8]

In tale prospettiva, si può fare riferimento al concetto di diaspora proposto da Richard Marientras nel 1985. Richard Marientras ha affermato che per alcuni la diaspora "se prouve dans le temps et s'éprouve par le temps" (225; "è provata nel tempo ed è testata dal tempo" [125;

[8] I saggi sul concetto di diaspora sono numerosi. Riconosco come letture fondamentali le seguenti: Armstrong, Bauböck, Butler, Cohen, Faist, Gabaccia, Marienstras, Rosoli, Tölölyan.

da qui in poi citerò la traduzione inglese del 1989][9]). Per Marientras, l'economia, da sola, "non crea necessariamente una diaspora" (125); un popolo deve, in qualche modo, mantenersi come gruppo distinto, aggiunge. Marientras, d'altra parte, non ritiene che la sopravvivenza del gruppo sia garantita dalla sua "originalità", ma piuttosto dal suo continuo "mantenimento del sentimento di appartenenza e della certezza dell'identità" (125). Marientras, a questo proposito, sottolinea con assoluta certezza l'importanza fondamentale della "decisione consapevole e [...] La determinazione del senso di appartenenza e di identità" (125). In conclusione, si osserva che il termine "diaspora" viene oggi utilizzato per descrivere qualsiasi comunità emigrata il cui numero raggiunge una soglia tale da renderla visibile all'interno della comunità ospitante. Tuttavia, per determinare con certezza che si tratti di una diaspora, è necessario attendere un periodo di tempo adeguato" (125).[10] In altre parole, la diaspora può essere definita come un fenomeno fluido, che trova la sua definizione nell'evoluzione stessa del fenomeno stesso. messa alla prova dal tempo" – e non un solo momento storico, statico che sia, con un apparente punto di arrivo, come può essere l'immigrazione storica italiana dal 1880 al 1924. L'eredità dell'identità italiana del periodo in esame, che si estende per oltre quarant'anni, è stata tramandata fino ai giorni nostri e attualmente gode del supporto di una varietà di fenomeni socio-culturali. Tali fenomeni includono: le produzioni artistiche, quali la letteratura, il cinema, il teatro, la pittura e altre forme d'arte; le ricerche prodotte in tutte le discipline; le numerose organizzazioni, ciascuna con una missione specifica, che possono effettivamente essere considerate parte della diaspora italiana nel contesto contemporaneo.

In effetti, per quanto riguarda questa nozione di fluidità con un'attenzione specifica agli italiani, è possibile fare riferimento al lavoro di Sam Baily sulla "diaspora aragonese". L'impiego del termine "diaspora" da parte di Bailey potrebbe costituire un'anticipazione nell'uso di tale concetto, applicato a una "dispersione italiana", come si propone di

[9] Vorrei sottolineare che la versione originale francese di questo libro è molto più lunga della traduzione inglese. L'edizione francese include saggi su casi geopolitici specifici che l'edizione inglese non contiene.
[10] Chiaramente, la definizione di diaspora di Armstrong del 1976, già citata, viene qui ripresa: "qualsiasi collettività etnica che non ha una base territoriale all'interno di una determinata polarità, cioè è una minoranza relativamente piccola in tutte le porzioni della polarità" (393).

definirla in questo contesto. L'impiego di Baily è datato al 1990, quando tenne una relazione alla conferenza annuale dell'American Italian Historical Association a New Orleans.[11] Due anni dopo, ne pubblicò una versione notevolmente elaborata in Studi emigrazione (1992).[12] Due caratteristiche rilevanti del saggio in esame evidenziano la necessità di problematizzare la nozione di "migrazione italiana" e la sua eredità. In primo luogo, si evidenziano le difficoltà insite nell'impresa. Baily opta per l'uso dell'espressione "rete sociale" rispetto alla più convenzionale "migrazione a catena"; la prima si riferisce a una rete di legami più "complessi e spesso multidimensionali", mentre la seconda implica una sequenza lineare e un legame diretto tra gli elementi (43n2). Riferendosi a una nuova tendenza negli studi sulla migrazione all'epoca della pubblicazione del suo saggio, Baily affermava inizialmente:

> Migration scholars have during the past decade increasingly emphasized the centrality of *social networks* to the migration process. These scholars view social networks as *an essential infrastructure* in the overall migration system, an *evolving collective mechanism* that links the larger economic and political structures in both *locations of origin and destination* with the individual migrants. (43; corsivi miei)[13]

Le caratteristiche multidimensionali di tali legami sono intrise di strutture economiche e politiche di classe. Inoltre, Baily suggerisce di considerare l'origine delle partenze e la geografia degli arrivi. Tale fenomeno, come è evidente, rientra in un meccanismo in fase di evoluzione che, in ultima analisi, esercita un impatto sull'individuo. Questo ci riporta alla nozione di pluralismo dell'invenzione e dell'interpretazione artistica di Fischer, che per sua stessa natura non può escludere il singolo artista e lettore/spettatore che ha trovato "una voce o uno stile che non viola le

---

[11] Ora, Italian American Studies Association.

[12] Nel suo saggio "Diaspore mobilitate e proletarie", John Armstrong si riferisce alla migrazione italiana in Francia del 1940 come segue: "Anche le *diaspore proletarie* prevalentemente polacche e *italiane* in Francia negli anni '40 impararono a parlare il francese in modo molto imperfetto" (406; corsivo dell'autore).

[13] Traduzione: "Nell'ultimo decennio gli studiosi di migrazione hanno sottolineato sempre più la centralità delle *reti sociali* nel processo migratorio. Questi studiosi considerano le reti sociali come *un'infrastruttura essenziale* del sistema migratorio nel suo complesso, un *meccanismo collettivo in evoluzione* che collega le strutture economiche e politiche più ampie nei *luoghi di origine e di destinazione* con i singoli migranti" (43).

[sue] diverse componenti dell'identità" (Fischer, 195). Il secondo aspetto della riconsiderazione di Baily della migrazione in termini di diaspora è la cronologia. All'interno di questa nuova prospettiva, che pone l'accento sulla rete e sui legami sociali, emerge la necessità di rivedere anche il concetto di cronologia. Nel considerare il fenomeno dell'immigrazione, in particolare le espressioni contemporanee come "flussi migratori" e concetti affini, è comune adottare una prospettiva storica. A titolo esemplificativo, si considerino i cosiddetti quarantaquattro anni di migrazione italiana negli Stati Uniti. In altre parole, è necessario fare un passo indietro, ignorando tutte le nozioni acquisite successivamente e, per maggiore certezza, la nozione di "ora".

Baily, infatti, sottolinea la necessità di un affinamento della metodologia che prenda in considerazione il dove e il quando. Egli asserisce che: "In primo luogo, è fondamentale ampliare e approfondire in modo più sistematico il nostro studio delle dimensioni critiche del tempo e dello spazio" (44). In altre parole, è necessario sfuggire alla concezione di un tempo statico e accettare il concetto di evoluzione dell'esperienza migratoria, al fine di comprendere appieno la relazione, ovvero il "legame", tra il passato e il presente, ovvero il "tempo", e il modo in cui questi legami si sviluppano a seconda della posizione geografica dell'individuo, ovvero lo "spazio". In questa fase iniziale, nella prima metà degli anni Novanta, Baily non è l'unico a concepire l'evoluzione dell'etnicità. Di seguito, si riporta l'affermazione di Gianfranco Rosoli: Nel suo ultimo saggio sulla diaspora degli Aragonesi (1992), Bailey ha analizzato una rete in Colorado fino alla quarta e quinta generazione. Questo ha consentito all'autore di valutare il significato a lungo termine della migrazione e, in particolare, la natura mutevole dell'etnia" (312). All'interno di questo quadro di "valutazione della [storia e] del significato a lungo termine della migrazione" in tutte le sue specificità, è possibile collocarla nel contesto della "natura mutata dell'etnicità" e, in ultima analisi, comprendere meglio l'eredità che si è sviluppata. Questo processo ci consente di comprendere, in una prospettiva diacronica, le manifestazioni e le articolazioni della nostra etnicità odierna in funzione della sua storia e del suo significato a lungo termine.

In definitiva, la questione verte sulla conglomerazione dello scorrere del tempo e delle interconnessioni dei vari eventi che si verificano nel corso della lunga cronologia, che evidenzia un'evoluzione delle nozioni. Questo fenomeno di interconnessione del tempo e degli eventi consente di rivedere il concetto stesso di cultura "diasporica italiana", che non si fonda più esclusivamente sulla storia, ma abbraccia tutte le manifestazioni e le articolazioni rilevanti del passato e del presente.

Opere citate

Anagnostou, Yiorgos. 2009. *Contours of White Ethnicity: Popular Ethnography and the Making of Usable Pasts in Greek America.* Athens: Ohio UP.

Anagnostou, Yiorgos, Yiorgos D. Kalogeras, and Theodora Patrona, eds. 2022. *Redirecting Ethnic Singularity: Italian Americans and Greek Americans in Conversation.* New York: Fordham UP.

Armstrong, John A. 1976. "Mobilized and Proletarian Diasporas." *The American Political Science Review* 70.2 (June): 393-408.

Baily, Samuel. 1992. "The village outward approach to the study of social networks: A case study of the Aragnonesi diaspora abroad, 1885-1989." *Studi emigrazione* 29.105 (March): 43-68.

Bauböck, Rainer. 2010. "Diaspora and transnationalism: What kind of dance partners?" In *Diaspora and Transnationalism: Concepts, Theories and Methods.* Rainer Bauböck and Thomas Faist, eds. Amsterdam: Amsterdam UP. 9-34.

Butler, Kim. 2001. "Defining Diaspora, Refining a Discourse." *Diaspora: A Journal of Transnational Studies* 10.2 (Fall): 189-219.

Cohen, Robin. 1997. *Global Diasporas: An Introduction.* Seattle: U of Washington P.

Faist, Thomas. 2010. "Cold constellations and hot identities: Political theory questions about transnationalism and diaspora." In *Diaspora and Transnationalism: Concepts, Theories and Methods.* Rainer Bauböck and Thomas Faist, eds. Amsterdam: Amsterdam UP. 295-322.

Fischer, Michael M. J. 1986. "Ethnicity and the Post-Modern Arts of Memory." In *Writing Culture. The Poetics and Politics of Ethnography.* James Clifford and George E. Marcus, eds. Berkeley: U of California P.

Gabaccia, Donna. 2000. *Italy's Many Diasporas.* Seattle: U of Washington P.

López, Gustavo and Ana Gonzalez-Barrera. 2014 "Afro-Latino: A deeply rooted identity among U.S. Hispanics." Pew Center Research. https://www.pewresearch.org/fact-tank/2016/03/01/afro-latino-a-deeply-rooted-identity-among-u-s-hispanics/. Accessed April 2, 2020.

Luconi, Stefano. 2011. "The Pitfalls of the 'Italian Diaspora'." *Italian American Review* 1.2 (Summer): 147-176.

Marienstras, Richard. 1985. "Sur la notion de diaspora." In *Les minorités à l'âge de l'État-nation.* Gérard Chaliand, ed. Paris: Fayard. 215-218. In English as "On the Notion of Diaspora." In *Minority Peoples in the Age of Nation-States.* Gérard Challiand, ed. London: Pluto Press, 1989. 119-125.

Patrona, Theodora. 2017. *Return Narratives: Ethnic Space in Late-Twentieth-Century Greek American and Italian American Literature.* Madison, NJ: Fairleigh Dickinson UP.

Prior, Ryan. 2019. "128 years later, New Orleans is apologizing for lynching 11 Italians." CNN. https://www.cnn.com/2019/04/01/us/new-orleans-mayor-apologizes-italian-americans-trnd/index.html.

Rosoli, Gianfranco. 1994. "The Global Picture of the Italian Diaspora to the Americas." In *The Columbus People: Perspectives in Italian Immigration to the Americas and Australia.* Lydio Tomasi, Piero Gastaldo, Thomas Row, eds. *Center for Migration Studies* special issue. Volume 11, Issue 3 (1994): 305-322.

Salvetti, Patrizia. 2017. *Rope and Soap: Lynchings of Italians in the United States.* Trans. Fabio Girelli Carasi. New York: Bordighera P.

Tamburri, Anthony Julian. 1991. *To Hyphenate or not to Hyphenate: the Italian/American Writer: Or, An* Other *American?* Montreal: Guernica.

_______. 2017. "The Coincidence of Italian Cultural Hegemonic Privilege and the Historical Amnesia of Italian Diaspora Articulations." In *Re-Mapping Italian America. Places, Cultures, Identities.* Carla Francellni and Sabrina Vellucci, eds. New York: Bordighera P. 53-75.

_______. *The Columbus Affair: Imperatives for an Italian/American Agenda.* New Fairfield, CT: Casa Lago P.

_______. 2022a. "Observations on Why Promotors of Italian American Culture Need to Know More: The Italian/American Experience of Religion." *Journal of Religion & Society.* Vol. 24: 1-8.

_______. 2022b. *Italian Diaspora Studies and the University: Professional Development, Curricular Matters, Cultural Philanthropy.* New York: Bordighera P.

_______. 2025. *Expanding Diasporic Identity: A Multi-directional Path to the New* Italian *Writer.* Cambridge, UK: Ethics P, 2025.

Tölölyan, Khachig. 1996. "Rethinking Diaspora (s): Stateless Power in the Transnational Moment." *Diaspora* 5.1 (Spring): 3-36.

Viscusi, Robert. 1990. "Breaking the Silence: Strategic Imperatives for Italian American Culture," *Voices in Italian Americana* 1.1 (Spring): 1-13.

Italian Migrants and Ethnic Schools in Brazil: The Case of Rio Grande do Sul (1875-1938)

Alberto Barausse
UNIVERSITÀ DEGLI STUDI DEL MOLISE

Abstract: This article challenges the thesis of classical historiography that Italian migrants showed little interest in their children's education. On the contrary, it highlights the emergence of a demand for schooling among Italians who settled in Rio Grande do Sul in the second half of the nineteenth century, both in rural colonies and in urban centres. From the 1870s on wards, migrants established ethnic schools combining elementary literacy with the transmission of cultural heritage. Initially led by family heads and settlers, these schools later involved parish priests, mutual aid societies, religious congregations, and consular teachers sent from Italy. Supported by subsidies and teaching materials provided by the Italian state, they compensated for the limits of the Brazilian public system and reinforced the Italianness of migrant communities. The study also interrogates broader issues: how did the multi-ethnic character of Rio Grande do Sul evolve under the rise of nationalist ideologies in Brazil and Italy? Were ethnic schools perceived as an obstacle to the Brazilian nation-building project? Based on diverse sources and framed within migration studies and the transnational history of education, the research reconstructs the heterogeneous and non-linear development of these institutions. Their decline after the First World War, and suppression under Vargas's *Estado Novo*, reveal the tensions between cultural pluralism and nationalist demands. Ultimately, Italian ethnic schools in Rio Grande do Sul represent a crucial yet little-known chapter in the history of migration and education.

1. INTRODUCTION AND METHODOLOGICAL PREMISES

The process of international mass mobility towards Brazil involved large groups of Italians beginning in the second half of the nineteenth century (Trento, 1989). The extensive body of research produced during the last two decades of the twentieth century, inspired by different historiographical approaches (Franzina, 2022), has shown how, on one hand, Italian migration responded to the projects of the Brazilian aristocratic classes, who sought alternative solutions for the replacement of enslaved labor following the abolition of slavery. On the other hand, it also reflected the aims of Italian elites, eager to provide alternative outlets for the lower classes, who were affected by the country's socio-economic backwardness and recurrent crisis (Rosoli, 1987;1993). Rio Grande do Sul, first as an imperial province and later as a state of the republican federation, was marked by a particularly intense migratory phenomenon with specific characteristics (Giron Slomp & Herédia Merlotti,

2007). It absorbed large numbers of immigrants in the process of territorial occupation, including Portuguese, Azoreans, Germans, Italians, and Poles (Pesavento, 1980). The migration phenomenon began in the nineteenth century, during the final phase of Pedro II's Empire, and continued after the proclamation of the Republic, which granted the individual states of the federation autonomous powers to legislate on land colonization (De Rosa, 1987). The most substantial Italian migration occurred between 1875 and 1897, when subsidized immigration was suspended by the Brazilian federal government. Nevertheless, arrivals continued, albeit on a smaller scale, in the following decades. The data presented in the table below allow for a clearer understanding of the migratory flows that took place between 1875 and 1915 – the year of the last decree on colonization (Horn Iotti, 2001) – as well as of the subsequent decline, which lasted until 1930.

Table 1. Italian migration flows to Rio Grande do Sul, Brazil (1875-1914)

Year	Italian migrants in Brazil	Italian migrants in RS	Foreign migrants in RS
1875-1879	12.532	8.579	11.019
1880-1884	28.201	8.973	10.636
1885-1889	169.053	26.133	29.692
1890-1894	248.047	21.591	52.370
1895-1899	320.972	4.613	10.437
1900-1904	197.462	2.336	5.182
1905-1909	114.006	1.687	12.893
1910-1914	123.149	2.256	51.735

Source: (Barausse, 2022b)

Italian migrants in the State of Rio Grande do Sul followed different trajectories, giving rise to both rural and urban settlements with distinct characteristics. Migration had already begun before the 1870s, when thousands of Italians from Uruguay and Argentina moved to the municipalities of southern Brazil, themselves affected by a severe crisis that forced many to emigrate. Italians thus settled in urban centers such as Pelotas, Bagé, Uruguayana, Rio Grande, Santa Vitória do Palmar, Alegrete, São Jerônimo, Cachoeira, and Jaguari. In 1893, Consul Legrenzi counted approximately 18,000 Italians distributed across Porto Alegre, Pelotas, Bagé, Uruguayana, Rio Grande, Dom Pedrito, São Gabriel, São Borja, Itaqui, Cruz Alta, Encruzilhada, Santo Antônio de Patrulha, Cachoeira, Livramento, Alegrete, Santa Vitória do Palmar, São Jerônimo, and Jaguari. This type of migration was largely characterized by workers and labourers with limited skills in logging and agriculture. Many engineers were employed in the construction and operation of roads, along with other professionals needed for the building of bridges and infrastructure, as well as doctors, pharmacists, and priests. In Porto Alegre, migrants were primarily engaged in commerce, though the presence of professionals such as photographers, music teachers, artists, sculptors, stonemasons, coffee makers, hoteliers, carpenters, blacksmiths, tinsmiths, boilermakers, millers, bakers, and gardeners was also significant.

Alongside urban mobility, rural migration took shape in the colonial areas made available by the Brazilian authorities to increase land productivity. The establishment of the Italian colonial zone was a consequence of the renewed colonization policy of the Imperial Government after earlier failures at the provincial level. In 1875, the Government promoted the settlement of rural colonies in the northeast of Rio Grande do Sul: Conde D'Eu and Dona Isabel (already demarcated), and a third colony, "Fundos de Nova Palmira" (later renamed Caxias). Two years later, a fourth colony, Silveira Martins, was founded to accommodate new arrivals, thus completing the initial core of Italian immigration in Rio Grande do Sul. The agricultural colonies were managed by the "Repartição Geral das Terras Públicas" and divided into square leagues of land, bounded by the so-called *linhas* and *travessões* (Giron Slomp & Herédia Merlotti, 2007). From a productive perspective, they were marked by the cultivation of beans, potatoes, maize, wheat, rye, barley, rice, tobacco and, above all, wine – though commercialization remained limited by poor transportation routes. Commercial and industrial activities were modest, including slaughterhouses, inns, tailoring and shoemaking, straw-hat production, beer and liquor brewing, brick and terracotta manufacture, and hydraulic mills (Perrod, 1883).

In both urban and rural contexts, forms of ethnic sociability quickly developed through the establishment of charitable and mutual aid societies, whose capital and membership varied according to local circumstances.

2. To the origins of Italian schools in the Imperial Province of Rio Grande do Sul

It was during this period that Italian migrants founded schools closely linked to their national and ethnic identity. Italian political authorities referred to them as "colonial schools" and later as "Italian schools abroad" while Brazilian authorities classified them as "private schools" or "isolated schools." The adjective "colonial" which current historiography of education replaces with "ethnic," did not imply a political subordination of Brazil. Rather, it reflected the designation given by Italian governmental and consular authorities to schools promoted by colonial settlements established under land colonization policies at the end of the Empire and in the early years of the Republic. The first Brazilian authorities with regulatory jurisdiction over schools in colonization areas were the "Inspectoria de Terras e Colonização". These schools initiated the educational process, combining basic literacy and cultural formation with the preservation and dissemination of Italianness. This national sentiment would resurface after the First World War and, under Fascist reforms, become particularly accentuated in the late 1920s and early 1930s. Some schools received financial support from the Italian government through the consular network, which supplied teaching materials and funds. This support intensified with the policies introduced by Prime Minister Francesco Crispi, who pursued a new emigration strategy. The reorganization of Italian schools abroad was part of Crispi's broader project of building a strong state and asserting Italy's role in international politics (Duggan, 2000; Levra, 1992). The modernization of Italy's diplomatic policy under Francesco Crispi – then Prime Minister and Minister of Foreign Affairs –aimed at closer engagement with emigrants. Law 5866 of 30 December 1888 established that Italy should not lose sight of its emigrants but rather guide them in their "new nation". Crispi's nationalism regarded emigration as a means of strengthening Italy's global presence, also through trade (Salvetti, 2002). Schools were thus conceived as instruments of national and civic revival, centred on patriotic values and the cult of the homeland (Barausse, 2022). The presence and configuration of educational institutions abroad varied across the destination countries of migration. The Royal Decree No. 6566 of 1889 approved the creation of Royal Italian Schools (especially in the Mediterranean) and Italian schools abroad, placing them under direct state management. It affirmed the secular nature of education, introduced grants for elementary schools run by associations or individuals, and allowed the opening of subsidized secondary schools. It was a period in which the budget for education subsidies increased. The objectives set by the new reorganization law were pursued through the distinction between government schools and subsidized schools, with funding provided by the ministries and managed by the consular authorities (Floriani, 1974). Given their orientations as "hearthstones of national education and patriotic sentiment" (Italian schools, 1891, p. 207), the schools to be established overseas were required to comply with governmental programs, which were appropriately adjusted to their specific geographical circumstances. The newly unified Italian foreign policy also included, from 1870 onward, administrative competence over Italian schools abroad. From that time, the consular structures were entrusted with the organization, promotion, inspection and systematization of schools. Plans were made to regulate and establish teaching programs and the textbooks to be used, as well as to conduct inspections in order to verify the function of the institutions. Beginning in 1888, the publication of the "Annuario delle scuole italiane all'estero" provided an important source for reconstructing this history, as it reported laws, decrees, and ministerial circulars issued over the years and, finally, the quantitative dimension of schools and enrollments. In addition, empirical verification is made possible through the analysis of the archival documents preserved in the Historical Diplomatic Archive of the Italian Ministry of Foreign Affairs. Through these tools, it is possible today, in the early twenty-first century, to trace the quantitative development of student populations. In particular, attention can be given to the enrollment trends in the schools established in Brazil, and specifically in the state of Rio Grande do Sul.

In the period between 1888 and 1930 the growth of enrollments in Italian schools established in the Brazilian state of Rio Grande do Sul was the second largest in the country, after those registered in the state of São Paulo.

Table 2 – Students in Italian Schools in Brazil, 1890-1930

Federative unit	**Periods**									
	1890 – 1891	**1896 - 1897**	**1904 - 1905**	**1909 - 1910**	**1913 - 1914**	**1921 - 1922**	**1922 - 1923**	**1924 - 1925**	**1927**	**1930**
Bahia	20	-	-	250	-	-	-	-	-	-
Minas Gerais	-	-	-	296	330	307	333	301	267	321
Paraná	-	-	752	596	786	704	1644	708	568	708
Santa Catarina	-	-	1681	1132	2261	1477	3195	2915	1032	2010
Pará	-	-	-	-	-	30	30	30	-	-
Pernambuco	-	-	-	424	424	656	656	656	409	61
Rio Grande do Sul	1468	2250	3213	2492	4310	3199	4628	4085	3315	3686
Rio de Janeiro	50	95	214	411	438	774	1072	901	334	101
São Paulo	515	1200	7275	6724	13307	5642	8248	10626	7012	6934
Espírito Santo	-	-	138	1053	1355	-	-	-	785	0
Mato Grosso	-	-	-	180	201	-	-	-	180	0
TOTAL	2053	3545	13273	13558	23412	12789	19806	20222	13902	13821

Source: Author's elaboration based on the "Annuario delle scuole italiane all'estero governative e sussidiate" (Yearbook of Italian Government and Subsidized Schools Abroad), published between 1890 and 1930.

Only recently, in the early twenty-first century, has the historiography of education recognized the need to establish a research agenda aimed at expanding knowledge of the phenomenon throughout Brazil (Ascenzi, Barausse, Luchese, & Sani, 2019).

Historians' interest in the educational and identity processes of Italian migrants stems from the demands expressed both by the evolution of educational historiography and by that of migration studies. New stimuli and new interpretative hypotheses have emerged from the perspectives of transnational history, which has sought to examine and conceptualise categories and identities, to uncover networks bound by ties stronger than those of social class or ideology, and to connect narratives and experiences that transcend time and place (Ossenbach & Del Pozo, 2011; Fuchs & Roldan, 2019). Building on historiographical perspectives opened up by "connected histories" and "histoire croisee", the field of educational history has also proposed to investigate more deeply those experiences that go beyond national borders and that shed light on the circulation of pedagogical ideas, movements and schooling initiatives on a global scale, thus avoiding a purely national framework (Ascenzi, Barausse, Luchese, & Sani, 2019; Castro, 2023).

Within this historiographical ferment, many of the contributions produced in recent years represent what has been described as an evolving open construction site (Barausse, 2022b). The studies conducted over the past fifteen years form part of research aimed at highlighting the interesting development of ethnic Italian schooling in several Brazilian states. In particular, reference can be made to the research activity organized by Italian and Brazilian groups, such as the *Research Group on History of Education, Immigration and Memory* (GRUPHEIM), affiliated with the University of Caxias do Sul and coordinated by Terciane Ângela Luchese. GRUPHEIM has developed research in collaboration with scholars from several institutional affiliations, both in different Brazil states and in Italy. Among the Italian institutions involved are the *Centro di documentazione e ricerca sulla storia delle istituzioni scolastiche, del libro scolastico e della letteratura per l'infanzia* (Ce.S.I.S.) – Research Center on the History of Schooling, Textbooks, and Children's Literature Group of Research – at the University of Molise, directed by Alberto Barausse and the *Centro di documentazione e ricerca sulla storia del libro scolastico e della letteratura per l'infanzia* (CESCO) – Research Center for the History of Textbooks and Children's Literature – at the University of Macerata, directed by Roberto Sani. The works of Ascenzi, Barausse, Luchese & Sani (2019), as well as those of Castro (2023), have surveyed the presence of early studies on Italian ethnic schools. An interesting corpus of research – including articles, monographs, and master's and doctoral theses on ethnic schooling – has been produced over the past fifteen years. Generally speaking, the scholarship of the last decade concerning ethnic schooling in Rio Grande do Sul refers to experiences developed between the second half of the nineteenth century and the 1930s. These studies relate to distinct temporal contexts of nation-state development in Italy and Brazil, yet they are rich in interconnections. For Italy, this production covers the moment when the newly unified nation-state, under the leadership of liberal elites, attempted – particularly with Crispi – to relaunch colonial policies within a framework that combined the need for a strong state with designs for colonial, political, or commercial expansion (Duggan, 2000). This was a phase marked by proposals for reform concerning the governance of emigration and the role of Italian schools abroad (Barausse, 2022c). It was then followed by a period of growing state intervention in the regulation of migratory phenomenon during the first decade of the twentieth century, culminating in the Fascist impulse to promote Italian projects abroad. For Brazil, the contributions also address a distinct time span in the history of Latin America, marked first by the final decades of the Empire and the onset of the republican federation. It was a period defined by the abolition of slavery and by the projects of colonization and immigration directed first by imperial, and later by federal and state, centres of power. This trajectory continued with the consolidation of the republican federation in the early twentieth century and reached the phase in which Brazil experienced the crisis of the *República Velha* and the transition toward Getúlio Vargas's *Estado Novo.*

From the pioneering studies on the capital of the state of São Paulo by Prado Eliane Mimesse (Prado, 2001,2010, 2014), followed by those of Franchini (2015) and Dell'Aira (2012), to the works of Claudia Panizzolo (2020) and Corrêa (2000, 2011) on Campinas; or to those on the condition of schooling in the state of Espírito Santo, to which

Simões (2014) and Franco (2014) have devoted attention; to the research conducted in the state of Santa Catarina, with contributions by Claricia Otto (2005, 2011, 2014), Norberto Dallabrida (1997, 2001, 2005, 2012, 2015), and Dos Santos Virtuoso (2008; Virtuoso & Rabelo, 2015); and finally to Minas Gerais, explored by Rodrigues (2009, 2014), Rio de Janeiro, investigated by Pagani (2012, 2014), and Paranà, where Falcade Maschio (2012, 2014, 2019) has focused her research on the colony of Colombo. Within this dynamic field is also situated the extensive research on Rio Grande do Sul, the context that has attracted most of the historical investigations on schooling, with contributions by Luchese (2007, 2008, 2010, 2012a, 2014, 2015, 2018), Rech (2014, 2015, 2018, 2019), Barausse and Bastos (2019), Grazziotin and Almeida (2013, 2014), Barausse (2016, 2017a, 2017b),Barausse & Luchese (2017), Castro e Barausse (2020), Rech and Barausse (2019), Castro (2021), Ciconetto Bernardi and Luchese (2020).

Altogether, these studies shed light on the different ways in which schooling was shaped by Italian ethnic initiatives within the broader framework of migration in various Brazilian states (Kreutz & Luchese, 2011). The process of Italian migration in states such as Minas Gerais, São Paulo, and Espírito Santo, for example, differed markedly from that experienced in Rio Grande do Sul and Santa Catarina, both in quantitative and qualitative terms. Likewise, the different types of schools promoted in colonial and migratory contexts have not yet been entirely clarified. Initial investigations have identified a plurality of educational agencies and forms of schooling; however, further research is still required to examine them in depth. What is known is that Italian schools were often organized in response to the absence of a public state school system in Brazil, that is to say, as an answer to the needs of immigrant families. At the same time, they also reflected Italian state policies aimed at maintaining connections with emigrants. The ways of organizing these schools varied across time and space and so too do the preserved sources. These histories can be reconstructed by drawing on a diversified documentary base, consisting of archival materials preserved both in Brazil and in Italy.

The first forms of schooling for Italian migrants in Rio Grande do Sul emerged in the first fifteen years of colonization, during the final phase of the Brazilian Imperial Regime. Research on its causes has pointed to a growing preliminary need for education, while also indicating the necessity of further studies to investigate both the literacy levels of the immigrants and their rates of school attendance (Luchese T. A., 2014). These questions become even more significant in light of the reports submitted by consular authorities, who regularly informed the Foreign Ministry about the development of the schools. During this period, schools were established in both rural and urban areas to address the scarce diffusion of Brazilian schools in the region. Luchese has documented the difficulties caused by the delay in the development of Brazilian state primary education in the colonial areas of Rio Grande do Sul, as well as the complexity of its causes. These problems were not only due to the shortage of qualified teachers and the deficiencies among the those already employed, but also to the difficulties of carrying out inspection services in a context marked by poverty and illiteracy (Luchese T. Â., 2015). This situation persisted despite the legislation on the occupation of the colonies, which, according to a regulation of 1867, provided for the establishment of schools as a public service. Attempts at improvement were made with a new law of 22 February 1876 (Giolo, 2007; Luchese T. Â., 2015, 114). The first schooling initiatives at the beginning of Italian immigration to Rio Grande do Sul were also supported by the Brazilian colonial administrations, namely the Inspectoria Geral de Terra e Colonização. Initially, the Brazilian imperial government selected teachers from among the colonists themselves. In this early period, extending at least until 1883, teaching assignments were given to migrants with higher levels of education. However, the fact that classes were conducted in Venetian dialect soon aroused serious concerns among Brazilian authorities about the risk of raising new generations of Brazilians completely alien to the culture and language of the country. For these reasons, in 1883 the first public teachers of the Portuguese language were appointed, though still in limited numbers (Luchese, 2015). The level of schooling remained, however, inadequate. As emphasized in a report submitted to the Italian parliament, "education in the colonies is truly pitiful" (Ministero degli Affari Esteri, 1880, 228).

Since the early 1880s, debates in the Italian parliament stressed the need to guarantee the development of schools so that settlers, "especially if a commoner", would not lose the use of their mother tongue. After all, the emigrant to Brazil was subjected to a well-known process: he "blends in with the people among whom he lives and is absorbed by them" (Ministero degli Affari Esteri, 1880). Italian deputies were made aware of the existence of Italian schools in Brazil. A school nucleus was also active in the city of Rio Grande, where for twelve years, beginning in 1865, a school was run by an Italian teacher, Giuseppe Morena from Deura in the province of Savona. Yet the instruction followed Brazilian government programs, and the teaching of Italian seemed to be "little thing", to extent that in 1877 the director decided to close the school (Ministero degli Affari Esteri, 1880, 229). In the capital city of Porto Alegre, teacher Adele Lazzari Bianchi had founded an elementary school where, for several years, she privately taught Italian to middle-class portalegrense girls. In Pelotas, another important urban centre of the state, evidence dates back to 1872 of the existence of an Italian school promoted by the Italian Union and Philanthropy Society and directed by an Italian teacher (Castro Brião de & Barausse, 2020).

In order to overcome the deficiencies of the public education system, other policies came into play. Barausse (2017b) and Luchese (2015) have verified, beginning in 1877 and 1884, there was a more intense participation of mutual aid societies, which signed contracts with teachers and sought the assistance of consular authorities for the acquisition of school supplies. In the urban context of Porto Alegre, Consul Pasquale Corte secured the patronage of the "Vittorio Emanuele II" Mutual Aid Society, established in 1877 (Le Associazioni, 2000), for the mixed elementary school attended by 26 pupils and founded by teacher Adele Lazzari Bianchi, in response to the growing demand for education generated by Italian immigration to the capital (Report Corte, 1884). Documentary sources reveal an undeniable demand for education from both from the colonial groups in rural areas and from immigrants in urban centers.

Reports produced by consuls during the 1890s indicate that many families in the colonial areas preferred to organize schools independently, to compensate for the absence of Brazilian public schools.

This choice was driven both by the lack of trust expressed toward existing public schools and by the practical difficulties caused by the distance of many colonial settlement, associational initiatives were mobilized to support schooling (Perrod, 1883, 316). In 1883, in the municipality of Dona Isabel, in the northeastern part of the state, the "Regina Margherita" Italian Mutual Aid Society – founded on September 20, 1882 – accepted the consul's proposal to start a school (Report Corte, 1884; Le Associazioni, 2000, p. 364). The following year, 1884, in another colonial center, Conde d'Eu, the newly established mutual aid society "Stella d'Italia", founded in March of that year, opened a school in the colony's headquarters, directed by the teacher Giovanni Puggina (Corte, 1984, 58-67). In the same district, called *linha geral,* another school was run by teacher Emilio Barni: "both teachers are very cultured and educated people and with the excellent teaching given by them well relevant is the profit of the pupils" (Report Corte,1884). How long did these initiatives last? Luchese and Kreutz (2010) speak of their ephemeral nature. The economic crisis that struck Brazil in the second half of the 1880s, caused by poor harvests and limited communication resources, heightened the settlers' difficulties in sustaining ethnic schools through autonomous means. In this situation, the commitment of consular authorities and the increase in resources allocated to the maintenance of schools were considered positive. Consular intervention supported the development of schools both in the urban context of the state capital and in the countryside, where migrant settlement was more intense. By the end of the imperial era and on the eve of Brazil's republican phase, the province of Rio Grande do Sul had a significant presence of Italian schools. In Porto Alegre, in 1889, the Italian schools were reinforced when the local Mutual Aid Society appointed the qualified teacher Dionigi Ronchi to direct a school for 60 students; in addition, an evening course was inaugurated, attended by 25 students. The Society also assumed responsibility for a small school with a few dozen pupils, under the guidance of another qualified teacher. In the northeastern colonial area of the state, school growth continued. In the municipality of Caxias, where the consul recorded the presence of nearly 20,000 Italians, there were eight Italian schools with 314 students. In the colonial area of Dona Isabel there were nine schools, though their significance varied. While the evaluation of the school run by the charitable society was positive, the judgment of those located in the colonial districts – the so-called *linhas* – was more nuanced. The total number of enrolled students reached 284. Although less populated, the province of Conde D'Eu had eight schools: one directed by the local charitable society and seven others located in the *linhas,* with a combined enrollment of 291 students. These schools were run either by settler teachers or by mutual associations. In the colony of Silveira Martins, known as the "Fourth Colony", there were three schools, subsidized with 1,500 lire enrolling 81 students. In the colony of Rio das Antas there was a single small school with 22 students, also supported by a subsidy of 1,500 lire. The schools of Encantado counted 40 students and were directed by a licensed teacher, with a subsidy of 500 lire. Finally, the schools in the urban centers of Pelotas, Rio Grande and Bagé were managed by their respective mutual aid societies, together enrolling 80 students; each received an allocation of 500 lire (Report Marefoschi, 1889).

The value of these schools was rather uneven, not only because of enrollment costs. Their methods were shaped by specific local needs: instruction often did not extend beyond the first two years of primary education, limiting students to "attend school to learn how to read and write". Plans to expand classes were concentrated mainly in the urban areas of Porto Alegre, Rio Grande and Pelotas, whereas "in the colonies it will not be easy, because parents do not send their children to school for more than two or three years". The consul emphasized:

> there is no doubt that these schools are affected by the uncertainty and instability characteristic of institutions maintained almost entirely by private initiative and supported with very limited means. The government subsidy is very useful in providing the institutions with stability, allowing students to attend the same schools and follow the same courses for a certain time. This subsidy, although modest, guarantees teachers a fixed allowance in addition to the small contributions received from students. The grant also entitles the Consulate to the opportunity and the responsibility of monitoring the progress of these schools through supervision, which is the only effective form of control, given the difficulty of finding individuals

with sufficient education to direct even the first classes of elementary schools, especially in the colonies (Report Marefoschi, 1889).

During the first phase of the Italian colonies in Brazil, the Italian government, through its consular authorities, sought to take advantage of the weaknesses of the Brazilian educational system. This is confirmed by the numerous reports that consuls and vice-consuls periodically sent to Italy, documenting the condition and development of schools in Brazil, particularly in the state of Rio Grande do Sul. The intervention of the consular authorities was ideologically linked to the need to promote the most effective means of preserving national identity, beginning with the Italian language (Report Marefoschi, 1889).

The vice-consul stationed in Pelotas, one of the southernmost cities in the state, stressed the importance of supporting the development of schools, especially in rural areas, where, despite significant difficulties, the local state authorities had managed to guarantee the presence and expansion of educational institutions. His observation is especially revealing, as it illustrates a distinct strategy for defending and promoting national identity. In his view, what proved particularly useful in this respect was the simultaneous diffusion of schools and the preservation of a certain degree of isolation of settler communities from contact with native Brazilians, since their mixture would inevitably result in the loss of national identity traits. This latter aspect paradoxically became one of the key criteria for defining the model of integration into the state (Report Acton, 1890).

3. The Development of Italian Ethnic Schools in the Republican State of Rio Grande do Sul at the End of the Nineteenth Century

The network of Italian colonial schools also contributed to the development of education in Rio Grande do Sul from the advent of the Republic and the promulgation of the 1891 Constitution until the First World War. In the new framework of the Brazilian Federal Republic, education was perceived as a crucial field for the progressive expansion of primary education, while secondary education largely remained in the hands of private institutions. The education policy developed by republican positivists during the First Republic (Tambara, 1995) integrated a broader strategy, with state action assuming the form of greater interventionism in the social sphere. This gave rise to a series of policies in which education increasingly played a central role, characterized by four elements: parliamentary initiatives, actions at the state government level, mediation with the Catholic Church, and the construction of a republican imaginary aimed at building a national consciousness (Corsetti, 1998). Within this framework, the school emerged as an essential tool to prepare the restructuring of Rio Grande do Sul society according to a positivist perspective (Didonet, 1975; Hentschke, 2015), in which education was conceived not only as an instrument for acquiring basic literacy and numeracy, but also as a means for the harmonious development of body, mind and ethics (Corsetti, 2007, 2008). The government of Rio Grande do Sul, under Júlio de Castilhos, began to implement measures such as Decree No. 89 of Feb. 2, 1897, aimed at reorganizing public education, including the creation of a more effective administrative structure beginning with a network of school inspectors.

Within this new perspective, albeit in a nonlinear fashion, the experiences of Italian schools persisted. In the early years of the Republican state, the development of Italian colonial schools was initially influenced by Francesco Crispi. The legislation on Italian schools abroad introduced under his government gave significant impetus to the establishment of schools sponsored by consular authorities. The annual report for 1890-91 noted the presence of 33 rural schools in the colonial areas of Rio Grande do Sul alone; while in 1889 the subsidies allocated to schools in the state amounted to 6,000 lire, within two years the figure had risen to 15,000 lire (Ministero Affari, 1889, 1890).

The policies adopted by Crispi's successor, Antonio di Rudinì, which sought to reduce the financial resources for subsidizing schools, only partially hindered their development. More decisive, however, was the lack of consistent commitment on the part of consular authorities to support the schools' growth in an organic way. Divergent ideological perspectives further shaped the situation. Some consuls, such as Pio di Savoia, expressed highly negative views about the role of Italian immigrants and the possibility of sustaining national identity abroad. According to him, schools had arisen not from attachment to the homeland and its language, but simply from "the need of having their children supervised while they go to the field work". At the same time, however, he conceded that the migration experience had led settlers to recognize that "it was necessary that their children learned something, so as to be a little braver against those who know more" (Report Pio di Savoia, 1894).

This tension between urban and rural immigrant communities persisted. In Pio di Savoia's judgment, the communities of Porto Alegre and Pelotas "did not deserve any attention" although their schools could serve as important instruments of "moralizing influence".

Urban immigrants, often employed in "crafts and small trades", were valued primarily for their economic contribution to commerce, but not considered deserving of sustained educational investment. For this reason, Pio di Savoia argued against establishing a stable school organization for what he described as "an excessively inconstant element, rather undisciplined, without any orientation". In his view, financial support should not be expanded; rather, the Italian government ought to return to providing "a real subsidy instead of the present system of actual maintenance" (Report Pio di Savoia, 1894).

From this perspective, Pio di Savoia introduced a radical reform of the distribution of subsidies to colonial schools in Rio Grande do Sul, which until then, according to him, had been administered in an "unwise and equitable" manner. Henceforth, schools would receive regular subsidies "in books, at the beginning of the school year, and a small cash prize at the end of the year". In addition, consular authorities set the standard contribution at 50 lire per year, alongside an incentive prize of 100 lire for the 12 schools deemed most deserving by a special committee chaired by the consul. To qualify, schools were required to meet precise criteria:

> a) The school must have been in existence for more than one year; b) the teacher must be a person of recognized honour; c) teaching must be conducted in Italian; d) the teacher must report to the consulate twice a year; e) the school year should not be shorter than ten months; f) the school day must not be shorter than three hours (Circular Pio di Savoia, 1894).

The implementation of these restrictive measures had serious consequences. Settlers' associations openly voiced their dissatisfaction, forcing the subsequent consul, Legrenzi, to petition the Ministry for the adoption of new measures. Even Legrenzi, though less pessimistic about the immigrant colonies, considered it necessary to prioritize rural schools, given the continuing tensions among the urban associations of Porto Alegre and Pelotas (Report Legrenzi, 1894). The effects of these restrictions became evident in the second half of the 1890s, when the number of schools declined significantly. The consul in Porto Alegre reported to the Ministry a total of 41 schools, down from 57. While schools in Porto Alegre and Pelotas survived thanks to facilities provided by the Mutual Aid Society Vittorio Emanuele II, those in Rio Grande and Bagé had dwindled and disappeared. The consul emphasized both the difficulties and the futility of Italian urban schools as tools to limit the spread of Brazilian ones (Report Dall'Aste Brandolini, 1898).

Italian schools founded during the last fifteen years of the nineteenth century thus displayed a highly heterogeneous profile, as shown by early surveys: colonial schools, rural schools, private schools promoted by mutual aid societies, parents or teachers in rural settlements, confessional parish schools, and schools run by religious orders. In many cases, schools were financed directly by peasant settlers; sometimes they received subsidies from the Italian government, and in other instances they were supported by municipal funds. This heterogeneity concerned their nature (associative or private), their organization (mixed or single-sex classes, enrolment fees, and forms of financing), their pedagogical models (day or evening classes, graded or ungraded structures, mnemonic versus intuitive methods, secular or Christian-inflected contents in history and geography), as well as the level of qualification of both schools and teachers.

4. The Development of Italian Schools in Rio Grande do Sul at the Beginning of the Twentieth Century until the End of the First World War

Between the end of the nineteenth century and the first decades of the twentieth, significant changes marked the economic and social development of Rio Grande do Sul. The slow process of modernization affected, in different ways, both important urban centers such as Porto Alegre and rural colonial areas. Italian migrant groups now appeared more permanently settled than temporarily, becoming increasingly embedded in the state's social and productive networks. Their numerical weight could no longer be ignored by the political and administrative authorities of Rio Grande do Sul, with Italian consular authorities reporting between 150 and 250,000 Italian residents. The development of schools in the state was shaped by the *castilhista* positivist approach, which promoted the gradual expansion of education in Brazil. This was implemented, albeit slowly, under the presidency of Borges de Medeiros, who relied on the new autonomous municipalities of the Italian colonial region – such as Bento Gonçalves and Garibaldi (formerly the colonies of Conde d'Eu and Dona Isabel) – and on the intendants who administered them, to respond to growing demands for schooling. New regulations introduced after Decree No. 874 of February 28, 1906, increased the responsibilities of municipal intendants as part of state efforts to expand the number of subsidized schools and classes (Alves, 1907).

Within this framework, there was also a rise in the number of religious schools and institutions. Following the expulsion of the French congregations, new orders such as the Sisters of St. Joseph of Chambéry, the Sisters of the Immaculate Heart of Mary, the Marist Brothers, and the Lasallian Brothers settled in Rio Grande do Sul. In 1915 they were joined by the Carlist and Passionist Priests (Giron, 2017; Luchese, 2015). These congregations invested heavily in schools and seminaries, broadening educational offerings, including for Italian migrant communities in remote colonial areas. As Consul De Velutiis pointed out, the French congregations represented a "great competition to ours, as they freely admit poor students, charging only those who can afford" (Report De Velutiis, 1906). By contrast, Italian ethnics schools continued to live "stunted lives". Settlers, confronted with economic crises exacerbated by droughts and locust infestations, often struggled to pay teachers, "who were poorer than them". The role of mutual aid societies was also unstable: "They rise, they break down and decay, easily, on behalf of the energy and good will of those who run them, and according to the moods of their associates and the conditions of their members", reported the consul (Report De Velutiis, 1906). Despite the growing competition from religious and state institutions, however, the first decade of the twentieth century was the most significant phase of quantitative growth for Italian ethnic schools. This expansion was made possible by new Italian policies characterized by greater state intervention in managing emigration. The establishment of the "Commissariato per l'Emigrazione" (Commissiner's Office for Emigration) in 1901 provided increased financial resources for Italian schools abroad. Brazil, and particularly Rio Grande do Sul, became a testing ground: from 1904 "maestri agenti" (teacher-agents), new professional figures tasked with promoting schools and Italianness in emigrant communities while also performing consular functions, were sent abroad (Barausse, 2021). This new framework was consolidated by the Tittoni Law l of 1910. In 1909, one of the most active consular agents, Luigi Petrocchi, submitted an updated report on schools seeking subsidies: there were 127 schools in total, of which 17 were confessional and 106 were run by teachers, while 3 were managed by mutual aid societies. Together, secular and religious schools enrolled 5,580 students (Report Petrocchi, 1909).

The financial provisions confirmed by Italian ministerial authorities were further reinforced by the enactment of Law No. 867 in December 1910, which organically reformed legislation on Italian schools abroad (Floriani, 1974; Barausse, 2022).

In the second decade of the twentieth century, Brazilian policy authorities also promoted two important processes. First, there was a real increase in the participation of municipalities in the Italian colonial region, resulting in the occasional and uneven expansion of the network of subsidized schools. Many private isolated schools, originally maintained by the community and offering instruction in Italian, were gradually transformed into subsidized schools supported by the state or municipalities. Some were even converted into municipal schools where Portuguese was incorporated into the curriculum. Recent studies point to growing settler demand for municipal schools, perceived as vehicles of social mobility, cultural prestige, and political distinction (Luchese T. Â., 2013, 2015; Werle, 2005).

A second important step was the introduction of a new elementary school model by decree in May 1909, which initiated the gradual transition from the traditional single-class structure – where one teacher taught students of different levels – to graded schools. These required at least 200 pupils and were organized into separate classes by level, each with its own teacher, under a single administration (Souza, 2023). In the Italian colonial region, graded elementary schools were established in Bento Gonçalves in 1910 and in Caxias do Sul in 1912, while Garibaldi only obtained recognition for a school group in 1926.

5. The Italian School Policies for Italianness between the two World Wars

At the beginning of the 1920s, after the events of the First World War and shortly before the rise of Fascism, the will to relaunch projects aimed at promoting national identity and culture in areas with a significant presence of Italian emigrants began to take shape. In this context, a programme for the revival of Italian schools abroad was outlined within a broader perspective of defending and promoting *Italianness*. This included, alongside the strengthening of schools, the diffusion of Italian culture and the fostering of closer relations with foreign countries. From 1920 onwards, under the Ministry of Foreign Affairs led by Carlo Sforza, the General Directorate for Italian Schools Abroad regained a more active role. At its head, Sforza appointed the intellectual Ciro Trabalza, historian of the Italian language, who shared the aspiration of a group of intellectuals oriented towards achieving a major cultural and educational renewal in Italian society through the structures of the state, considered the priority instruments of national pedagogy (Barausse, 2015).

In the period between the crisis of the liberal institutions and the first phase of Fascism, up to 1925, the main concern of ministerial authorities was to determine the most appropriate forms of reorganization of the school system in the Americas. The goal was to strengthen the network of schools, considered essential both for promoting Italianness and for preventing the loss of national identity traits – a phenomenon defined by experts as the "rapid denationalization process" (Report Alemanni, 1923). During the first half of the 1920s, however, the number of Italian schools decreased, accompanied by a change in their characteristics. Consular agents on mission in Rio Grande do Sul, as well as other consular authorities, reported a significant reduction in the number of secular schools, paralleled by the growth of religious schools, in addition to the expansion, in both rural and urban areas, of schools promoted by the Brazilian State in line with an intensification of nationalist aims (Report Seghetti, 1922-23; Report Bompard 1925). In continuity with the school policies of the previous decade and under the guidance of the Directorate General for Italian Schools Abroad, the orientation was to provide a more efficient didactic reorganization, to support the recruitment of teachers with specific training, to mediate with religious authorities in order to involve the Italian clergy, and to promote the collaboration of local communities through active participation in religious associations linked to *Italica Gens,* a federation of Catholic religious congregations (Promemory, 1923). The educational question also became the object of a diplomatic intervention in 1924, on the eve of the visit by the Italian ambassador to Brazil (Pro-Memory, 1924). In essence, during this first phase of Fascism, through the preparation of a comprehensive programme, government leaders and high-ranking ministerial personnel focused on fostering greater involvement of local communities, mainly through collaboration with religious institutions. This approach aimed to consolidate the educational institutions entrusted with guaranteeing both the expansion and the defense of the Italian national identity.

A few years later, the consul of Porto Alegre, Luigi Arduini (1925), spoke of a real "debacle", of a "disastrous situation". In particular, Arduini denounced "the current conditions, unfortunately far from thriving, in our schools", with special emphasis on the state of "abandonment" and "carelessness" into which "all small laic schools" in the colonial area had fallen. These schools, subsidized by the royal government and located mostly in rural zone, were considered "little bastions of *Italianità!*" At the same time, Arduini reiterated the poor "effectiveness, utility and scope" of the teaching activities carried out by institutions sponsored by religious congregations, "most of them of French origin and mentality", in promoting the national language (Report Arduini, 1925).

The consular authority did not perceive opportunities for "progress" but rather stressed the need to establish a true "barrier" through a series of measures. These included greater financial commitment, support for schools in the colonial area managed by secular teachers, the involvement of Italian church personnel, and the wider dissemination and circulation of school supplies and textbooks (Report Arduini, 1925).

The period between the late 1920s and the beginning of Second World War constitutes the concluding phase of the experience of Italian schools in Rio Grande do Sul. It was not, however, a phase marked by linearity, but rather by contradictions and growing conflict shaped by changes occurring within both states. These changes were destined to provoke a bitter clash between two competing nationalization campaigns. In Italy, Fascism, beginning in 1926, increasingly assumed the features of a totalitarian regime. In 1928, two significant changes occurred: the dissolution of the "Commissariato per l'Emigrazione" (Commissariat for Emigration) and the administrative reorganization of the Ministry of Foreign Affairs. The office in charge of managing schools and Italians abroad was renamed the "General Directorate of Schools and Italians Abroad" and Mussolini appointed as its new head the plenipotentiary Minister Piero Parini, secretary of the Fasci Italiani all'Estero (Italian Fascist Abroad) (Garzarelli, 2002; Knox, 1982). This appointment marked a turning point, orientating the development of ethnic schools towards the regime's propaganda abroad (Gentile, 2002; La Rovere, 2002). Entrusting the DGSIE to Parini (Floriani, 1974, 76-77; Pretelli, 2010, 76-77; Parini, 1935; Franzina & Sanfilippo, 2003; Bertonha, 2001) signaled the politicization of the entire emigration sector, including the school system (Pretelli, 2010). The reinforcement of Fascism in Rio Grande do Sul coincided with the arrival of a new generation of consuls more aligned with the regime, who took office at the Consulate General of Italy in Rio Grande do Sul: Manfredo Chiostri, Mario Carli, Guglielmo Barbarisi and Santovincenzo Magno. Historiography often presents their role in homogeneous terms; in fact, their approaches were markedly different (Bertonha, 2001; Grassi Orsini, 1998; Barausse & Luchese, 2018). Until the early 1930s, however, Italian consular authorities sought to avoid initiatives that might have led Brazilian political leaders to view Italian schools as harmful or "dangerous for the formation of a national [Brazilian] conscience". As Consul Chiostri wrote in a January 1930 report, it was considered preferable to maintain the *status quo*. In line with his predecessors, he noted the "denationalization process that unfortunately hangs over our collectivities, from which not even the German groups – better organized from a school point of view – were exempt" (Report Chiostri, 1930). By this time, the number and distribution of schools were strongly conditioned by the drive of Brazilian state policies to expand public education. The process of nationalization of schooling in Brazil received new impetus between 1930 and 1937, when Flores da Cunha, appointed by Getúlio Vargas, headed the administration in Rio Grande do Sul. Flores da Cunha introduced several measures aimed at reorganizing the school system: in 1935, he created the Secretary of State for Education and Public Health (SESP), regulated the teaching career, introduced new criteria for dismissal and transfer of teachers, expanded the school network and facilities, and increased both students attendance and teacher appointments. According to Bastos and Tambara, "in 1930, there were 718 teachers, with 2,131 municipal schools and 1,320 private schools; in 1937, the number of school units increased to 5,346, of which 902 were state schools, 2,807 municipal schools and 1,637 private schools (Câmara Bastos & Tambara, 2014, 86-87).

The expansion of public schools, subsidy policies, and the restrictions imposed under the *Estado Novo* regime on ethnic schools led to their progressive extinction, even before the official closure decree of 1942. It should nevertheless be recalled that the principle of freedom of education – vigorously defended by local positivists – had previously made it possible, in the absence of adequate public institutions, for ethnic schools to flourish (Kreutz, 2003). Although the issue of nationalization was present in the press and debated among intellectuals and local leaders, it did not yet result in restrictive or punitive legislation during those years. Relations between Flores da Cunha's and immigrant communities, particularly Italians and Germans, remained cordial. Thus, Piero Parini and Ambassador Cerruti were warmly received by both Brazilian political authorities and the Italian immigrant communities during their visits in December1931 (Rech & Barausse 2019) and 1932 (Barausse & Luchese 2015, 452).

But the great fascist offensive in the colonies abroad "brought about a reinforcement in the construction of a new identity, using evident symbols drawn from the new homeland in its modern, orderly and progressive model" (Costantino de, 2009, 11). A new Italy was thus projected, and the emigrants of that nation were redefined "Italians abroad" (Giron, 1994, 83). Among the demonstrations that involved both the diplomatic and political authorities and the Italian community in Rio Grande do Sul – and in particular that of Porto Alegre in the 1930s – special attention was given to the visits made by Piero Parini in December 1931, during the final phase of the consular mission of Manfredo Chiostri, and by Ambassador Cerruti in 1932 (Barausse & Luchese, 2017, 452). Both events were intended to have a strong resonance, especially in relation to the impulse for the reorganization of schools and Italian language courses.

Received at the headquarters of the "Dante Alighieri Society", Piero Parini delivered a speech defending the Fascist project. He emphasized the new logic with which Italians were regarded – since the late 1920s, no longer as mere immigrants, but as "Italians abroad". This conceptual shift reflected the orientation of Fascist vision regarding emigrants, stressing the need for a resumption of "Italianità" and for renewed efforts to spread the Italian language (Rech & Barausse, 2019, 536-537; *A chegada do diretor geral dos fascios italianos no exterior*, 1931).

Within this framework, we observe the beginning of the reorganization of Italian schools in Rio Grande do Sul under the guidance of the new consul Mario Carli, a figure closer to Fascist orientations and to Parini's directives. With Carli, who arrived in March 1932, the Fascist stance towards schools was made explicit, particularly in the state capital. The drive for the development of schools was inscribed within a broader strategy that, as we shall see from the first half of the 1930s, aimed at centralizing under consular control all Italian organizations – Mutual Aid Associations, *Fasci italiani all'estero*, *Dopolavoro*, *Dante Alighieri* – as well as the promotion and restructuring of Italian schools, newspapers, Italian language and culture courses, radio programs, monuments, and public festivities. All of these were conceived as coordinated strategies for the diffusion of Fascist discourse and the construction of a sense of belonging to the "great Italy", to "Italianità", and, ultimately, to Fascism (Barausse & Luchese, 2017, 459). The new consul's orientation was characterized by the centralizing style with which the representative authority of the Italian state and government in Rio Grande do Sul intended to reorganize the entire social and cultural life of Italian community, ensuring effective Fascist control. In 1933, a new school was inaugurated thanks to the contribution of the *Dante Alighieri Society*. In the urban context of the Capital, consular authorities further favored a process of reorganization of existing schools, especially those linked to the mutual aid associations (As escolas ítalo-brasileiras em Porto Alegre. Origem, organização, atividade, 1936). With different curricular characteristics or degrees of proximity to the Consulate, these institutions were progressively reorganized under a singular consular umbrella, coordinated by a unified educational directorate. The central figure of this process was Professor Luigi Ledda, directly appointed in Rome by Piero Parini. Ledda supported the consul during the reorganization and subsequently assumed the post of director of the Italian school in Porto Alegre, a position he held from 1 January 1934 until his departure from the *gaúcha* capital in 1938 (Barausse, 2019). The reorganization project developed along several lines. First, the institutionalization of a didactic directorate was established in order to centralize and unify the coordination of activities under a single structure. This was accompanied by the prospect of increasing the number of schools; consolidating a calendar to ensure the effective conduct of the school year; introducing a weekly timetable; standardizing textbooks; expanding student enrollment and monitoring school attendance; establishing regular inspection services and pedagogical guidance for teachers; supplying schools with the necessary and appropriate teaching materials; and organizing of a calendar of celebrations and joint festivities with Brazilian authorities. Together with these measures, the structuring of a common curriculum was defined, which provided for teaching of both Italian and Portuguese (Report Carli, 1932, 3; Report Carli, 1933). The new *curriculum* envisaged "putting Italian schools in a position to maintain the mother country's language, history and customs". To this was added the request that Italian be made compulsory in secondary colleges – on the model of French – while ensuring that second-and third generation students would not feel disadvantaged by ignoring "indigenous cultural elements", indispensable for a career and for continuing their studies in courses where Italian was not included. The process also involved the collaboration of the "gaúchas" authorities, who provided, free of charge, teachers of Portuguese for these schools (Report Carli, 1932, 2).

The reorganization project was supported by an incisive press campaign, both in the ethnic and Brazilian press (Rech & Barausse, 2019). To strengthen the centralizing character of the initiative, plans were also made for the creation of a new federative association capable of bringing together the eight existing Italian societies in the capital, thereby ensuring more direct control and securing additional financial resources (Report Carli, 1933). After nearly a year of negotiations, the reorganized schools changed their institutional character and assumed the name *Italian-Brazilian schools* (Barausse & Luchese, 2017). They were inaugurated on 6 March 1933, an event widely emphasized in the local press (*A reorganização radical das Escolas Italianas*, 1933).

The development of these schools was accompanied by extracurricular initiatives designed to sustain and consolidate them. Among the many planned measures were the creation of a School Patronage and a school medical inspection service (introduced in 1933), the construction of a sports field (*Campo Sportivo Italo Balbo*), and the organization of summer camps, named *Campeggio Mussolini.* In these camps, students from both Porto Alegre and rural schools spent part of their holidays participating in activities centered on discipline, recreation and sports (Report Carli, 1933).

The reorganization process, however, advanced only slowly in the first half of 1933. The Italian consul encountered strong internal resistance, particularly when centralization required the dissolution of the committee of the "Dante Alighieri Society". A special commissioner was sent to address accusations of maladministration concerning the *Italica Domus* Society and its social assets (Crocetta, 1934).

The implementation of a more organic and systematic strategy was entrusted to Consul Guglielmo Barbarisi. Step by step, he managed to ease the conflicts generated by the strained relationship with the local "Dante Alighieri Society" and to bring the entire network of associations within the consular orbit. He reorganized the *Fascio* and the National Association of Combatants, and in this framework took charge of ensuring the necessary provisions and resources for the consolidation of the schools. Upon his arrival, Barbarisi faced a precarious situation: few teachers, poorly paid salaries, and a lack of material and classrooms. A few days after taking office, on 1 June 1934, he modified the framework of local teachers and, more importantly, secured from the Ministry the appointment of four permanent teachers (Rech & Barausse, 2019, 542). By the end of 1934, the four Italian-Brazilian schools – "Dante Alighieri", "Umberto I", "Elena di Montenegro" and "Vittorio Emanuele II" (reactivated) – were functioning in accordance with the reorganization plan. In 1936, in addition to improving these institutions, Barbarisi founded a new school in a working-class neighborhood of Porto Alegre (*As escolas ítalo-brasileiras em Porto Alegre. Origem, organização, atividade*, 1936). The institution was named "Rosa Maltoni, august mother of our beloved Duce" (Report Ledda, 1935). Unlike the other schools, it was not linked to Italian associations in the capital but maintained exclusively by the consulate. At the beginning of the 1937 school year, Porto Alegre counted five primary schools, representing the majority of the seven Italian schools operating in Rio Grande do Sul. Two additional schools were located in Caxias do Sul and Pelotas. At the same time, the consular authorities sought to intervene in the colonial areas, the most significant initiative being the foundation of the new Italian school "Príncipe de Piemonte", inaugurated in Caxias in August 1936 (*L'inaugurazione della sede della nuova scuola italiana in Caxias*, 1936). According to the consul, the institutes present in the capital and in Caxias responded adequately to government expectations: both the urban Italian schools and that of Caxias do Sul were described as "born with the sacrifice of our Charitable and Mutual Aid Societies, small and modest institutions where discipline and order are model" (*As escolas ítalo-brasileiras em Porto Alegre. Origem, organização, atividade*, 1936). Before leaving his post for a new assignment, Barbarisi was able to present a far more positive quantitative picture than at the beginning of the 1930s. He proudly reported that the number of enrolled students had more than quintupled during his tenure, rising from 120 in 1933 to 625 at the beginning of the 1937 school year (Rech & Barausse, 2019, 543). The teaching staff reached 12 members, of whom 4 were permanent and 8 temporary, with the addition of 6 Brazilian teachers assigned to teach Portuguese (Report Barbarisi, 1936). Even the government authorities of Rio Grande do Sul expressed moderate approval of the progress achieved, as highlighted by the local press on the occasion of the official visit of the State Secretary of Education, Otello Rosa, to the "Dante Aligheri" and "Rosa Maltoni" schools in July 1936 (*A visita do secretário da Educação aos colégios Dante Alighieri e Rosa Maltoni*, 1936).

6. Crisis in Italo-Gaúcho Relations and the Closure of Italian Schools

With the *Estado Novo* coup of 1937, Getúlio Vargas deposed Flores da Cunha and appointed General Manoel de Cerqueira Daltro Filho, who governed between 17 October 1937 and 19 January 1938, when he died in office. He was succeeded by General Osvaldo Cordeiro de Farias (Maestri, 2010, 321), who remained until September 1943, when he left the position to join the Brazilian Expeditionary Force sent to fight the Axis in Europe. Cordeiro de Farias was followed by Ernesto Dornelles, who governed until the end of the *Estado Novo*. The five years in which Cordeiro de Farias was at the head of the government of Rio Grande do Sul proved crucial and decisive for the nationalization campaign (Pagani , 2005; Dal Molin, 2005). Practices of "Brazility" were widely disseminated and implemented, including in education. The nationalization of education was interpreted as a continuation of the revolution initiated in 1930 (Barausse & Luchese, 2017, 456). According to Quadros, the intervention of the Brazilian state in education, beginning in 1937, unfolded across four dimensions: 1) an extensive and detailed jurisprudence on education; 2) the technical and administrative restructuring of SESP/RS; 3) policies to expand the state education network, including the construction of schools, the recruitment of teachers and staff, and the increase in student enrollment; and 4) closer guidance, supervision and inspection of school activities (Quadros, 2014, 120).

The nationalization of education thus resulted in comprehensive reform, whereby the state assumed control of schools in Rio Grande do Sul, with particular emphasis on the Technical Section of the General Directorate of Public Instruction and the Center for Research and Educational Guidance (CPOE / RS) (Câmara Bastos & Tambara, 2014).

During the *Estado Novo* (1937-1945), the policies of Cordeiro de Farias and of the Secretary of Education José Pereira Coelho de Souza, focused squarely on the nationalization of education (Câmara Bastos & Tambara, 2014). The aspiration was to forge the "new" Brazilian citizen, identified with the homeland and national unity. Yet, as Gertz warns, this nationalization campaign "did not reach in a linear and uniform way all groups, and there were significant differences in the evaluation of the various foreign populations that were in Gaucho territory" (Gertz, 2005, 146).

The most acute phase of the crisis in Italo-Brazilian relations was managed by the Italian consular authorities in continuity with previous strategies, optimistically grounded in the defense of *Italianness*. For the new consul, Santovincenzo Magno, the school issue was functional to "an ever broader and deeper assertion of Fascist Italy". Specifically, he insisted that the development of elementary schools should be organically linked to other associations, seen as part of a single material space, the future "Casa d'Italia". Schools were thus included in a program that also encompassed the "fasci all'estero", Fascist aid organizations, and the Church through religious orders active in the colonial areas: "We must not forget that every fascio, school, missionary must obey the exterior and a single command which is the ever wider and deeper affirmation of Fascist Italy" (Barausse & Luchese, 2017, 465).

Reports sent to the General Directorate of Italians and Schools Abroad confirm the extensive use of content designed to promote Fascist education in the Italian schools still active in Rio Grande do Sul (Carignani, 1938). The new school director, Mariano Berlingeri, extolled the "redemptive work of the Fascist school" against which, in his view, the policies of local authorities – as well as the actions of Portuguese teachers appointed by the Secretary of Education – seemed to operate (Report Berlingeri, 1938).

The effects of the Brazilian nationalization campaign were felt with increasing intensity in the 1938 school year. The Italian consul reported a sharp decline in enrollment, attributing it to the propaganda campaign carried out by local newspapers and political authorities. Italian teachers opposed the nationalization process "encouraged by zeal and combative spirit, giving the colony the tangible proof that their children in their schools would find all the moral, intellectual and material assistance and only schools of the Fascist regime were capable of giving such a brilliant example" (Prospect, 1938).

By Decree No. 7212 of April 1938, the federal *interventor* in the state ordered that ethnic schools teach physical education, civic education, and manual labor in accordance with official guidelines. Portuguese, history, geography and civic education were to be taught during school hours by teachers appointed by the Department of Education and paid by private primary schools where instruction was given in a foreign language. Schools that resisted or failed to comply with these requirements were to be closed. The decree also mandated the registration of all private primary schools. Complementary regulations were introduced by Decree No. 7247 of April 1938, providing instructions for the registration of schools with the General Directorate of Public Instruction (Kreutz, 2003).

At the federal level, Decree 406 of May 1938 targeted rural schools, requiring the exclusive use of Portuguese didactic material, the display of the national flag during festivities, and the appointment of teachers and principals born in Brazil. The curriculum was to include Brazilian history and geography, and children under the age of fourteen were prohibited from receiving instruction in a foreign language. In December 1939, Decree No. 1006 instituted supervision and censorship of schoolbooks. Decree No. 1545 of August 1939 directed the Secretaries of Education to open schools in immigrant-settled areas. These provisions reinforced the inspection of schools, the teaching of Brazilian history and geography, civic education to promote patriotism, and the explicit prohibition of foreign languages in public activities. In March 1940, Decree No. 2072 established the *Brazilian Youth* as mandatory in schools, while Decree No. 3580 of September 1941 prohibited the import or printing of foreign-language textbooks for primary schools (Kreutz, 2003).

With the compulsory registration of foreign private schools established in 1938 by Cordeiro de Farias and Coelho de Souza, 2,418 schools were registered, of which 241 were permanently closed for failing to comply with Decrees 7212 and 7247. Italian-Brazilian schools were among those definitely closed, despite having been reorganized along Fascist lines. A 1939 report recorded frequent complaints by teachers against political catechesis, noting that "they were obliged to cross their arms and watch impassively the absorption of ideological exotisms by children". Although relatively few in number, these schools were described as centers of Fascist ideological formation. Inspectors reported the presence of Fascist textbooks, symbols, and uniforms, teachers sent by the Italian government, notebook entries, and the fact that "the children would greet the masters with the Fascist salute and sing the *Giovinezza*" (Report Coelho de Souza, 1939). All of these elements violated Brazilian requirements, and as a result all schools were closed in May 1938, with no reopening permitted. Despite this, federal *interventor* Coelho de Souza repeatedly stated that there were no problems of nationalization among Italian descendants and that public schools were valued by Italian immigrants and their children.

Confronted with the intensification of nationalist policies, Italian consular and diplomatic authorities suggested adopting a cautious stance so as not to provoke harsher reactions from Brazilian officials. As recent research by Barausse and Luchese (2017) and Barausse and Rech (2019) has shown, however, the Italian consular authorities underestimated both the determination and the capacity of Brazilian political leaders to enforce the new provisions. In particular, the Italian ambassador's initiatives suggested a "wait-and-see" approach in the hope of negotiating directly with the federal government for adjustments to the decrees – an expectation which, in Rio Grande do Sul, proved illusory.

Works Cited

A chegada do diretor geral dos fascios italianos no exterior. 1931, December 16. *Correio do Povo*, p. 7.

A reorganização radical das Escolas Italianas. 1933, March 1. *A Federação*, p. 4.

A visita do secretário da Educação aos colégios Dante Alighieri e Rosa Maltoni. 1936, August 1. *Jornal da Manhã.*

As escolas ítalo-brasileiras em Porto Alegre. Origem, organização, atividade. 1936, September 17. *La Voce d'Italia.*

Ascenzi, A., Barausse, A., Luchese, T. Â., & Sani, R. 2019. History of education and migrations: crossed (or connected or entangled) histories between local and transnational perspective. A research "agenda". *History of Education & Children's Literature, XIV*(2), pp. 227-262.

Barausse, A. 2017. Le scuole italiane nel Rio Grande do Sul attraverso le carte consolari tra la fine dell'Impero e l'inizio della Repubblica (1875-1893. In A. De Ruggiero, V. B. Heredia , A. Barausse, A. De Ruggiero, V. B. Herédia, & A. Barausse (Eds.), *História e narrativas transculturais entre a Europa Mediterrânea e a América Latina* (Vol. 1, p. 195;248). Porto Alegre: Edipucrs.

_______. 2019. As fontes para uma história das práticas educativas nas escolas italianas no Rio Grande do Sul (Brasil): da colonização ao período varguista. *Linhas, 20*(44), 126-153.

_______. 2022. "Esportare la lingua e la cultura del Belpaese". Le scuole italiane all'estero dall'Unità ai primi anni del fascismo (1861-1925). *History of Education & Children's Literature, XVII*(2), 89-143.

_______. 2022. Innovazione didattica e promozione dell'identità nazionale nelle scuole italiane del Rio Grande do Sul/Brasile negli anni della grande colonizzazione (1875-1901. In A. Ascenzi, & R. Sani (Eds.), *L'innovazione pedagogica e didattica nel sistema formativo italiano dall'Unità al secondo dopoguerra* (pp. 79-135. Roma: Edizioni Studium.

_______. 2022. Processi di scolarizzazione etnica italiana nei contesti migratori in Brasile: un primo bilancio storiografico tra dimensione locale e trans-nazionale della ricerca. In R. Radunz, & V. B. Herédia Merlotti, *Imigração e emigração* (pp. 133-184. Caxias do Sul: Educs.

Barausse, A., & Luchese, T. Â. 2017. Nationalisms and schooling: between italianity and brazility, disputes in the education of italian-gaucho people (RS, Brazil, 1930-1945. *History of Education & Children's Literature, XII*(2), 443-475.

_______. 2018. Uma história da educação dos (i)migrantes italianos entre o local e o transnacional: entrecruzando documentos e olhares investigativos. In A. Karsburg, & M. Vendrame (Eds.), *Variações da micro-história no Brasil: temas, abordagens e desafios* (pp. 171-203). São Leopoldo: Oikos Editora, E-book,.

Bertonha, J. F. 2001. Emigrazione e politica estera: la diplomazia sovversiva di Mussolini e la questione degli italiani all'estero 1921-1945, *Altreitalie*, 23, 2001, pp. 39-60. *Altreitalie*(23), 39-60.

_______. 2001, *O fascism e os imigrantes italianos no Brasil.* Porto Alegre: EdiPUCRS.

Câmara Bastos, M. H., & Tambara, E. A. 2014. A nacionalização do ensino e a renovação educacional no Rio Grande do Sul. In Quadros, *Uma gota amarga: itinerários da nacionalização do ensino no Brasil.* Santa Maria, RS: EduFSM.

Cantalupo. 1934. *Telegram by the royal Ambassador Cantalupo of February 6, 1934.*

Castro Brião de, R., & Barausse, A. 2020. "Una società senza scuola è un corpo senz'anima": As escolas italianas de Pelotas/RS mantida pelas sociedades de mútuo socorro no século XIX. *História da Educação, 24*. doi:DOI: http://dx.doi.org/10.1590/2236-3459/92488

Corsetti, B. 1998. Controle e ufanismo: a escola publica no Rio Grande do Sul (1888-1930. *Historia da Educação- ASPHE, 2*(4).

Corte, P. 1884. *Le colonie agricole italiane della provincia di Rio Grande del Sud del Brasile all'esposizione nazionale di Torino* . Montevideo: Stamperia a vapore della "Nacion".

Costantino de, N. S. 2009. A construção da identidade no Brasil Meridional:i talianos na capital do Rio Grande do Sul. *Revista Cordis*(2), 1-14.

Crocetta, B. 1934, Januari 27. Per una questione morale. Le vicissitudini della Dante Alighieri culminate con l'atto violento e arbitrario del 23 luglio 1933. *La Verità*, p. 1.

Dal Molin, C. 2005. *Mordaça verde amarela: imigrantes e descendentes no Estado Novo.* Santa Maria: Pallotti.

De Rosa, L. 1987. L'emigrazione italiana in Brasile: un bilancio. In G. Rosoli (Ed.), *Emigrazioni europee e popolo brasiliano* (pp. 153-167). Roma: Centro studi emigrazione.

Duggan, C. 2000. *Creare la nazione. Vita di Francesco Crispi.* Roma-Bari: Laterza.

Floriani, G. 1974. *Scuole italiane all'estero: cento anni di storia.* Roma: Armando.

Frago, A. V. 1998. Por una historia de la cultura escolar: cuestiones, enfoques, fuentes. *Congreso de la Asociaciòn de Historia Contemporànea. Actas ...* (pp. 167-183. Valladolid: Universidad de Valladolid.

Franzina, E. 2014. La storiografia italiana e l'emigrazione in Brasile. In E. Franzina, *La terra ritrovata. Storiografia e memoria della prima imigrazione italiana in Brasile* (pp. 97-124). Genova: Stefano Termanini Editore.

_______. 2022. Um balanço da historiografia da imigração. In R. Radunz, & V. B. Herédia Merlotti, *Imigração e emigração* (pp. 21-48). Caxias do Sul: Educs.

Franzina, E., & Sanfilippo, M. Eds. 2003. *Il fascismo e gli emigrati. La paraboola dei fasci italiani all'estero (1920-1943).* Roma-Bari: Laterza.

G. L. Rech, E. A. 2015. Professor Gino Battocchio e as aulas gratuitas de italiano nos ginásios da capital do RS . In V. H. Merlotti, & R. Radunz, *140 anos da imigração italiana no Rio Grande do Sul.* Caxias do Sul: Educs.

Garzarelli, B. 2002. Fascismo e propaganda all'estero: le origini della Direzione generale per la propaganda (1933-1934). *Studi Storici*(2), 481-482.

Gentile, E. 2002. *Fascismo. Storia e interpretazione.* Roma-Bari: Laterza.

Gertz, R. E. 2005. *O Estado Novo no Rio Grande do Sul, Passo Fundo, UPF, 2005, p. 146.* Passo Fundo: UPF.

Giron Slomp, L., & Herédia Merlotti, V. B. 2007. *História da Imigração Italiana no Rio Grande do Sul.* Porto Alegre: Est Edições.

Giron, S. L. 1994. *As sombras do littorio: o fascismo no Rio Grande do Sul.* Porto Alegre: Parlenda.

Grassi Orsini, F. 1998. Diplomazia e regime, cit., pp. 63-87. In V. Pellegrini, & Pellegrini (Ed.), *Amministrazione centrale e diplomazia italiana (1919-1943): fonti e problemi* (pp. 63-87). Siena: IStituto Poligrafico dello Stato.

Horn Iotti, L. 2001. *Imigração e colonização: legislação de 1747-1915.* Caxias do Sul: UCS.

Il Regio Console Generale d'Italia Comm. Guglielmo Barbarisi lascia Porto Alegre. 1937, April 30. *La Voce d'Italia*, p. 4.

Il Regio Console Generale d'Italia Comm. Guglielmo Barbarisi lascia Porto Alegre. 1937, aprile 30. *La Voce d'Italia*, p. 4.

Julia, D. 1996. Riflessioni sulla recente storiografia dell'educazione in Europa. *Annali di Storia dell'educazione e delle istituzioni scolastiche*(3), 119-147.

Knox, B. M. 1982. Parini Piero , pp. 393-394. In P. V. Cannistraro, *Historical Dictionary of Fascist Italy* (pp. 393-394). Greenwood Press.

Kreutz, L. A. 2003. A educação dos imigrantes no Brasil. In E. M. Lopes, & L. M. Faria de Filho, *500 anos de educação no Brasil* (pp. 347-370). Belo Horizonte, MG: Autêntica.

L'inaugurazione della sede della nuova scuola italiana in Caxias. 1936, August 27. *La Voce d'Italia*, p. 3.

La Rovere, L. 2002. "Rifare gli italiani": l'esperienza di creazione dell'uomo nuovo nel regime fascista. *Annali di Storia dell'educazione e delle istituzioni scolastiche*(9), 51-58.

Le Associazioni. 2000. In *Cinquantenario della colonizzazione italiana nel Rio Grande del Sud* (pp. 364-397). Porto Alegre: Posenato Arte e Cultura.

Le colonie brasiliane Conte d'Eu e Donna Isabella. Rapporto dell'Avv. Enrico Perrod R. Console a Porto Alegre. 1883, vol. XIX, Parte I,). *Bollettino Consolare*, pp. 277-320.

Le Società Italiane di Porto Alegre hanno destituito della dignità di Console il comm. Mario Carli. 1934, February 24. *La Verità*, p. 1.

Levra, U. 1992. *Fare gli italiani. Memoria e celebrazione del Risorgimento.* Torino: Comitato di Torino dell'Istituto per la storia del Risorgimento italiano.

Luchese, T. A. 2014. *Historia da escola dos imigrantes italianos em terras brasileira.* T. Â. Luchese, Ed.) Caxias do Sul: Educs.

Luchese, T. Â. 2015. *O processo escolar entre imigrantes no Rio Grande do Sul.* Caxias do Sul: Educs.

Luchese, T. Â., & Kreutz, L. 2010. Educação e etnia: as efemeras escolas étnico;comunitarias italianas pelo olhar dos consules e agentes consulares. *História da Educação, 14*(30), 227-258.

Maestri, M. 2010. *Breve História do Rio Grande do Sul da pré-história aos dias atuais.* Passo Fundo: EdUPF.

Ministero Affari, E. 1889. *Annuario delle scuole coloniali per l'anno finanziario 1888-1889.* Roma: Tipografia di Gabinetto del Ministero degli Affari Esteri.

Ministero Affari, E. 1890. *Annuario delle Scuole coloniali per l'anno finanziario e scolastico 1889-1890.* Roma: Tipografia delle Mantellate.

Ministero degli Affari Esteri. 1880. *Relazione al Parlamento sulle scuole italiane all'estero.* Roma.

Pagani , M. F. 2005. *O nacionalismo.* Caxias do Sul: Maneco.

Parini, P. 1935. *Gli Italiani nel mondo.* Milano: Mondadori.

Perrod, E. 1883, March. Le colonie brasiliane Conte D'Eu e Donna Isabella. Rapporto dell'avv. Enrico Perrod. *Bollettino Consolare, 19*, 297-300.

Pesavento, S. J. 1980. *Història do Rio Grande do Sul.* Porto Alegre: Mercado Aberto.

Pretelli, M. 2010. *Il fascismo e gli italiani all'estero.* Bologna: Clued.

Quadros, C. 2014. O discurso que produz a reforma: nacionalização do ensino, aparelhamento do Estado e reforma educacional no Rio Grande do Sul (1937 - 1945. In Q. org.), *Uma gota amarga : itinerários da nacionalização do ensino no Brasil,* (pp. 191-231). Santa Maria, RS: EdUFSM.

Rapporto del R. Console cav.avv. Edoardo dei conti Compans de Brichanteau (25 marzo 1892). 1893. In M. d. Esteri, *Emigrazione e Colonie. Rapporti di RR. Agenti Diplomatici e Consolari pubblicati dal R. Ministero degli Affari Esteri* (pp. 122-123). Roma,: Tipografia Nazionale di G. Bertero.

Rech, L. G., & Barausse, A. 2019. Schooling of Italian immigrants in Porto Alegre/RS (1928-1938). *History of Education & Children's Literature, XIV*(2), 527-557.

Rosoli, G. 1987. Le relazioni tra Italia e Brasile e la questione dell emigrazione (1889;1896). In G. Rosoli, *Emigrazioni europee e popolo brasiliano. Atti del Congresso Euro Brasiliano sulle migrazioni (1985: São Paulo).* Roma: Centro Studi Emigrazione.

Rosoli, G. 1993. G. Rosoli, L'emigrazione italiana nel Rio Grande do Sul, Brasile meridionale 105-122. *Altreitalie, 10*(2), 105-122.

Sani, R. 2011. *Sub specie educationis. Studi e ricerche su istruzione, istituzioni scolastiche e processi culturali e formativi nell'Italia contemporanea.* Macerata: EUM.
Trento, A. 1989. *Do Outro lado do Atlantico: um século de imigração italiana no Brasil.* São Paulo: Nobel.

Archival Sources

Carignani. 1938. [Educational program for the 2nd elementary class of the Umberto I School of the teacher Ada Carignani April 25, 1938. In Archivio Storico diplomatico del Ministero degli Affari Esteri [henceforth ASMAE], Archivio Scuole [henceforth AS], AS 1936-1945, busta [b.] 62, fascicolo [f.] Porto Alegre].
Circular n. 392 of 20 February 1894 to the Consular Agents, to the agents of the Official Consulate of Italy and to the Italian teachers in the State of Rio Grande do Sul. In ASMAE, AS, 1889-1910, busta [b.] 343.
Promemory. 1923. [Promemory for His Excellency the Sub Secretary of Italian State. Italian school in America, February10, 1923. In ASMAE, AS 1923-1928, b. 702, f. Studi per riforme ordinamento Scuole italiane nel Levante e in America].
Promemory. 1924. [Pro-Memory for His Excellency the Ambassador General Badoglio, Cultural Schooling Program for the States of South America (with specific attention to Brazil), February 1st, 1924. In ASMAE, AS 1923-28].
Prospect. 1938. [Prospect of students and teachers on April 20, 1938. In ASMAE, AS 1936-1945, b. 63, f. *Porto Alegre 1936-1937*]
Report of Alemanni. 1923). [Report of Alemanni, V. 1923. In ASMAE, AS 1923-1928, b. 702, f. Studi per riforme ordinamento Scuole italiane nel Levante e in America]
Report Corte. 1884. Report of Consul Corte, P. July 15. In ASMAE, AS 1868-1888, b. 218 P-S, f. Porto Alegre.
Report Marefoschi. 1889. [Report of Consul Marefoschi, M., July 26, Archivio Storico Diplomatico del Ministero degli Affari Esteri ASMAE, AS CAT III B 1889-1910, b. 339, f. 5 183/55
Report Acton. 1890. [Report of Vice-Consul Acton, E. May 1890. In ASMAE, AS, CAT.III B, 1889-1910, b. 339, f. *183/55*]
Report Brichanteau. 1891. [Report of Consul Brichanteau, E.C. In ASMAE, AS, CAT.III B, 1889-1910, b. 339, f. 183/55]
Report Pio di Savoia. 1894. [Report of Consul Pio di Savoia, R. February 18, 1894. In ASMAE, AS, CAT.III B, 1889-1910, b. 339 Carte sciolte].

Report Legrenzi. 1894. [Report of Consul Legrenzi August 8, 1894. In ASMAE, AS, CAT.III B, 1889-1910, b. 339 Carte sciolte].

Report Legrenzi. 1895. Report of Consul Legrenzi, A. January 1895. In ASMAE, AS, CAT.III B, 1889-1910, b. 339 Carte sciolte.

Report Brandolini Dell'Aste. 1898. [Report of Consul Dall'Aste Brandolini. April, 29 1898. In ASMAE, AS, CAT III 1889-1910, B, b. 343, f. Rio Grande do Sul]

Report De Velutiis. 1906. [Report of Consul De Velutiis, F. May 6, 1906. In ASMAE, AS, 1889-1910, b. 343, f. Rio Grande do Sul].

Report Petrocchi. 1909. [Report of Consular agent Petrocchi, L., January 15, 1909. In ASMAE, AS, 1889-1910, b. 343, f. Rio Grande do Sul].

Report Ancarani. 1909. [Report of Consular Agent Ancarani, U. January 10, 1909. In ASMAE, AS, 1889-1910, b. 343, f. Rio Grande do Sul].

Report Della Ragione. 1909. [Report of Consular Agent Della Ragione, G. January 10, 1909. In ASMAE, AS, 1889-1910, b. 343, f. Rio Grande do Sul].

Report Bompard, C. 1925. November 18. In ASMAE, AS, 1923-28, b. *637,* f. Porto Alegre.

Report Arduini. 1925. [Report of Consul Arduini, L. September 1925. In ASMAE, AS 1923-28, b. *637].*

Report Chiostri (1930. [Report of Consul Chiostri, L., January, 7 1930. In ASMAE, AS 1929-1935, b. 785, f. *Parte Generale.*]

Report Carli. 1932. [Report of consul Carli, M. October 4, 1932. In ASMAE, AS 1929-1935, b. 785, f. Porto Alegre, sf. Scuole italiane].

Report Carli. 1933. [Report of Consul Carli, M. May, 20. In ASMAE, AS 1929-1935, b. 785, f. Porto Alegre 1934-35].

Report Ledda. 1933. [Report of Director Ledda, L. Telespresso of May 20, 1933 *Sistemazione scolastica Porto Alegre.* In ASMAE, AS 1929-1935, b.785, f. Porto Alegre 1934-35, sf. Scuole italiane].

Report DGSIE. 1921. [Report of General Direction of Italian School Abroad s.d. [but from 1921]. In ASMAE, AS 1888-1920, b. *437*].

Report Ledda. 1935. [Quarterly report of Ledda, L. June, 8, 1935. In ASMAE, AS 1929-1935, b. 785, f. Porto Alegre].

Report Barbarisi. 1936. [Report of Consul Barbarisi, August 10, 1936. In ASMAE, AS 1936-1945, b.63, f. Porto Alegre 1936-37]

Report Coelho de Souza. 1939. [Report presented to Ex. Sr. Dr. J. P. Coelho de Souza, D. D. Secretary of Education and Public Health by the director of the administrative section, in charge of services related to the nationalization

of education 1939. Public Instruction - Maço 17 - caixa 8, Arquivo Histórico do Rio Grande do Sul (henceforth AHRGS)].
Report Berlingeri. 1938. [Report of Didactic Director Berlingeri M. on the situation of the schools on April 20, 1938. In ASMAE, AS 1936-1945, b. 62, f. *Porto Alegre 1938*].

Tra incubo e nostalgia: immaginario eco-centrico e transculturazione nella poesia di John Ciardi

Sabrina Vellucci
UNIVERSITÀ DEGLI STUDI ROMA TRE

Abstract: Nella letteratura italiano/americana degli ultimi decenni del ventesimo secolo l'evoluzione delle rappresentazioni dell'ambiente, sia naturale che urbano, testimonia una costante attenzione per questioni quali l'ingiustizia ambientale, l'inquinamento delle risorse, la devastazione degli ecosistemi. Contraddicendo il pregiudizio che vede questa cultura distante da preoccupazioni ecologiste, alcuni componimenti di John Ciardi mostrano come il retaggio diasporico abbia contribuito a forgiare diverse modalità di relazione e nuove forme espressive a contatto con il territorio americano. Nello scambio tra i diversi mondi dell'esperienza (im)migratoria, ovvero nel processo di transculturazione fra il contesto rurale italiano e quello urbano statunitense, il concetto di eco-nostalgia (Hopkins 2020) e l'estetica immanentista del numinoso (Lioi 2009) mettono in crisi il modello dell'American Dream prospettando l'attivazione di risorse culturali inedite, in continuità con l'altro dall'umano.

Nella letteratura di autrici e autori statunitensi di origine italiana degli ultimi decenni del ventesimo secolo l'evoluzione delle rappresentazioni dell'ambiente, sia naturale che urbano, testimonia una costante attenzione per questioni quali l'ingiustizia ambientale, l'inquinamento delle risorse, la devastazione degli ecosistemi.[1] Tale diffuso interesse indica l'opportunità di colmare una lacuna nel discorso teorico-critico intorno a questa letteratura, che pure negli ultimi anni si è molto animato sulle due sponde dell'oceano, ovvero finalmente anche in Italia.

D'altra parte, la convinzione che le tematiche ecologiste fossero distanti dalla cultura italiana americana sembra essere stata piuttosto radicata. Ne è testimonianza l'introduzione a un numero speciale della *Environmental Review* dedicato alla storia ambientalista degli Indiani d'America. Nel suo breve prologo, lo storico Richard White osservava che molti lavori scientifici sui Nativi Americani e l'ambiente esistono perché

[1] Si vedano, ad esempio, le poesie di Diane di Prima (in particolare quelle raccolte in *Loba* e *Revolutionary Letters*), le poesie e i saggi della compianta Lucia Perillo, la raccolta *Waging Beauty as the Polar Bear Dreams of Ice* di Daniela Gioseffi; il memoir di Susanne Antonetta, *Body Toxic*, e quello di Louise DeSalvo, *Breathless: An Asthma Journal*; i romanzi di Denise Giardina, ambientati nella regione mineraria del West Virginia, e naturalmente, *Underworld*, il romanzo capolavoro di Don DeLillo che fa del concetto di "waste," elevato a oggetto di riflessione filosofica, il fulcro della narrazione.

nella cultura popolare i Nativi sono divenuti sinonimo di "ecologia." Senza questo legame, scriveva White, "a journal issue on Indians and the environment would be no more likely than one on Italian-Americans [*sic*] in nature or Chinese-American environmental thought" (White, 101).

Il paradosso enunciato da questo studioso chiarisce che, nell'immaginario collettivo della metà degli anni Ottanta, gli italiani americani e la "natura" (qualunque fosse il significato attribuito alla parola) erano due entità pressoché inconciliabili. Una tale generalizzazione si basava probabilmente sul fatto che la maggior parte degli americani di origine italiana risiedeva (e tutt'oggi risiede) in aree urbane, e sul fatto che i quartieri etnici delle grandi città – le ormai leggendarie "Little Italy" – hanno avuto un ruolo fondamentale nella costruzione sociale dell'identità italiano/americana. Tuttavia, a partire dagli anni Novanta, il concetto di ambiente è stato riformulato per includere i luoghi in cui gli esseri umani abitano e nei quali svolgono attività quotidiane. L'ambiente non è più, quindi, inteso solo come il territorio geofisico, ma anche come il paesaggio costruito delle città, dove risiede più dell'80% della popolazione statunitense. Inoltre, già negli anni Ottanta, gli attivisti per la giustizia ambientale hanno iniziato a richiamare l'attenzione su come l'impatto dell'inquinamento delle risorse e della devastazione degli ecosistemi sia direttamente proporzionale alle disuguaglianze di classe, razziali ed etniche.[2]

Inoltre, come osserva Anthony Lioi (141), per gli immigrati provenienti soprattutto dall'Europa del Sud e dell'Est, giunti sul continente americano a cavallo tra la fine del diciannovesimo e l'inizio del ventesimo secolo, la partecipazione alla storia razzializzata del Manifest Destiny e della cosiddetta "Nature's Nation"[3] rimane una questione aperta. È opportuno, perciò, domandarsi se e in che modo l'ambiente della diaspora – lo scambio tra vecchi e nuovi mondi dell'immigrazione – abbia dato vita a una nuova poiesi culturale; ovvero interrogarsi sulle differenze generate dal retaggio italiano nell'opera di poeti e narratori

---

[2] Ho trattato questi temi, anche in relazione alla poesia di John Ciardi, in maniera più estesa nel volume *Italian American Poetics of Place* (Vellucci 2024).

[3] La definizione è stata coniata da Perry Miller nel suo *Nature's Nation* (Cambridge, MA: The Belknap Press, 1967).

che hanno conosciuto gli Stati Uniti come ambiente diasporico. Quali sono gli effetti di tale eredità nell'incontro con le presenze non-umane o altre dall'umano sul suolo americano? E, soprattutto, in che modo tali incontri hanno plasmato o riformato l'idea di "America" – il Sogno Americano – nelle opere di questi autori e autrici?

Nella poesia *Mystic River* di John Ciardi, l'incontro con ciò che Lioi designa con il termine latino "numina" – gli spiriti del luogo, espressioni della potenza o della volontà divina della natura – determina un'estetica teofanica e immanente, distinta dalla tradizione angloamericana di scrittori e poeti quali Ralph Waldo Emerson, Emily Dickinson e T.S. Eliot. La voce poetica in questo caso nasce dall'incontro con una creatura che, in quanto incarnazione del divino, determina un radicamento dell'io lirico *nel* luogo e la rigenerazione della cultura – ossia la formazione di una nuova origine o di un'origine alternativa a partire dalla cultura negata di quel mondo contadino che non aveva trovato dimora né in Italia né negli Stati Uniti.

Pubblicata sul *New Yorker* il 22 aprile 1950, e inclusa nella raccolta *As If* (1955), *Mystic River* stigmatizza l'avversione puritana per i numi del Nuovo Mondo attraverso la partecipazione dell'io lirico agli spiriti del luogo, ovvero rappresenta la rivalsa dell'immigrato non bianco sul senso di supremazia morale della cultura WASP – un'eco della concezione puritana degli eletti – che qui è posta di fronte al fallimento materiale e spirituale della propria civiltà. La poesia è divisa in tre parti. La prima, composta da cinque strofe di sei versi con schema rimico ABABCC, introduce il fiume contaminato dalla devastazione ambientale della "civiltà di limo e acque nere" iniziata dai puritani, "gli esploratori religiosi" che lo avevano nominano "Mysticke" con inconsapevole ironia.

> The dirty river by religious explorers
> Named Mysticke and recorded forever into its future
> Civilization of silt and sewerage, recovers
> The first sweet moon of time tonight. A tremor
> More thought than breeze, more exhalation than motion
> Stirs the gold water totem, Snake of the Moon. (Ciardi 1975, 32)

L'ironia è rafforzata dalla modalità in cui si compie l'esperienza della rivelazione a cui il nome del fiume allude, che qui non si manifesta in un astratto mondo ultraterreno, ma appare come il concreto riscatto del fiume sul disastro causato dai colonizzatori, annunciato già nell'enjambement del terzo e quarto verso della prima strofa con il recupero della "prima dolce luna," e dell'io lirico che con esso si identifica. Persino l'uso dell'aggettivo 'sweet' può essere letto come parte della critica dell'autore ai valori estetici della cultura protestante anglosassone. Come osserva Lioi, in una nota alla sua traduzione del *Paradiso*, Ciardi avrebbe deplorato la scelta dei precedenti traduttori dell'opera dantesca che avevano reso gli aggettivi 'dolce' e 'amaro' con 'buono' e 'cattivo': "This is a disservice because it replaces sensory adjectives with moralistic terms that suggest an alienation from the senses that is anathema to Dante's poetics" (Lioi, 145-146).

Nella seconda strofa il fiume è descritto attraverso la voce (e la lingua) dei primi coloni come piacevole, dolce/mite, salubre, pescoso e navigabile:

> "A most pleasynge gentle and salubrious river
> Wherein lieth no hindraunce of rock nor shoal
> To the distresse of nauvigation, but ever
> Aboundaunce of landynge and of fisherie, and withal
> Distillynge so sweet an air thorough its course
> Sith it runneth salt from the sea, fresh from the source (Ciardi 1975, 32)

Eppure, tanta abbondanza sarà distrutta ("But what the Gods will have they first destroy") e nella quarta strofa si torna al presente in cui "la luna danza sull'acqua contaminata," i pesci sono fuggiti e, come nella *Waste Land* eliotiana,[4] gli dèi sono morti:

> Still Mystic lights the wake of Gods—the moon
> Dances on pollution, the fish are fled
> Into a finer instinct of revulsion
> Than Gods had. And the Gods are dead,

---

[4] Si vedano i riferimenti alle terre non più fertili del Re Pescatore e all'inquinamento del fiume Tamigi nella terza sezione, "The Fire Sermon" (vv. 173-195) (Eliot 2001, 11). T.S. Eliot è tra gli autori anglofoni riconosciuti da Ciardi come modelli, insieme a William Butler Yeats, Stephen Spender e Archibald MacLeish.

Their sloops and river rotted, and their bones
That scrubbed old conscience down like holystones (Ciardi 1975, 32)

Nella loro terra antica, ancora illuminata dal fiume, non cresce più nulla, solo un campo di pattinaggio e il chiosco degli hot dog. La morte degli dèi equivale a un suicidio ecologico causato dal tradimento del fiume e dall'indifferenza verso la sua implorazione, come leggiamo negli ultimi versi della quinta strofa:

Powdered imperceptibly. Their land
Is an old land where nothing's planted
Beside the rollerdrome and hot dog stand –
Still Mystic lights the wake of Gods, still haunted
By the reversing moon. "Let me be clean,"
It cries and cries, but there are years between. (Ciardi 1975, 33)

Nella seconda parte, sono descritte le conseguenze della devastazione che colpisce anche gli abitanti della zona. L'io lirico racconta la propria esperienza del fiume durante l'infanzia a Medford, nel Massachusetts, lo stesso luogo in cui John Winthrop aveva costruito un approdo, come si legge nel terzo verso. A questo illustre padre fondatore della Massachussetts Bay Colony si deve la definizione della colonia puritana come "City upon a Hill,"[5] che in seguito avrebbe designato la città di Boston e, successivamente, sarebbe stata fatta propria dalla retorica dell'eccezionalismo americano arrivando a indicare per estensione tutti gli Stati Uniti.

A Medford, a sei miglia da Boston, all'epoca un sobborgo ai margini della campagna, la famiglia Ciardi si era stabilita nel 1919 a seguito della morte del padre in un incidente d'auto. Dalla Little Italy del North End, la madre, le tre figlie e il più piccolo, John, che all'epoca aveva tre anni, si trasferiscono in un quartiere operaio di etnia mista (in una proprietà che il padre e lo zio avevano acquistato al numero 84 di South Street, affacciata sul fiume Mystic). Il luogo assomigliava più al paesaggio rurale italiano delle origini della madre che alle strade del North End. All'inizio degli anni Venti, Medford era, nei ricordi di Ciardi, "una

[5] L'immagine è tratta dal "Discorso della montagna," nel *Vangelo secondo Matteo* 5,1-7,29.

città semi-rurale frondosa, melliflua e tentacolare" (Cifelli 11). Come nota John Paul Russo (453), "una delle ragioni per cui Ciardi scrive così spesso di natura e immanenza dello spirito può risiedere nel fatto che, durante l'infanzia, il cortile della sua casa si apriva sulla campagna e sul fiume Mystic che lo attraversava." L'autore ricorda di aver nuotato nel fiume, che arrivava da un estuario sul Charles e percorreva circa sette miglia fino a Mystic Lakes, ed era un corso d'acqua "così pulito da poterci bere" (Cifelli 11). Per tutto il decennio 1920, dalle vecchie chiatte abbandonate su cui era solito giocare, il giovane John osservò i costruttori ammassare le case l'una accanto all'altra e l'inquinamento del fiume diventare un problema:

> Most of the town became crowded, ugly. By 1930 the red flags of foreclosure were nailed up on house after house—a squalid time. And the river had gone dirty, not quite an open sewer, but too dirty to use. It even stopped freezing over in the winter; I don't know why. It had been a festive rink through all of my first winters in the twenties, and then even the ice stopped forming. [...] I often think that in an earlier age, I might have felt about that river as Thoreau felt about his pond and his canoe ways. It made me feel, among other things, that most of the good things were long ago. (Cit. in Clemente 216)

Cifelli (11) nota che "nella sua immaginazione egli collegò la morìa dei pesci del fiume alla scomparsa del padre, un'associazione che si insinuò, a suo dire, in molte poesie degli anni successivi."

Il contrasto tra il sogno rappresentato dalla Città sulla Collina e la realtà brutale delle morti causate da violenza, malattia e povertà descritte nelle tre strofe della seconda parte di *Mystic River* non potrebbe essere più stridente:

> And I have stoned and swum and sculled them all[6]:
> Naked behind the birches at the cove

---

[6] Il verso riecheggia "And I have known the eyes already, known them all— [...] And I have known the arms already, known them all—" (Eliot 1917, 12) in *The Love Song of J. Alfred Prufrock*, un'altra nota poesia di Eliot, imperniata sull'incapacità del protagonista di interagire con il proprio ambiente. Il riferimento a un componimento canonico del modernismo angloamericano sembra suggerire, come osserva Lioi (146), che i discendenti di quella civiltà dovrebbero riconoscere e assumere su di sé la responsabilità della loro cultura nel disastro ambientale del Nuovo Mondo.

Where Winthrop built a landing and a yawl
And tabloids found a famous corpse of love
Hacked small and parceled into butcher's paper,
Joe La Conti stumbled on an old pauper

Dying of epilepsy or DT's,
And I came running naked to watch the fit.
We had to dress to run for the police.
But did we run for help or the joy of it?[7]
And who was dying at the sight of blood?
Weeks long we conjured its traces in the mud

And there was no trace. Later above the cat-tails
A house frame grew, and another, and then another.
Our naked bank bled broken tiles and nails.
We made a raft and watched the alewife smother.
But there our play drank fever, and Willie Crosby
Went home from that dirty water and stayed to die. (Ciardi 1975, 33)

Il fiume stesso diventa un macabro scenario di morte: sulla sua sponda un senzatetto si spegne a causa del delirium tremens; i pesci soffocano per via dell'edificazione scriteriata, a seguito della quale la "riva nuda sanguinava piastrelle rotte e chiodi" – un'immagine in cui la personificazione del fiume, annullando la distinzione tra umano e non-umano, trasmette efficacemente l'entità della devastazione. Infine, il poeta ricorda il suo compagno di giochi, Willie Cosby, morto a seguito dell'ingestione dell'acqua inquinata del fiume.[8]

La terza e ultima parte costruisce un'esperienza numinosa in cui il protagonista si unisce al fiume e alle sue creature per superare il mortifero retaggio puritano e raggiungere uno stato di illuminazione:

---

[7] In *Lives of X* (1971), Ciardi descriverà una trafficata arteria cittadina che scorreva parallelamente al fiume, la Mystic Valley Parkway. All'incrocio tra questa e Winthrop Street si verificavano spesso incidenti, al punto che il giovane Ciardi, "curious to see spilled blood, could run from his house at the sound of a crash. Usually he could beat the ambulance to the scene" (Kennedy 26).

[8] La voce poetica fa riferimento a un evento traumatico realmente accaduto durante l'infanzia dell'autore, il quale proverà anche in seguito, nel componimento "Two Saints" (*Lives of X*), a elaborare la perdita del suo amico.

So I know death is a dirty river
At the edge of history, through the middle of towns,
At the backs of stores, and under the cantilever
Stations of bridges where the moon drowns
Pollution in its own illusion of light.
Oh rotten time, rot from my mind tonight!

Let me be lit to the bone in this one stir,
And where the Gods grew rich and positive
From their ruinous landing, I'll attend disaster
Like night birds over a wake, dark and alive
Above the shuttered house, and, bound and free,
Wheel on the wing, find food in flight, and be

Captured by light, drawn down and down and down
By moonshine, streetlamps, windows, moving rays.
By all that shines in all the caved-in town
Where Mystic in the crazy moon outstays
The death of Gods, and makes a life of light
That breaks, but calls a million birds to flight. (Ciardi 1975, 34)

L'incontro con le presenze divine dell'acqua e degli animali del luogo si fonda sulla storia e sulla dialettica di un figlio di immigrati, che, come il fiume, corre "ai margini della storia, attraverso il centro delle città, / sul retro dei negozi e sotto gli sbalzi / dei ponti." Nel clima intellettuale presieduto dai bramini di Boston, in cui la cultura d'origine del poeta è vista come degenerata e malata,[9] l'alleanza dell'io lirico con il mondo altro dall'umano e l'adozione del punto di vista di quest'ultimo appare il tentativo di combattere la violenza della cultura di matrice anglosassone con la forza della natura e delle culture preesistenti all'"approdo rovinoso" degli dèi bianchi europei. L'identificazione con le creature naturali e con gli spiriti del luogo suggerisce che la divisione tra natura e storia/cultura, caratteristica del canone della letteratura ambientalista statunitense del primo periodo, non è più sostenibile. La

[9] La retorica di molta letteratura riformista degli ultimi decenni dell'Ottocento (ne è un esempio il noto *How the Other Half Lives: Studies among the Tenements of New York* [1890] di Jacob A. Riis) dipingeva gli italiani come i più degenerati tra i nuovi arrivati europei: "Often illiterate, considered not-quite-white and accepting of the lowest standards, they were seen as passive subjects, unable and unwilling to change the environmental conditions surrounding them" (Morello & Culhane).

sofferenza della natura coincide con la sofferenza della cultura. Il vecchio, il ragazzo, i pesci e il fiume sono collegati. La luce della luna, che riesce a neutralizzare l'inquinamento, è tutt'uno con quella proveniente dai lampioni e dalle finestre della cittadina in rovina. Il protagonista stesso ne è illuminato "fino al midollo," mentre, in quanto parte di "questa mescolanza," si identifica con gli uccelli notturni, scuri e vitali, che trovano cibo attraverso il volo, attirati dalle luci e dal fiume. Sopravvissuto alla morte degli dèi, il Mystic fa di questa luce una vita che, pur ardua (o folle, come la luna del terz'ultimo verso), richiama in volo un milione di uccelli – un'immagine evocativa della storia migratoria di cui è partecipe l'io lirico.

Non stupisce, perciò, che Ciardi trovasse negli uccelli un soggetto particolarmente congeniale e che a questi abbia dedicato diversi componimenti. In un'intervista dichiarò: "I like to watch birds. I do not miss looking at a bird if I can help it. We sometimes have quite an active bird life in our hemlock thicket outside the breakfast home window" (Cifelli 314).[10] Erano per l'autore poesia in movimento e, al contempo, simboli del poeta stesso. I componimenti dedicati ai volatili sono tra le sue opere migliori in virtù della loro vivacità, dell'attenta osservazione e del senso di meraviglia che li anima. In *As I Would Wish You Birds* (dalla raccolta *In Fact*), Ciardi ha catalogato e tipizzato con l'occhio di un ornitologo una mezza dozzina di specie (gattucci, ghiandaie, colibrì, tacchini, pavoni, struzzi, dodo) prima di concentrare la sua attenzione sul gabbiano, "ultimate bird / everywhere everything pure wing and wind" (Ciardi 1962, 37). Il ritmo serrato dei versi di *Gulls Land and Cease to Be* cattura invece con sguardo cinematografico l'immagine di un gabbiano che plana:

> Spread back across the air, wings wide,
>   Legs out, the wind delicately
> dumped in balance, the gulls ride
>   down, down, hang, and exactly
> touch, folding not quite at once
>   into their gangling weight, but
> taking one step, two, wings still askance,

[10] Si veda anche la poesia "Bird Watching" (Ciardi 1962, 28).

reluctantly, at last, shut,
twitch one look around
and are aground. (Ciardi 1997, 45)

I gabbiani sono protagonisti anche di *Orders*, quindici distici non rimati che si concentrano sul loro essere "stranamente a casa" nell'habitat "impossibile" del deserto, in luoghi come il Grande Lago Salato dello Utah o il Deserto Rosso del Wyoming. L'iniziale angoscia provocata dalla loro vista, mentre seguono gli aratri, "beccando gli animaletti che emergono dalle zolle rivoltate" (Ciardi 1962, 10), porta la voce poetica a osservare che "disfa quasi la natura, il loro essere lì / […] distanti mille miglia dal mare." Finché non vede "il mare sul punto di ritirarsi" e si rende conto che "deve essere il sale a ingannarli." I versi seguono la meditazione, che oscilla tra la repulsione e l'apprezzamento di ciò che la presenza incongrua di queste creature può in definitiva suggerire:

Gulls in Wyoming, Utah, follow the plows,
picking the small jet lives from the turned furrows.

It half unfastens nature, their being there
a mile up and a thousand in from the sea.

[…]

At home where all mind trespasses and prays
And the impossible is a habitat –

[…]

I think they're queerly lost by a right instinct.
Or else they're only waiting, their instinct sound,

to be on hand when the next ocean starts here.
I wish they'd go to sea where they belong

and let the hawks and buzzards have the desert
in their own terms, as if it meant to last.

And then again I'm glad they're queerly home:
their presence teaches possibility

[...]
another range. [...] (Ciardi 1962, 10-11)

Anche la raccolta *In the Stoneworks* (1961) comprende poesie in cui la natura e gli uccelli sono osservati da vicino,[11] come *The Bird in Whatever Name*, incentrata su una varietà che vive in simbiosi con il rinoceronte africano, nutrendosi delle sue larve e dei suoi pidocchi. La poesia è parte di un gruppo di componimenti, tra i quali *Thoughts on Looking into a Thicket*, che celebrano "le manifestazioni più bizzarre del principio di affermazione della vita nella natura" (Cifelli 312).

Nella prefazione all'antologia *Mid-Century American Poets* (1950), Ciardi scrisse che "i periodi d'oro della poesia sono sempre stati quelli in cui il poeta aveva la sensazione di essere saldamente radicato in una tradizione nativa" (Ciardi 1950, ix). Tali affermazioni hanno rafforzato l'idea che egli cercasse le proprie radici nella cultura italiana e riuscisse a fondere questo retaggio con quello della poesia anglo-americana. La tensione, mediata "attraverso l'arte e la cultura rinascimentale," era riflesso di un autore gratificato dal riconoscimento della componente italiana della sua poesia (Russo 2009, 453), pur essendo sempre rimasto ambivalente nei confronti della tradizione italiano/americana. Come nota Russo, Ciardi si stupiva del suo legame con l'America italiana, rispetto alla quale si sentì sempre piuttosto distante. Pur non essendosi mai spinto fino a un vero e proprio rifiuto, egli non si avvicinò neppure a una convinta accettazione, ma rimase in una posizione che potremmo definire interlocutoria per tutta la sua carriera. Tra il 1950 e il 1951, vinse una borsa Fulbright che gli consentì di visitare l'Europa per la prima volta e di trascorrere sei mesi in Italia. Nel 1956-1957 trascorse un anno in Italia, presso l'American Academy, come vincitore del Premio Roma per la poesia: già noto traduttore dell'*Inferno* dantesco, Ciardi stava allora lavorando al *Purgatorio*. Durante questi soggiorni, scrisse poesie ispirate dalla sua esperienza italiana, come quelle che compongono *Fragments from Italy*, una sequenza di otto poesie che si muovono tra la Calabria, il Mar Mediterraneo, Roma e Napoli (Ciardi 1955, 135-

[11] Nel 1959 Ciardi aveva intitolato una raccolta per bambini *The Reason for the Pelican* (recentemente tradotto in italiano da Annalisa Macchia e Luigi Fontanella come *Il perché del pellicano* [Medusa Edizioni, 2024]); nel 1985, intitolerà una delle sue ultime raccolte *The Birds of Pompeii*.

143), e altre, pubblicate in seguito, quali *An Apartment with a View*, *Roman Diary: 1951*, *A Conversation with Leonardo* e *Addio* (Ciardi 1997, 500-501, 502, 431-32, 429). La permanenza a Roma sembra quindi aver spinto Ciardi a riconoscere la sua eredità diasporica e a riconnettersi con la cultura dei suoi avi[12] e con la propria italianità – un risultato notevole per uno scrittore che aveva espresso con forza il suo sentirsi "americano." A questo proposito è significativo un episodio riguardante la recensione di una poesia sull'Italia e su Mussolini, che Ciardi aveva pubblicato sull'*Atlantic Monthly*. In quell'occasione, riporta lo stesso autore, il poeta Robert Lowell riconobbe nel componimento

> the best Italian American poem he had ever seen. And I thought, "Does this son of a bitch think he is more American than I am?" Where does he think I was brought up? Because my name is Ciardi, he decided to hyphenate the poem. Had it been a Yankee name, he would have thought, "Ah, a scholar who knows about Italy." Sure he made assumptions, but I can't grant for a minute that Lowell is anymore American than I am.[13]

Tuttavia, come si è visto in *Mystic River*, la sua adesione alla cultura statunitense non era sempre stata così convinta. Nell'ambiente culturale bostoniano dominato dall'élite dei bramini, in cui il retroterra del poeta figlio di immigranti era disprezzato, l'alleanza con il mondo altro dall'umano – e l'abbracciarne il punto di vista – era un tentativo di contrastare la sopraffazione della cultura statunitense attraverso il potere della natura e delle civiltà che preesistevano al calamitoso sbarco dei bianchi. L'autore sarebbe tornato su questa materia in "The River," una riflessione sul ruolo del fiume Mystic nella tratta degli schiavi, inclusa in *Lives of X*, una raccolta contenente diversi componimenti autobiografici. In questo poema, il fiume "sporco" riappare sotto forma di fantasma, avendo subìto una morte "santificata" (in conseguenza della colonizzazione cristiana) al pari dei suoi primi abitanti e dei loro simboli sacri: "Is there a longer death than rivers die / out of the

---

12 I genitori erano originari di Manocalzati, in provincia di Avellino.

13 Cit. in Linda Caetura, ed., *Growing Up Italian*. New York: Morrow and Co., 1986, 150 (Tamburri, Giordano, Gardaphé 6-7).

sainted valley of their first, / following the mist-blown tribes and their totems" (Ciardi 1971, 19).

Ciardi concepiva quindi il sacro come inscindibilmente radicato nel luogo. Il suo rapporto con il fiume e la città, con i pesci e gli uccelli è spesso immaginato come un viaggio iniziatico, caratterizzato da una crisi, un passaggio in un mondo ultraterreno e un ritorno dopo aver acquisito un potere spirituale. Le immagini di un'Italia "archetipica," ispirata alla cultura del meridione dei suoi genitori, sono influenzate dalla visione di un mondo rurale in cui "tutto era significativo e allo stesso tempo misterioso" (Giordano 305). In questa visione, esisteva un legame segreto tra l'uomo e la natura, caratterizzato da sentimenti di meraviglia, rispetto e timore. Nella poesia "Daemons," l'io lirico respinge le superstizioni esteriori delle quali nella contemporaneità si è perso il significato profondo, avendo dimenticato: "how the soul breathes / from plant, beast, and man, and must / be propitiated" (Ciardi 1966, 11-12). Qui come altrove, l'opera di Ciardi illustra il processo di transculturazione che, in diversi testi canonici della letteratura italiano/americana del ventesimo secolo, ha trasformato un sentimento di "eco-sospetto" in "eco-nostalgia" (Hopkins 116). Tale fenomeno, risultato del passaggio dalla miseria della vita rurale nel Sud Italia all'altrettanto brutale repressione urbana di cui molti emigranti fecero esperienza nei grandi agglomerati degli Stati Uniti, suggerisce una visione in cui "la natura, un tempo spietata, appare ingentilita e sotto controllo, [...] e in cui la prosperità o almeno la stabilità economica è stata finalmente raggiunta" (Hopkins 137).

Durante i suoi viaggi in Italia, Ciardi mostra simpatia per gli abitanti dei piccoli centri del Sud più che per quelli delle grandi città. *S.P.Q.R. A Letter from Rome* esprime rabbia e delusione nel trovare la terra dei genitori esotica e aliena. Sentimenti paragonabili ispirano *Naples*, il ritratto grottesco di un uomo pingue seduto in un caffè bombardato contornato da nuvole di mosche, che gradualmente è identificato con la stessa città – e con l'Europa intera – in rovina: "And all of ruined Europe fell about him. [. . .] When he waved his arm / to brush away the flies / a column fell. When he waved it back / another" (Ciardi 1955, 143). L'Italia sembra attrarre il poeta soprattutto come terra della Grande Madre Mediterranea, incarnata dal ritratto amorevole di Nona Domenica Garnaro, protagonista del primo frammento ambientato in un paesino calabrese (Ciardi 1955, 135). In un componimento successivo, *An Inscription for Richard Eberhart*, Ciardi trova nelle antiche rovine romane e negli scavi di Pompei il punto di partenza per una riflessione sulla propria esistenza, che infine trasforma l'Italia in un'esperienza rigenerante, resa nei termini dell'ambiente vegetale e animale: "I have slept on ruined Rome and wakened green / with the squeal of birds and the power-hum of bees / sealed in the air like amber" (Ciardi 1959, 86).

Nel mostrare i limiti del Sogno americano, le poesie di John Ciardi presentano il retaggio diasporico come elemento capace di forgiare diverse modalità di relazione e nuove forme espressive a contatto con il territorio 'americano.' Prospettano, insomma, l'attivazione di risorse culturali inedite, in continuità con le civiltà native e con elementi che appartengono alla sfera dell'altro dall'umano. In ritardo rispetto ai conflitti del diciannovesimo secolo per la costruzione del Paese e rispetto alla storia razzializzata dell'ambientalismo, l'immaginario eco-centrico italiano/americano che emerge da questi componimenti sembra poter offrire un'origine alternativa da cui iniziare a ricostruire la storia del rapporto tra umani ed ecosistemi del e nel Nord America.

OPERE CITATE

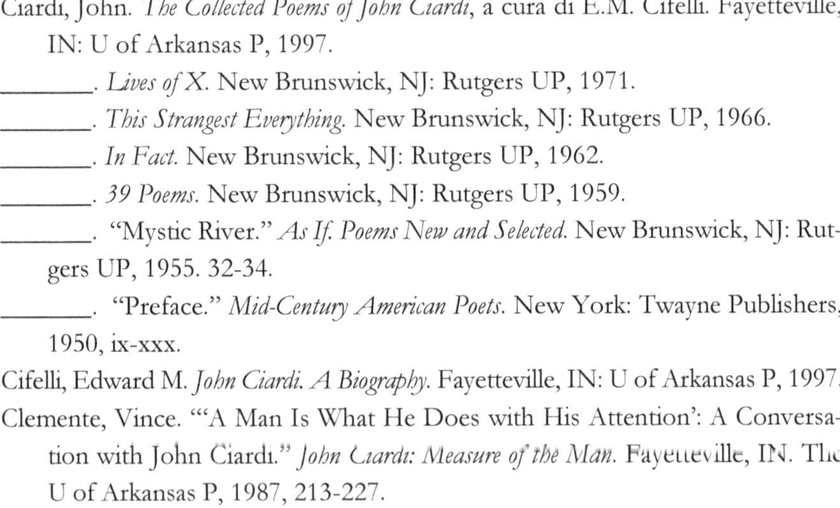

Ciardi, John. *The Collected Poems of John Ciardi*, a cura di E.M. Cifelli. Fayetteville, IN: U of Arkansas P, 1997.

_______. *Lives of X*. New Brunswick, NJ: Rutgers UP, 1971.

_______. *This Strangest Everything*. New Brunswick, NJ: Rutgers UP, 1966.

_______. *In Fact*. New Brunswick, NJ: Rutgers UP, 1962.

_______. *39 Poems*. New Brunswick, NJ: Rutgers UP, 1959.

_______. "Mystic River." *As If. Poems New and Selected*. New Brunswick, NJ: Rutgers UP, 1955. 32-34.

_______. "Preface." *Mid-Century American Poets*. New York: Twayne Publishers, 1950, ix-xxx.

Cifelli, Edward M. *John Ciardi. A Biography*. Fayetteville, IN: U of Arkansas P, 1997.

Clemente, Vince. "'A Man Is What He Does with His Attention': A Conversation with John Ciardi." *John Ciardi: Measure of the Man*. Fayetteville, IN. The U of Arkansas P, 1987, 213-227.

Eliot, T.S. "The Love Song of J. Alfred Prufrock," *Prufrock and Other Observations.* London: The Egoist Ltd, 1917.

_______. *The Waste Land*, a cura di M. North. New York: Norton, 2001.

Giordano, Fedora. "An Archetypal World: Images of Italy in the Poetry of John Ciardi," in Rizzardi A. (a cura di), Atti del Settimo Convegno Nazionale AISNA, "Italy and Italians in America." *RSA. Rivista di Studi Anglo-Americani* 3.4-5 (1984-1985): 305-313.

Hopkins, Sienna. "From Rural *Miseria* to Urban Repression: Environmental Injustice and Eco-Nostalgia in Italian American History and Literature." *Italian American Review* 10.2 (2020): 114–147. https://doi.org/10.5406/italamerrevi.10.2.0114.

Kennedy, X. J. "John Ciardi's Early Lives," in Clemente V. (a cura di), *John Ciardi. Measure of the Man.* Fayetteville: U of Arkansas P, 1987. 24-31.

Lioi, Anthony. "Real Presence: The *Numina* in Italian American Poetry." *MELUS* 34. 2 (Summer 2009): 141-156.

Lipsitz, George. *How Racism Takes Place.* Philadelphia: Temple UP, 2011.

Morello, Stefano & Kerri Culhane. *The Lung Block. Uno slum di New York e la sua comunità di immigrati italiani dimenticati* (27 agosto 2021). https://storymaps.arcgis.com/stories/182aa239f6ff4ad88d8f50c245e1ca80.

Russo, John Paul. "The Nostoi of John Ciardi and Jorie Graham," in Camboni M., De Angelis V.M., Fiorentino D., Petrovich Njegosh T. (a cura di), *USA: Identities, Cultures, and Politics in National, Transnational and Global Perspectives.* Macerata: EUM, 2009. 453-466.

_______. "Where Your Gods Are, There Your Home Is: A Motif in Italian American and Italian Canadian Poetry." *Oltreoceano* 14 (2018): 133-147.

Tamburri, Anthony Julian, Paolo Giordano, and Fred L. Gardaphé (a cura di), *From the Margin. Writings in Italian Americana.* West Lafayette, IN: Purdue UP, 1991/2000.

Vellucci, Sabrina. *Italian American Poetics of Place: An Environmental Perspective.* Lanham, MD: Fairleigh Dickinson UP, 2024

White, Richard. "American Indians and the Environment." *Environmental Review*, 9.2 (Summer, 1985), Special Issue: American Indian Environmental History: 101-103.

Dreams beyond Nostalgia: Louisa Calio's Search for Roots

Elisabetta Marino
UNIVERSITÀ DEGLI STUDI DI ROMA TOR VERGATA

Abstract: Primarily by exploring her poetry collections *In the Eye of Balance* (1978) and *Journey to the Heart Waters* (2014), this essay focuses on the creative output of Louisa Calio, one of the most compelling contemporary American artists of Italian descent. As will be shown, Calio addresses the tension between nostalgia for one's roots and the desire to embrace the American dream – a theme common among authors with an ethnic background – by recognizing universal roots in Africa that have the potential to dissolve differences.

Louisa Calio is a multimedia artist and performer of Italian ancestry, whose poems and narratives have appeared in prestigious anthologies, journals, and collected volumes. Her works have been translated into Italian, Sicilian, Korean, Russian, and Tigrinya. She has often combined poetry and visuals – as in her two exhibitions *A Passion for Africa* (2007) and *A Passion for Jamaica* (2008) – and has received several awards, including the Connecticut Commission of the Arts Award and Grant to Individual Writers, the Barbara Jones and Taliesin Prizes for Poetry (Trinidad & Tobago), and first prize in the 4th *Concorso di Poesia Internazionale – Messina Città d'Arte*. Her profile is included in Barbara Love's seminal *Feminists Who Changed America 1963–1975*, in recognition of her "greatest contribution to feminist spirituality" (Love 2006, 68).[1] By focusing on her creative output – especially her poetry collections *In the Eye of Balance* (1978) and *Journey to the Heart Waters* (2014) – this essay sets out to investigate the artist's inspiring and distinctive interpretation of the dream of belonging, around which so many poems and narratives written by American authors of immigrant descent have developed. As will be shown, far from indulging in the conventional depiction of nostalgia for a lost land of origin and a much-fantasized past, or in the exploration of the struggle toward Americanization featured in many works produced by writers of her generation,

1 Louisa Calio also taught English and Creative Writing and organized intergenerational seminars involving elderly participants and students from diverse backgrounds. She has brought the arts into jails, hospices, public schools, and hospitals. She was the co-founder and first executive director of City Spirit Artists, Inc., and currently serves on the Advisory Board of *Arba Sicula*. From 2002 to 2013, she directed the Poets and Writers Piazza for Hofstra's Italian Experience. She is also a certified Sivananda yoga instructor.

Calio succeeds in moving beyond binary oppositions by nurturing a different dream: one that acknowledges common, universal roots in Africa, the place where humankind is believed to have taken its first steps. By revealing unexpected correspondences and connections, and by unsettling well-established hierarchical perceptions, including those between citizen and immigrant/refugee, man and woman, and humankind and the natural world, Calio cultivates and envisions a more expansive dream: a peaceful world with neither boundaries nor partitions. In her quest – both individual and collective – a crucial role is played by a thorough reassessment of femininity, through the rediscovery of powerful dark mothers.

Stanislao Pugliese has emphasized Calio's unique position, noting "a sensitivity to multiculturalism and ethnic diversity that is sometimes lacking in Italian American culture" (quoted in Amatulli). His view is echoed by Cinzia Marongiu, who argues that, although "proudly anchored to her Italian American roots," the artist "takes a more diverse approach to cultural and literary backgrounds than typical in Italian-American tradition" (Marongiu 2023, 90). In her numerous essays and interviews, Calio herself has expanded on her Sicilian-Neapolitan heritage on her mother's side, and her Sicilian roots on her father's, highlighting two factors that have contributed to shaping the course of her life and career: the welcoming and inclusive environment of her household, and the artistic talent of her "tribe" (Dossena 2020), as she defines her extended family.[2] As a child, she never experienced the cultural dilemma faced by other contemporary Italian American poets, such as Maria Mazziotti Gillan,[3] nor did she feel compelled to adjust her behaviour and linguistic choices depending on whether she was inside or outside the invisible boundaries of her ethnic niche. Born on an auspicious day – July 4 – Calio was raised surrounded by Mickey Mouse, Davy Crockett, and other all-American

[2] Lina Unali underscores the pivotal role played by what she terms "the extended family of parental figures" (Unali 2007, 73), a defining feature in the works of several Italian American writers. As she explains, "the original grid of father-mother elementary relations is enlarged in order to actively embrace all other family relations: grandfather, grandmother, uncle, aunt, sister, brother, even in-laws" (73).

[3] In "Public School No. 18, Paterson, New Jersey," for example, Mazziotti Gillan writes that, at home, her words were "smooth in [her] mouth" (Mazziotti Gillan 2006, 16), while at school she grew silent, fearing that sentences in Italian might "sprout from [her] mouth like a rose" (16). She also conveyed both a sense of shame and an urge to blend in.

icons, while being Italian, for her, was as natural as breathing (Marino 2011, 1). In a 2016 interview with Alok Mishra, she also stressed that, given the multicultural fabric of American society, she grew up "feeling part of many cultures and people [...] a child of the universe" (Mishra 2016). Unquestionably, Calio is fully aware of the ordeals many Italian immigrants had to endure in order to carve out a better life in the Promised Land of opportunities. As she revealed to Tiziano Thomas Dossena, when her maternal grandfather, Rocco Marchesani, began his American venture at the age of 14, he had to leave behind not just his mother country and native language, but also "a language of feeling repressed in order to survive and fit into a foreign culture with a complex history of slavery, Native American abuse, and British roots" (Dossena 2020). Nonetheless, trauma apparently did not travel from his generation to the next. As a child, Calio was encouraged to wholeheartedly embrace a plurality of perspectives and traditions: different dialects from all corners of the peninsula, various social classes, clashing views, and divergent aspirations would meet around her grandmother's kitchen table. Even Catholicism – a staple feature of Italian American subjectivity – merged with the agnosticism and Protestantism adopted by some of her family members[4] (ibid.). Calio likens culture to "a delicious prism" (Mishra 2016), to the clothes one decides to wear: "some we try on and wear a while and others we discard quickly. For some of us, we try on several cultures at once, while others may find one only fits in this life time" (ibid.). It is not surprising, therefore, that multimediality (intimately linked to the ability to capture the nuances and complexities of phenomena), fluidity, and syncretism are hallmark qualities of her work.

Artistic inclinations run in Calio's family; her maternal grandfather, who had a passion for opera, created fine wooden furniture and sculptures, often commissioned by celebrities and prominent figures such as Marilyn Monroe and the Rockefellers. A poet and a musician, her grandmother Luigia worked in the clothing industry, and her son (Calio's father) followed in her footsteps, becoming a fashion designer executive for Ralph Lauren's women's wear after serving in WWII. Her

[4] Calio describes her grandmother as a "a pagan of sorts whose father converted to Protestantism" (Dossena 2020).

aunt Christina was an opera singer, while her mother Rosa was a skilled storyteller, an empowered female figure whose aspirations went beyond the mere tending of the household.

Since her early years, Calio has associated creativity with the capacity to heal traumas and recompose fractures, even harmonizing the "warring parts" (Calio 2015, 33) within herself. To elucidate her theory, she recalls two insightful episodes from her childhood. At five, she won a drawing competition with her first piece of art: a sketch of a boy riding a bicycle. What initially seemed a casual subject turned out to be a memory of a time when, as an infant, she fractured her skull after being hit by a young cyclist: "I now believe this was the way I processed a trauma, transforming a destructive experience into a creative one, as art can do" (Dossena 2020). Some years later, to cope with the abuse perpetrated by a nun, she found solace in the soothing lines of John Donne's "No Man Is an Island" (ibid.), which had a therapeutic effect. Even though no *postmemories*[5] stemming from her cultural background haunted her, Calio always felt different from "the carefree all-American girl, all bubble gum and popcorn" (Calio 2015, 33). Her potent yet initially mysterious attraction to Africa – first felt in her youth[6] – became increasingly clear in the '60s and '70s, during her college and graduate school years: she befriended students of Ethiopian, Sudanese, and Eritrean ancestry, participated in their struggles and protests, identified with "darker others"[7] (Calio 2017), and undertook her first journey to West Africa in 1974, which proved to be an eye-opening experience. As Calio underlined in a 2015 interview, her Italian origin prompted her to

[5] The term *postmemory* was coined by Marianne Hirsch in the context of Holocaust survivors and their legacy of pain, to indicate "the experience of those who grow up dominated by narratives that preceded their birth, whose own belated stories are evacuated by the stories of the previous generation shaped by traumatic events that can be neither understood nor recreated" (Hirsch 1997, 22).

[6] As a child, Calio used to repeatedly draw a large eye, similar to that of Horus; she also performed rituals to the sun (Dossena 2020) and imagined herself as "an Egyptian priestess dancing to Middle Eastern music," while dreaming of "Bedouins in long billowing robes riding across the dunes on Arabian horses" (Calio 2017).

[7] After all, as Stefano Luconi has pointed out, "Italian Americans and African Americans initially shared a mutuality of non-whiteness" (Luconi 2021, 4). The question of Italian American *whiteness* has long stirred heated controversy. As Fred Gardaphé has noted, "For Italian Americans, 'making it' has come with a high price tag. It has cost them the language of their ancestors – the main means by which history is preserved and heritage passed on from one generation to the next. They have had to trade in or hide any customs that have been depicted as quaint, but labelled as alien, to prove equality to those above them on the ladder of success. Italian Americans have become white, but a different kind of white than those of the dominant Anglo-Saxon culture. Italian Americans have become whites on a leash" (Gardaphé 2004, 125).

explore deeper connections, namely those that bind humankind together, in a context where "gli dei sono vivi" (Calio 2015, 2), *gods are alive.*

Inspired by E.A. Wallis Budge's *The Egyptian Book of the Dead* (1895), Calio embarked on a quest that ultimately led to her first poetry collection, *In the Eye of Balance*, which also evolved into a successful traveling performance. In the preface to the volume – complemented by ten paintings and drawings by Terry Lennox – Calio explains that the poems included in the book chronicle her *initiation*, her "conscious understanding of [her]self as a woman, an artist, and an individual with a strong interest and love for foreign cultures and world affairs"[8] (Calio 1978, i). She also encourages readers to seek a balance between intellect and intuition, inviting them to follow her on a path toward "a wonderful renaissance" (ii) – one that enables everyone to determine which aspects of our collective past to retain and which to discard, such as fixed gender roles and stereotypical prerogatives. As Calio emphasized in an interview with Rosa Amatulli, "the feminine is all-inclusive, which means we see ourselves in all others, regardless of gender, race, religion, or class" (Amatulli 2023). In her effort to undermine hierarchies, reconcile opposites, and foster "fluidity and openness" (Calio 1978, ii), the artist invites each person, regardless of sex, to acknowledge the feminine within themselves and to allow it to develop.

In the Eye of Balance is divided into three parts, a number emblematic not only of the Holy Trinity, but also of the synthesis achieved through the dialectical tension between thesis and antithesis. In the opening poem, "Portrait of an Artist as a Young Woman" (a title that clearly strives to complete what Joyce had left unaddressed), Calio sketches the persistent gap between the male artist – who, like Icarus and Daedalus, is entitled to push himself beyond set boundaries, soaring through the skies – and his female counterpart, portrayed as a caged bird. The poet's chosen imagery is reminiscent of a passage from Mary Wollstonecraft's feminist treatise *A Vindication of the Rights of Woman* (1792),[9] in which

[8] In the preface, she also draws the readers' attention to her multicultural education and openness to learning: I studied Jung, Tantra, Taoism and most deeply, the Dogon, whose cosmology seemed to reflect clearly the means of unifying the oppositions I lived in" (Calio 1978, i-ii).

[9] In Kate Chopin's *The Awakening* (1899), the metaphor of the caged bird is also employed to signify women's subjection.

young ladies, "taught from their infancy that beauty is woman's sceptre" (Wollstonecraft 1891, 82), cannot but roam their "gilt cage" (ibid.), unaware that, despite its allure, it is, in fact, a prison. Conversely, the artist imagined by Calio is fully cognizant of her constrained condition and of the pain it entails, as her wings keep striking the bars until they bleed; yet she remains determined to resist: "I begin again, and again and again / Though my wings be clipped from the start" (Calio 1978, 3). It is worth noting that, in her attempt to rectify gender imbalance, Calio provocatively symbolizes male agency through two icons of delusional power – Icarus and Daedalus – while venturing into the realm of mythology, a repository of "male-devised stories which invariably portray woman as the Other" (Gubar 1979, 301), as Susan Gubar observes.

In two of her critical essays – "A Rebirth of the Goddess in Contemporary Women Poets of the Spirit" (1984) and "The Poet as Initiate: Re-emergence of the Darkmother in Women's Poetry in the 1970s" (2005) – Calio traces the gradual awakening to "a mystical feminine revelation" (Calio 1984, 50) among several women writers of the 1960s and 1970s, building on the legacy of Emily Dickinson, Virginia Woolf, Sylvia Plath, and Anne Sexton, who had undertaken a similar exploration of the self, albeit often unknowingly and with limited success. In these essays, Calio proposes a compelling alternative to both Eve, the fallen woman, and Mary, the immaculate virgin and *mater dolorosa*: "the half of the divine consciously omitted in traditional worship of the Father God" (ibid.), epitomized by the Egyptian Isis. Calio clarifies that Isis is a "powerful and inspired dark mother who dared to call upon the sun god, Ra, for her equal place, as well as for the healing of her beloved, Osiris, and their child, Horus"[10] (Calio 2005, 334). She is at once loving and disdainful, compassionate and resolute, peaceful and wild, embodying the full range of feminine possibility. As Lucia Chiavola Birnbaum contends, dark mothers, including the broad spectrum of black Madonnas, "counte[r] racism and sexism and connot[e] nurturance of the 'other' in

[10] After Set killed Osiris, he desecrated and dismembered his body, which was then reassembled by Isis – his sister and wife – who also restored him to life. By gathering the scattered parts of her husband and making him whole again, Isis becomes an emblem of female agency and of the unity between male and female, reclaimed from fragmentation. Isis, Osiris, and Horus may be interpreted as an earlier, more balanced and harmonious trinity, in contrast with later patriarchal religious structures.

contrast to the violence toward the 'other' that has historically characterized established religious and political doctrines" (Chiavola Birnbaum 1993, 12). The unusual hue of these ancestral deities (ranging from pitch black to tawny) recalls the color of the soil and is therefore connected with fertility rites and regeneration.

Given what has been argued so far, it is not surprising that Isis is a recurring presence throughout *In the Eye of Balance*. In the second poem of the collection, "Chant: Through the Rites of Isis," Calio compares and contrasts the "domestic tranquillity" (Calio 1978, 5) still yearned for by most men, with the emerging "raging female soul" (5) determined to recover her voice[11] and ignite a revolution:

Shedding the yoke of centuries
She begins anew
As the snake who sheds its skin
Close to the secrets of the earth, she stays
Leaving behind the guilt
Leaving behind the myths
Leaving behind the lies
To rot and decay. (5)

Described as "unsweet," "unpalatable," and "unladylike" (6) (the opposite of what is conventionally attributed to her gender), Isis personifies a dynamic blending of opposites, "not quite masculine, not quite feminine / Not quite in between" (6). The poem "Isis II" ends with an invitation to "reshape humanity" (37) on more equitable terms, recognizing shared traits over differences.[12] This idea is further explored in the final section of "Foreign Affairs," where the puzzle of one's life is pieced together through sympathy for others, as we are all interconnected – members of an extended human family:

---

[11] The significance of breaking the silence is forcefully conveyed in the poem "The Voice," where the "scattered powers" (Calio 1978, 7) of the female protagonist are finally reclaimed. Her voice is "no longer the small whispers / Of leaves tossed in summer's breeze" (7) but, like a howling wind, is retrieved "from the secret pockets of men / Who thought it theirs" (7). Here too, an African icon of power is invoked as a source of renewed inspiration: "Sheba magnificent Ethiopian" (7).

[12] In "Aesthetic Theory," Calio also claims "I am a multitude" (Calio 1978, 62), thus echoing Walt Whitman and Jean Toomer, whose mystical work she discovered at twenty.

We are told we are separate
We common commoners from a common start
Sharing in the common lot;
In contemplating your life
I find the key to mine. (43-4)

The collection culminates in the final poem entitled "Snow White – You Little Witch," a reimagining of the traditional fairy tale in which the young protagonist, instead of falling under the spell of a malignant witch, turns out to be the victim of a jealous and manipulative king, who concocts the sleeping potion to control her. He even spreads rumors that the witches had spellbound the maiden, thus triggering a ferocious hunt: "The kingdom hunted witches and / Brutalized, burned, beheaded them" (64). Rather than fostering fierce retaliation, however, the venerable and dignified witches envisaged by Calio – representing the suppressed qualities of every Snow White after patriarchy's intervention – serve as redeeming forces for all, even the wicked king:

Wiser in time
The witches grew a disguise
Came to free Snow White
The dumb King and the kingdom. (64)

An international conference organized by the American Italian Historical Association in Cleveland, in 1997, proved to be an epiphanic moment in Calio's career and personal growth. Entitled "Shades of Black and White: Conflict and Collaboration Between Two Communities," the event brought together several scholars and artists – including Lucia Chiavola Birnbaum and myself – to discuss the intertwined histories of Italian Americans and African Americans. As Calio remarks, "I felt I finally came home and found an inclusive community of Italian American writers who could speak my inclusive language" (Dossena 2020).

The poems she began to compose after her second journey to Africa, in 1978, were later gathered into a new illustrated anthology eventually released in 2014: *Journey to the Heart Waters*, "a memoir in verse"

(Marongiu 2023, 94). Calio had traveled to Khartoum, the capital of Sudan, to join forces with her Eritrean-born partner in efforts to ease the precarious situation faced by many Eritrean refugees who, at the time, were fighting for independence from the Ethiopian rule. Once more, after this experience, important fragments of her life's mosaic seemed to fall into place at last, acquiring new significance. As the artist observes in the "Prologue" section of the volume, "I had no idea my Sicilian Aunt, Mariann Calio, had made a similar journey to Africa at about the same age (28 years old) or how close Sicily was to Africa historically, as well as geographically" (Calio 2014, 9). Part of her extended family had moved to Tripoli in the 1920s to work as translators for the Italian government, following a stream of Italian laborers who had emigrated to Libya after the Italian unification, lured by the prospect of better work opportunities – replicating the American ventures of their compatriots. In Cinzia Marongiu's view, "Calio challenges the binary conception of cultural belonging and embraces a broader and more complex vision that surpasses the rigidity of belonging exclusively to one culture or another" (Marongiu 2023, 104). Moreover, the *Other* is transformed into a mirror image of herself, through which her past can be more clearly deciphered and her present understood. In the artist's words, "I had a profound empathy for the trauma of culture loss, and the Diaspora of the Eritrean people. This put me in closer touch with what my ancestors had experienced" (Calio 2014, 10). In line with her reasoning, even though the collection is neatly divided into three distinct parts – poems of arrival; the memory of what inspired the journey; the actual journey – the arrangement of the poems rejects chronological linearity, which would conform to the logic of mutual exclusion. In *Journey to the Heart Waters,* time is ritualistic, mythical, and therefore circular and recurring, following a spiral movement: "the experiences in Sudan would open me to a higher vision, beyond the confinements of ordinary time and limiting duality" (10).

References to the communal experience of Italian Americans are scattered throughout the anthology. The memory of her grandfather, wrongly accused of being a fascist, surfaces in "The Call. Flashback USA 1976," alongside the harrowing ache he felt "beyond the loss of Italy / or the disappointments of America" (Calio 1978, 31). The courage and resilience of her immigrant grandparents are evoked in "Amarat – a Khartoum Suburb," where Calio wonders whether she could have been "as brave as they / During their first days in America / With no way back home" (54). Her "ancestral diaspora" (67) is hinted at in "Today I Walk with a Soldier." Nevertheless, the scope of the collection remains more comprehensive, returning once again to the investigation of the feminine and deeper roots. As Calio underlines, when she arrived in Khartoum – a multicultural crossroads – she "met all [her] ancestral fears in the form of an immigration officer who was offended that [she] was a woman who dared to travel alone" (Calio 2008, 179). In "Arrival – Khartoum Airport (January 1978)," in fact, she exposes her vulnerability to patriarchal unwritten laws, which initially prevent her – "the only woman in pants across a desert land"[13] (20) – from moving freely and fully developing her potential. The feeling that women, chaperoned wherever they might roam, are "not seen as fully human" (9) – as she points out in the "Prologue" – is palpable. Locked in the "dark portable prisons" (20) of their burkas, they can only catch sight of the world through "grid work screens that chop their vision" (20): "Their absence makes such a notable presence" (20).[14] They are cruelly reduced to grotesque caricatures of themselves, as in the life-size placards carried by students protesting against the "old law" (22) enforced by fundamentalist parties. These weird and monstrous replicas,

> [...] appea[r] mummified,
> Not a glimpse of human flesh
> Under endless wraps of white cotton gauze
> Hands are covered with black gloves
> Feet enclosed in thick, black leather shoes
> Baby coffins.[15] (22)

The Black Madonnas of the eponymous poem are their powerful counterparts, embodying women's hidden strength – their capacity to

---

[13] The line appears in one of the sections of "Bhari" and is repeated, identically, a few pages later, in "Black Madonnas" (25).

[14] The two lines are included in the same section of "Bhari."

[15] These lines come from another section of "Bhari."

regenerate, like seeds buried in the ground, waiting for the right time to break the silence in which they are shrouded:

> I see your essence, no matter how veiled
> Waiting like a seed to germinate
> Like the seed I've carried from my ancestors
> Flowering in its own timing. (24)

Calio adopts an original ecofeminist viewpoint by linking her resistance to women's submission with her rebellion against colonialist[16] and exploitative drives which, in turn, invariably produce separation and conflict. Noël Sturgeon claims that ecofeminism "articulates the theory that the ideologies that authorize injustices based on gender, race, and class are related to the ideologies that sanction the exploitation and the degradation of the environment" (Sturgeon 1997, 23). Accordingly, in "Khartoum Telatta, a Refugee Camp,"[17] the artist grants wounded and violated Mother Earth – with whom veiled women (both literally and figuratively) collectively identify – the chance to tell her own side of *his*tory, denouncing oppression while promoting unity in respect of diversity.

> My name is Eritrea, South Africa, Somalia, Iraq
> My name is America, before and after the European…
> I am an Eritrean,
> Though I was told by your country
> I am to be Ethiopian. […]
>
> Wars are interminable separations
> My children are all refugees or dead.
> Who will pay this blood debt? […]
>
> We remain locked in the jaws of separation
> Each regretful act justified by past dreadful deeds
> Ever recreating the patterning of pain. […]

---

[16] Geraldine Moane also maintains that, "given that colonialism operates in a patriarchal context, it is clear that colonialism is itself a gendered process" (Moane 1999, 33). See also Marongiu 2023, 92.

[17] The poem was previously published in *Birthed from Scorched Hearts: Women Respond to War* (2008), under the title "Eritrea, My Ithaca."

Today I will call myself human being.
Will you join me?
All the colors make one light
Why stay in the dark? (69-70).

Natural imagery contributes to the envisioning of a renewed world where boundaries are but a faint memory, and the primeval idea of the unity of humankind, in harmony with the environment, prevails over modern antagonism, hatred, and abuse. Hence, the feminized and ever-changing desert is transformed into a symbol of endurance and defiance: "A desert cannot be owned or possessed / in this respect, she is closest to our essence"[18] (17). The Nile, a recurring protagonist in Calio's lines and childhood fantasies, not only restores the fertility of the soil, but also epitomizes the possibility of uniting what appears separate – "the two Niles / blending to one" (18).

Calio's dreams beyond nostalgia and her quest for an all-encompassing subjectivity, female empowerment, and communal roots in Africa find another possible expression in *Lucia Means Light*, an autobiographical novel soon to be published by the artist which serves as a fitting conclusion to this essay.[19] The choice of her protagonist's name, Lucia Libra, is thought-provoking: as the title suggests, Lucia means "light," and also invokes the saint who protects eyesight – meaningfully enabling both the character and the readers to perceive reality beyond biases and misconceptions. Her surname, Libra, may signify Lucia's quest for balance in a still unbalanced world, and, as a constellation, indicate Calio's intention to elevate human life to a higher dignity, by connecting it to the cosmos and the whole. Set in the 1960s and 1970s, the narrative revolves around Lucia's exploration of the deepest parts of herself, led by her spirit guide Marimba (named after the African musical instrument) – a constant presence since childhood – and by her African American friend Nova Freeman. Nova's *liberating* surname – Freeman – underscores emancipation, while the concepts of novelty and innovation, as well as a reference to the stars, are em-

[18] These lines, along with those that are quoted immediately afterwards, are found in "Bhari."

[19] I wish to express my deepest gratitude to the author for granting me the opportunity to read the draft of the manuscript and for permitting me to cite from it.

bedded in her given name. The novel, in which Isis is also mentioned several times, ends with Lucia's journey to Africa and with the realization that not only does light "depen[d] on darkness to exist" (Calio 2025, 198), but that light itself is "beyond color or shade or race or gender [...] light [is] who we really are" (277), thus encapsulating Calio's central message of spiritual and communal oneness.

Works Cited

Amatulli, Rosa. 2023. "In Search of Her Deeper Roots: An Interview with Louisa Calio." *Strade Dorate*, May 17, 2023. https://www.stradedorate.org/2023/05/17/in-search-of-her-deeper-roots-an-interview-with-louisa-calio/.

Birnbaum, Lucia Chiavola. 1993. *Black Madonnas: Feminism, Religion and Politics in Italy*. Boston: Northeastern UP.

Birnbaum, Lucia Chiavola, ed. 2005. *She's Everywhere! An Anthology of Writing in Womanist/Feminist Spirituality*. New York: iUniverse.

Calio, Louisa. 1978. *In the Eye of Balance*. New York: Paradiso Press.

_______. 1984. "A Rebirth of the Goddess in Contemporary Women Poets of the Spirit." *Studia Mystica* 7 (1): 50–59.

_______. 2005. "The Poeta's Initiate: Re-emergence of the Darkmother in Women's Poetry in the 1970s." In *She's Everywhere! An Anthology of Writing in Womanist/Feminist Spirituality*, edited by Lucia Chiavola Birnbaum, 334–45. New York: iUniverse.

_______. 2008. "In Search of a Larger Truth: Eritrea My Itaca." In *Birthed from Scorched Hearts: Women Respond to War*, edited by MariJo Moore, 179–83. Golden, CO: Fulcrum.

_______. 2014. *Journey to the Heart Waters*. New York: Legas.

_______. 2015. "Poems by Louisa Calio." *Journal of Italian Translation* 10 (1): 30–34.

_______. 2017. "My Italian/Sicilian Soul." *Ovunque Siamo* 1 (2). https://ovunquesiamoweb.com/archive/vol-1-issue-2/louisa-calio/.

_______. 2025. *Lucia Means Light*. Unpublished manuscript.

Dossena, Tiziano Thomas. 2020. "Poetry Is a Way of Knowing… Exclusive Interview with Author Louisa Calio." *L'Idea Magazine*, December 20, 2020. https://lideamagazine.com/poetry-is-a-way-of-knowing-exclusive-interview-with-author-louisa-calio/.

Gardaphé, Fred. 2004. *Leaving Little Italy: Essaying Italian American Culture*. Albany: State University of New York Press.

Gubar, Susan. 1979. "Mother, Maiden and the Marriage of Death: Women Writers and an Ancient Myth." *Women's Studies: An Inter-disciplinary Journal* 6 (3): 301–315.

Hirsch, Marianne. 1997. *Family Frames: Photography, Narrative, and Postmemory*. Cambridge: Harvard UP.

Love, Barbara J., ed. 2006. *Feminists Who Changed America, 1963–1975*. Urbana: U of Illinois P.

Luconi, Stefano. 2021. "Italian Immigrants, Whiteness, and Race: A Regional Perspective." *Italian American Review* 11 (1): 4–26.

Marino, Elisabetta. 2011. "Lo straordinario talento creativo di Louisa Calio, tra America, Italia e Africa." *In Limine* 7: 1–7.

Marongiu, Cinzia. 2023. "Navigating the Heart's Waters with Louisa Calio: Discovering Roots and Bonding with Nature." Translated into Italian by the author. *Journal of Italian Translation* 18 (2): 88–113.

Mazziotti Gillan, Maria. 2006. *Talismans/Talismani*. Empoli: Ibiskos Ulivieri.

Mishra, Alok. 2016. "Louisa Calio. Interview by Alok Mishra." *Ashvamegh* 17. https://ashvamegh.net/louisa-calio-interview-alok-mishra/.

Moane, Geraldine. 1999. *Gender and Colonialism: A Psychological Analysis of Oppression and Liberation*. Basingstoke: Palgrave MacMillan.

Sturgeon, Noël. 1997. *Ecofeminist Natures: Race, Gender, Feminist Theory, and Political Action*. New York: Routledge.

Unali, Lina. 2007. "Family Ties and a Sense of the Past in Italian American Women Writers." In *American Solitudes: Individual, National, Transnational*, edited by Donatella Izzo, Giorgio Mariani, and Paola Zaccaria, 71–79. Rome: Carocci.

Wollstonecraft, Mary. 1891. *A Vindication of the Rights of Woman*. London: T. Fisher Unwin.

Breaking "the Chrysalis": The American Dream in Pascal D'Angelo's Son of Italy

Francesca D'Alfonso
UNIVERSITÀ DEGLI STUDI DEL MOLISE

Abstract: This study explores the narrative structure and thematic complexity of *Son of Italy* by Pascal D'Angelo, positioning it as a work that transcends its role as a mere testimony of Italian immigration to the United States. It argues that the novel develops a dual-layered narrative: on the one hand, a first-person account oscillating between past and present; on the other, an introspective reconstruction of personal experience in real time. The protagonist, a poor boy from the Abruzzese mountains, confronts both the illusions and the brutal realities of the American Dream, in the end transforming his marginal condition through literature and self-cultivation. The evolving perception of America – from a mythologized land of opportunity to a site of exploitation and alienation, and finally to a place of personal rebirth through literary success – constitutes the central thread of the narrative. The article further situates *Son of Italy* within the broader framework of 1920s American literature, emphasizing its distinctive voice and the author's insistence on "truth" as both a poetic and existential imperative. Ultimately, D'Angelo's work is interpreted as a *Bildungsroman* of the immigrant experience, articulating not only the traumas of displacement but also the potential for creative transcendence.

1. *Son of Italy* is not simply an immigrant novel. Its distinctive feature lies in the complex and psychologically demanding trajectory of its protagonist's introspective journey. The narrator's voice resonates on every page, not merely because of its dominant tone of authenticity, but also owing to the stylistic qualities that characterize D'Angelo's prose: each word seems carved into the hard rock of the mountains of Abruzzo. This stylistic trait transforms the reading of *Son of Italy* into a meditative experience in which past and present ceaselessly seek points of contact and dialogue. From a narratological perspective, the novel operates on two levels. The first is articulated through a first-person narrator who recalls his past both in the light of the present and through the lens of accumulated experience. The second is represented by immediate, first-person experiences that are recreated, as if in real time. The opening lines of the novel already foreground the distinction between those who act and those who narrate:

> As I glanced back over the time-shadowed sky of my infancy, I seem to see a vast expanse of mist that gives no light to any early events.

> But here and there looms a faint pyramid of recollection that can apparently never fade. Toward them I grope, almost in a twilight of memory, seeking to bring out what really happened to me while I passed through the little world of inevitable childhood and poverty. (D'Angelo 2003, 7)

Thus, childhood is revisited in a "twilight of memory", a space where literature is conspicuously absent: a primitive world in which the only available culture is that of material experience. As Dennis Barone observes, "On the first page of the autobiography, the poet describes his Abruzzi home as a place of fear" (Barone 2023, 6) – a fear intertwined with the primordial harshness of a landscape that offers no concessions to human proportions. It is in this context, above all, that the image of silence prevails: the only possible dialogue for little Pascal (still "Pasquale" at this stage) is with nature itself, with the landscape and the heights of Mount Majella. The first chapters convey the clear perception of a community whose cultural immobility and ingrained sense of social resignation prevent it from imagining rebellion or envisioning life beyond the confines of its village – a place where words such as progress, reform, social justice, and democracy remain unknown. With a few deft strokes, D'Angelo conveys this reality to the reader; at the same time, he signals that from childhood the narrator sought to break the boundaries of a tradition rooted in sociocultural paralysis. Against resignation, the young Pasquale does not hesitate to react: this becomes evident when his father offers him the possibility of changing his life – by deciding to emigrate to the United States – thus nurturing his hopes and sense of renewal.

Together with his father, eager to live a life aligned with his inner aspirations, the protagonist looks to America as a promised land, the locus of a possible social redemption. This trajectory culminates in the image that closes the novel: a poor, semi-literate child, without cultural resources or adequate language to express his feelings, transformed into a celebrated figure in literature: "The literary world began to take me up as a great curiosity and I was literally feasted, welcomed and stared at. Letters of congratulation and appreciation came from various sections of America: from Boston to 'Frisco" (168). Significantly, the novel concludes with thoughts addressed to D'Angelo's parents. The writer is not only happy for himself, but imagines the pride of parents who, through his success, have been symbolically redeemed. The son's literary triumph appears to compensate for the father's failure: "And sweeter yet was the happiness of my parents who realized that after all I had not really gone astray but had sought and reached a goal far from the deep-worn groove of peasant drudgery" (168).

If we examine the fifteen chapters of the novel in the light of the epilogue, it becomes evident that Pascal D'Angelo's aim was not merely to recount the anguish and suffering of an Italian immigrant – an approach often characteristic of immigrant writing of the period. Rather, his intention was to foreground the arduous yet, in many respects, miraculous path that led him from a small remote village in the Abruzzi to the streets of New York and, ultimately, to the heart of American publishing and journalism. From this perspective, the final pages retrospectively illuminate the preceding fourteen chapters as a process of self-heroization. The letter addressed to the editor of *The Nation*, the subsequent recognition of the author, and the literary fame he briefly enjoyed in the 1920s function as a symbolic recompense, redeeming the hardships that culminate in the epilogue. Equally significant is the fact that the narrative, conceived as an autobiography, concludes not with the oblivion that followed in D'Angelo's real life, but with the affirmation of literary success. In this sense, the letter serves as the definitive seal of triumph: at last, the poet's voice is heard:

> *Oh! Please hear me! I am telling the truth. And yet who knows it? Only I. And who believes me? Then let my soul break out of the chrysalis of enforced ignorance and fly toward the flower of hope, like a rich butterfly winged with a thousand thoughts of beauty.*
>
> *Remember, without any expenses on your side you can help me! This is what I want: to be one sharer (though honorary) of the prize, the honor of the prize, a winner of the prize! For I have no friends who can help me in the literary world. I am a poor worker but a rich defender of truth.* (167, italics in the text)

The emphasis here falls insistently on the word *truth* – a term that does not allude to a metaphysical absolute, nor merely to the factual accuracy of the story. Rather, here *truth* signifies the poet's inspiration, an inner vocation that is inscribed day after day in his soul and nourished by a fundamental and indestructible *truth*. It is no coincidence that, in his introduction to the novel, Carl Van Doren – who recognized the value of Pascal D'Angelo's poetry – underscores several times that he was impressed by "[D'Angelo's] authenticity" (Van Doren 1924, x). Van Doren also acknowledges his pleasant surprise upon reading *Son of Italy*, describing it as a unique and extraordinary testimony, an autobiographical novel that ought to be read as "the record of enormous struggles against every disadvantage. [...] And *A Son of Italy* [sic] unquestionably belongs with the precious documents of the literature of Pascal D'Angelo's adopted country" (Van Doren, x).

A close examination of Van Doren's introductory pages reveals that, while exalting the "truth" that characterizes the autobiography, there is also, to a certain extent, a distancing from the literary value of the work, which is situated within the context of other writings whose "precious" contribution forms part of the American literature devoted to the stories of emigration. From a certain point of view, the critic's attitude is understandable: the 1920s marked a high point for the American novel.[1] At the very moment when D'Angelo published *Son of Italy*, for example, William Faulkner (1897-1962) brought out his first novel, *Soldiers' Pay* (1926) inaugurating a literary career that would produce a series of masterpieces. Similarly, beginning in 1923, Ernest Hemingway (1899-1961), published a number of short stories that revealed his talent as an innovator of American fiction, followed by *The Sun Also Rises* (1926) and *A Farewell to Arms* (1929), novels that secured his consecration in the pantheon of American literature.[2] The general silence surrounding D'Angelo's figure can also be explained by the powerful emergence of a remarkable generation of American writers, among them F. Scott Fitzgerald, John Steinbeck, John Dos Passos, Thomas Wolfe, and Erskine Caldwell, whose popular success, rein

[1] On the lively cultural debate and the varied socio-political discourse that characterized these years, see Rideout 1970, in particular 106-224.

[2] On the impact of Hemingway's narrative on the American novel in the first half of the twentieth century, see Bradbury 1984, 74-80. On Hemingway's technique, Bradbury observes: "In Hemingway's novels and stories of the Twenties verbal and emotional economy unite to form an existential, central modern style, a complex formal attenuation comparable to period tendencies in painting" (77).

forced by critical acclaim, secured for their works a central and enduring place within the panorama of American literature.[3] Nevertheless, to consider *Son of Italy* merely as a testimony of emigration, a document of interest only to archives, would be unduly reductive. Pascal D'Angelo's work, in my opinion, must be regarded as far more than this.

2. Moving to a textual analysis, it may be observed say that, from a structural point of view, *Son of Italy* can be divided into three distinct sections. The first five chapters delineate the Italian phase, a trajectory marked by extreme poverty, loneliness, and social abandonment. On a strictly geographical level, Cauze – the small cluster of houses and huts where the D'Angelo family resided – appears as a hamlet situated at the very periphery of the world, isolated from political and cultural currents. In the novel, the writer reproduces this reality by underscoring the distance separating his humble dwelling from the rest of Italy. The valley's most important center, Sulmona, is only briefly mentioned, primarily as the birthplace of Ovid and for its historical resonance; D'Angelo offers little further detail. What emerges clearly, however, is that Sulmona is perceived by the child Pascal as an almost unreachable city, especially when contrasted with Introdacqua, the small town around which his village gravitates.

The opening chapters of *Son of Italy* thus convey the image of a desperately isolated community, devoid of sociocultural rootedness, living under the shadow of Mount Majella with no prospect of change. If Sulmona is distant, the rest of Italy appears utterly alien, a political entity irrelevant to the inhabitants of Cauze, where life proceeds unchanged, bound to the immutable rhythm of the seasons. The sole certainty seems to be the gaze of the mountain which, like a magnetic pole, ties the shepherds and peasants of the valley to a destiny of immobility and imperturbable silence. The beginning of the second chapter highlights this intimate bond between community and mountain, which all the inhabitants of the valley revere as their majestic mother and fundamental point of reference:

---

[3] As becomes evident when reading the pages of *Son of Italy*, Pascal D'Angelo was largely indifferent to the aesthetic debates and artistic controversies of the modernist movement both in the United States and in Europe. For further discussion, see Bradbury and McFarlane 1991, 151-190.

> The hamlet where I was born on January 20, 1894, is comprised of a small group of stone houses near Introdacqua, and not very far from the old walled city of Sulmona. Introdacqua nestles at the head of a beautiful valley whose soft green is walled by *the great blue barrens of Mount Majella. The mother mountain looms to the east of us and receives the full splendor of the dawn.* We are proud to call ourselves the sons of *the majestic Majella.* And our race, the ancient Samnites, is said to have sprung from those sunny altitudes and spread their power over all Italy, making even Rome tremble. (17, italics mine)

In this passage, the narrator's lexical choices and sentence structure reveal the deliberate construction of an identity that seeks to present itself to the reader as the authentic voice of a vanished world, one that at the time of his autobiographical writing still dominates his imagination. The temporal distance between *then* – the child of Cauze, unaware of the world beyond the mountain chain – and *now* – the mature author recounting the stages of his biography in American English, a language not originally his own – is effectively annulled. Past and present converge: the author's roots retrospectively legitimize his present and confer meaning upon his human and artistic journey. Indeed, in linguistic segments such as "We are proud", Pascal D'Angelo emphasizes the unifying function of his voice, seemingly forgetting nothing of his origins. Moreover, Introdacqua itself is transfigured through the mythologizing discourse of memory: "Introdacqua is a beautiful town and nature seems to have squandered beauty on the surrounding vistas. The people are very quiet and extremely peaceful" (20). Thus, even decades after his departure for America, the Majella continues for the narrator to embody the figure of the "mother", the epicenter of the recreated world. Yet these words are uttered by a writer who now identifies himself as part of the American literary panorama.

The proud affirmation of roots emerges most clearly in the historical and cultural references he invokes: the walled city of Sulmona, resonant with its Roman past; the pride of belonging to the homeland of Ovid, the great Latin poet; and the evocation of the Samnites, remembered for their power and prestige. These elements collectively construct a narrative of "lofty" origins, a celebration of the greatness and unparalleled beauty of his native land. On one level, such references serve to dignify the narrator's self-image; on another, however, the exaltation of the past and the majestic portrayal of the Abruzzese landscape stand in stark contrast to the material deprivation and abandonment of villages located at the margins of civilization. It is no accidental that the narrator, while extolling scenes of natural splendor, simultaneously depicts the darker side of the mountain community, one governed more by prejudice than by rationality. In this tension, he discerns a latent affinity with Evil. Indeed, the emergence of witchcraft and other folk narratives of malign forces – expressions, in fact, of superstition – transform the woman branded as a witch into the scapegoat for the calamities and diseases that afflict the entire village. In other words, as D'Angelo suggests, the small community of Cauze displaced the causes of its misery and abandonment onto an "external" figure who inhabited the margins of society:

> Like a promontory of fright overshadowing a craving sea of beggars, loomed *a strange woman* in our town. She had come from the *weird barrens of the mountains,* before I was born, and had made her home among us. She was gazed at, but scarcely seemed to see anyone as she passed through the crooked streets of our town. *Yet a shudder ran through the hearts of all who beheld her, especially the mothers with small children.* (27-28, italics mine)

The narrator does not dramatize the theme of witchcraft as a folkloric residue of backwardness, rooted in a tradition that attributes every misfortune of the community to the malign influence of an external agent whose sole function is to harm others. Rather, D'Angelo offers a more nuanced and humane interpretation: as a shepherd tending his family's goats, little Pascal discovers that the woman feared as a witch – invested by collective imagination with an almost supernatural aura – is in reality a destitute and marginalized figure condemned to suffer more than the others by the extremity of her poverty. Encountering her unexpectedly on the rugged slopes of the Majella, the boy instinctively perceives that the old woman is not a diabolic presence but merely a victim of exclusion, her eccentric behavior a reflection of her social abandonment:

> With a gasp of horror I stopped short. There in front of me, tall and erect, stood the fearsome witch.
>
> I had the impulse to turn and scamper down the mountain, abandoning all, sheep, goats, staff.
>
> But as I looked up at her, I felt a strange feeling of pity. There was no hatred, no anger in her grey eyes. There was an animal fear. I have seen it in the eyes of young helpless birds. Her arms were very thin and bony, one of her feet had been wounded, probably on the sharp stones of the mountains, and she had tied a woolen rag around it .(40)

Thanks to his acute sensitivity, the young protagonist reads in the woman's eyes a trace of humanity invisible to the rest of the community. The little shepherd thus distinguishes himself from those around him: despite the prejudices instilled in him by adults, he transcends their fearful and hostile perception, which is grounded less in reason than in inherited malice. What emerges is a natural force of solidarity that spontaneously leads him to compassion. This empathetic impulse recalls not only the moral horizon of George Eliot's novels – entirely oriented toward the value of "human sympathy" – but also the words of Dostoevsky, who in *The Idiot* (1868) – often considered his masterpiece – affirms: "Compassion was the most important, perhaps the sole law of human existence" (Dostoevskij 2008, 242). Little Pascal, as this episode demonstrates, seems to embody this law intuitively, well before his initiation into literature, thus foreshadowing the ethical dimension that will later nourish his artistic vocation.

3. Far removed from the great currents of thought and untouched by the rapid socio-historical transformations of the early twentieth century, the protagonist's village only comes into contact with the broader socioeconomic and geopolitical context when two decisive words enter the common vocabulary: *America* and *emigration.* For the inhabitants of the Abruzzese valleys, these terms acquire an unequivocally positive resonance, evoking the promise of a new life in another world, of social and economic advancement, and thus of an alternative to the miserable existence that characterizes the towns and hamlets around Mount Majella. Therefore, the narrative reaches a crucial diegetic turning point

as the immobile, cyclical time of the community is suddenly disrupted by the historical time of progress.

On the narrative level, this encounter with History culminates in the decision of little Pascal's father to emigrate, joining a group of fellow villagers in their departure for New York, in search of a life of renewed hope. It is particularly noteworthy that the word *America* makes its first appearance in the fourth chapter, the chapter of decision and separation:

> One evening, when I was fifteen, I found my mother crying softly but bitterly. As soon as I entered our hut she wiped her eyes and tried to assume a calm expression. To my repeated questions she shook her head. I asked where my father was. She pointed out toward the fields. (45)

Here the novel juxtaposes two perspectives. On the one hand, the father embodies hope, adopting a realistic outlook that perceives only desolation around him and, consequently, regards emigration as the sole possibility of rescuing himself and his family. On the other hand, the maternal perspective dramatizes the trauma of change, animated by an instinctive premonition that the husband's venture in America is foredoomed to failure. For the adolescent protagonist, the mother – figure of silence and resignation – embodies attachment to the earth, a chthonic and primordial presence, both sensitive and determined, unwilling to relinquish the little she possesses for the uncertain promise of prosperity abroad:

> Then I begged her to please tell me what it was that oppressed her. She sighed deeply and whispered, "Your father has decided to go away."
> Alarmed I exclaimed, "Where to?"
> "To America." (47)

Although it is not the first time that the young protagonist hears the word *America*, now that he is directly involved, he seeks to grasp what may be concealed within this toponym – something that, at first sight, signifies only separation from his family, estrangement from his roots, and even the sensation of being lost in a space dominated by an indefinable nothingness: "I felt a wild pain, for I dearly love my father. To America! I had heard much of that strange place in which people we knew had vanished and had never returned. Had never returned! And my own father! After all, I was a young boy, and could not keep back the tears" (47).

In short, Pascal's tears join those of his mother in an embrace of understanding and solidarity that seems to bind them forever: "[...] she, with a mother's divine art, softly calmed me. And smiling in my eyes, she begged me to go to the gentle dreams. So, slowly, together we went up the ladder into our unlit bed" (47-48). However, from this initial rejection, marked by pain and fear of his father's American future – a future imagined through the tales he had heard – the adolescent gradually begins to accept the project of emigration as the only possible path toward freedom from want and economic independence for the entire community. Day by day his attitude evolves, until he finally perceives the New World as the sole chance of attaining social dignity, if not mere survival. His mother's position also contributes to this change of perspective: "In the evening my mother had been smiling so much and had made many wonderful promises of the new happy life we would lead when my father returned from America laden with riches. I began to think that this new land was quite a desirable place" (50). Thus Pascal resolves to accompany his father on his journey to America. Having listened to so many words and stories of emigration, he becomes convinced that he too must experience the New World – this Promised Land – at his father's side. The image of America, which had first appeared as a horizon of separation and loss, is progressively reshaped into the mythical representation of a nation where even the humblest may aspire to enrichment, dignity and happiness.

A second dramatic turning point follows upon the first diegetic rupture (the father's decision). The fifteen-year-old Pascal's determination to leave with his father entails a separation that admits no reunion. The mother, through her instinctive intuition, perceives the truth of this irreversibility: "Sobbing, she threw her arms about me and pressed me to her breast. In the darkness of her tight embrace, eyes closed, I wept. We both wept there on the steps. She kissed my lips again and again. Her warm tears fell on my face. I was sobbing, *'I will return soon, we will return soon'. But no. Her* [sic!] *mother's fears foretold the truth. I never returned*" (52, italics mine). The merging of mother's and son's tears signifies a union in grief, an act of shared mourning for a journey that, as the narrator later confirms with a sense of retrospective guilt, would indeed be "into the unknown" and without return. In this way, the autobiographical voice inscribes the pain of separation at the very core of its myth of departure: an inaugural trauma that shapes the narrative's articulation of emigration as both necessity and destiny.

4. Significantly, given the centrality of the transition from one world to another, the second part of the novel begins with the arrival in the United States of Pascal D'Angelo, his father, and the group of fellow villagers from the Majella valleys. The narrator carefully reconstructs the preparations for departure, a process that from a social perspective involves the entire community. Euphorically, neighbors and relatives bid farewell and celebrate those who set out for the New World, interpreting their departure as the first stirrings of life in a society long imprisoned in socioeconomic paralysis, incapable of awaking from centuries of immobility and silence. Within the intimate sphere of the family, however, the contrast remains vivid: the mother's resignation – since the departure is experienced as a form of mourning – stands in opposition to the father's anxious eagerness to leave and to his warm approval of Pascal's decision to join him on the American adventure:

> Quickly we set about making plans for leaving. My father had wished to take me along even before my decision, but hated to separate me from my mother, though he thought of me all the time. Nor did he oppose my desire to accompany him.
>
> My mother, soon resigned, began to make us various pairs of socks, both of cotton and of wool shorn from our neighbors's lambs.
>
> [...]
>
> We heard of many others in the town who were leaving. Some of them had rich *compari* and relatives. Dinners were being given in their honor before their departure. As for us, we were growing more and more eager each day. (53)

With just a few lines, the narrator succeeds in conveying the magnitude of a phenomenon of profound social and cultural resonance, one that would have an extraordinary impact on the Abruzzo-Molise hinterland, a region otherwise removed from the political debates, industrial transformations, and economic changes that Italy was experiencing at the dawn of the twentieth century (Cf. Villari 2011, 45-77 and *passim*). From the perspective of the sociology of emigration, Chapter V is crucial not only for its depiction of a decisive turning point in the life of the protagonist and his family, but also for what it reveals about the mechanisms of recruitment and the preparations for reception upon arrival in New York. What emerges is the collective nature of the migratory process: the emigrant never departs blindly or in isolation, but as part of a network of individuals recruited locally, often linked by shared work experience, common expectations, and even cultural affinities. This dynamic is captured in the narrator's observation: "With a few others in our town, my father arranged to go to work in America for a foreman on the state roads who was a fellow-townsman" (54).

A fact that clearly emerges from these pages is that, at the beginning of the twentieth century, emigration was structured through networks of intermediation between those already established in the United States and those who, still in their native villages, wished to turn transform their lives in socioeconomic terms. Yet this system of mediation was marked by a fundamental misunderstanding: intermediaries rarely clarified that employment in road construction, for instance, meant enduring months of bitter cold and engaging in labor far more exhausting than agricultural work. Employment conditions often verged on slavery, governed by relentless schedules and by a labor system that allowed no exceptions in terms of humane treatment. For the majority of those preparing to leave their homeland, however, America simply meant relocating to a geopolitical space where wealth was perceived as immediately accessible. This conviction nourished the illusion that, once on American soil, economic well-being could be attained with relative ease and less toil.

As the subsequent chapters of the autobiography reveal, the image of America as a Promised Land – a space of freedom and prosperity for all – was illusory. Equally deceptive was the notion of a society in which both state and private enterprises were prepared to provide genuine opportunities for advancement to all, regardless of origin, language, or ethnicity. Indeed, as the narrator notes at the beginning of Chapter V, the collective euphoria was fueled by the idea that emigration would eradicate poverty and hunger, and that the wages sent home would eventually benefit the entire community. Those who departed were thus celebrated with a kind of naïve conviction that every inhabitant of the village would share in the fruits of their labor abroad.

From a narrative standpoint, however, the most striking element is the journey from Cauze to Naples, which represents, on the diegetic level, the protagonist's first experience of initiation. Removed from the protective enclosure of the mountains of his childhood, young Pascal begins to glimpse the wider world beyond that natural barrier and to broaden his horizon of knowledge. At the same time, he begins to perceive that there exists a reality far richer than that of his native village. In short, for Pascal, the journey to the boarding dock becomes a narrative of discovery: for the first time, he travels by train; for the first time he sees the sea; for the first time he encounters people who do not belong to the small, enclosed world of Cauze; and, above all, for the first time he boards a steamship[4]:

> Finally I saw a thrilling sight. We had just come out of a tunnel and were speeding at a high, rare altitude towards the plains of Campagna. Sparkling and flashing in the distance and spreading right across the world was something all in motion. At first I was frightened. Then I thought, "The sea! That must be what they call the sea!" (55)

The narrator underscores the sense of amazement provoked by his first vision of the sea. Because of his heightened sensitivity to every manifestation of the cosmic and natural order, Pascal perceives the expanse of water as a reality that addresses not only the senses but also the spirit.

---

[4] The ship was the *RMS Cedric*, owned by the British Company White Star Line, with a tonnage of more than 20,000. In 1916 the liner was requisitioned for the transportation of British troops to Egypt and Palestine. It returned to passenger service only in 1919, after a number of accidents and mishaps involving other ships. The *Cedric* was built in the Belfast shipyards and inaugurated in August 1902; it officially entered service on 11 February 1903 with its maiden voyage from Liverpool to New York.

What is conveyed implicitly to the reader transcends the simple astonishment of a child confronted with an unfamiliar spectacle. The boy intuits in the immensity of the sea a primordial force whose mystery no human ingenuity can fully subdue. This intuition is promptly confirmed by the narrative: "The voyage was a nightmare, interposed with moments of strange brilliance. We passed the Azores which looked like toy islands and windmills. No sooner had they vanished under the horizon than a tremendous storm rolled into us" (56-57). The first impressions Pascal records of his vision and encounter with the open ocean show how the forces of nature find their most striking expression in the mass of water that seems to diminish, if not annul, the majestic greatness of the *RMS Cedric*.

However, with regard to the crossing from one continent to another, what emerges more than anything else is the hero's artistically acute personality. Pascal proves to be a perceptive observer of the elements of nature, whether they reveal themselves in destructive violence or in serene tranquility. Considering the poetic temperament of the protagonist, his perpetual attention to the sky, clouds and the stars reveals an upward gaze that embodies his spirituality, his desire to elevate himself, and his refusal to be bound by material constraints. In many respects, the crossing thus marks the transition from a boy who lives from hand to mouth to the poet who, though only embryonically represented, appears already instinctively engaged in the pursuit of spiritual fulfillment. In purely spatial terms, one might conclude that the axis of horizontality (matter) and that of verticality (spirit) here achieve a form of fusion and precarious harmony, anticipating the protagonist's arrival in America. Indeed, while the encounter with the vastness of the ocean highlights an ambivalence – at once peaceful and rebellious, life-giving and death-dealing (the level of horizontality) – the boy's upward gaze proleptically reveals to the reader the *poet who will become*: Pascal D'Angelo, who will eventually inscribe in words his tensions, his aspirations, and his striving for a higher representation of his own condition and of his relationship to the world.

5. The opening of Chapter VI assumes the epic tone of a discovery destined to mark the protagonist's life indelibly. For Pascal, it is as

though he were crossing a threshold into a reality utterly different from all that he has known. The very use of the conjunction 'And', with which this phase begins, suggests a desire to link the new scene to all that precedes it: the hopes and imaginings that accompanied the voyage across the ocean and, earlier still, the preparations for departure. From a narratological and linguistic perspective, the incipit – "And this is America, I thought" – is characterized by striking semantic density. It conveys the presence of a reflective self who has long anticipated this moment, whose thoughts flow in a circular psychological rhythm that ultimately gestures toward myth: the recurring conviction that in this virgin land beauty and happiness lie within reach:

> And this is America, I thought. During our way over on the ship I had seen golden heaps of clouds and rainbow vistas toward which we sped, and I had come to believe that they were perhaps the portals of America.
>
> But this place was out in a forest, a soft murmuring woodland of enormous trees, straight and majestic. In our country large forests are a rarity. And trees were practically all planted by the hands of man. But these giant trees were monuments. And as the sunlight poured through them I felt small and helpless – almost lost. (61)

The first representation of America thus reveals the *a priori* mythologization of those lands and that nation by the narrator, who remains unaware that the hard life he has left behind will not be replaced by the happier life fashioned by his vivid imagination. Pascal's astonished gaze serves to highlight the contrast between the enormity of America – especially with regard to the natural landscape – and his small village. Now, confronted with the monumental scale of America, he perceives himself almost as a Lilliputian facing a universe inhabited only by giants. Yet this initial sense of euphoria quickly dissolves. Only a few days after beginning work, the newly arrived group from Italy – including Pascal and his father – encounters the brutal reversal of the "American myth". Far from fulfilling the promise of prosperity, America reveals itself a place harsher and more devastating than the reality of the Abruzzese mountains. This realization marks a crucial passage: the movement from positive expectation to the recognition that all the images constructed around the New World were no more than illusions.

In many respects, the chapters that follow demonstrate that, from the perspective of the team of emigrants from the Abruzzi, *Son of Italy* unfolds as a tragic narrative. Indeed, if we consider the daily reality of Italian laborers, it is difficult to escape the conclusion that this is, at bottom, a story of failure: "Our original gang was of the family type, all quiet, hard-working men. We had known each other more or less in Introdacqua. But by the time we were settled in Hillsdale we were like very close relatives" (62). Confronted with the challenges of a new social environment and subjected to labor conditions that are both impersonal and hierarchical, the one positive element that emerges is the solidarity forged among the emigrants. This ethnic-cultural convergence, rooted in shared origins, grows stronger over time rather than weakening, and remains unmarred by ill will. As for the narrative technique, it should be noted how each character encountered by the protagonist is characterized by a few very precise and literarily effective details. Since they hail from the same area of the Abruzzi region, the young hero finds himself, at least in principle, in familiar surroundings, within a small community where his native dialect is spoken and where no one contemplates learning English. This "conservative" tendency can be read as a form of cultural self-defense, an attempt to preserve identity in the face of dislocation. Yet it is precisely against this backdrop of linguistic and cultural immobility that Pascal begins to feels the limits of his mother tongue. The recognition of these limits sparks a deeper reflection on the meaning he wishes to assign to his life – even if, at first, he does not perceive English as a language destined to shape his identity or define his sense of being:

> None of us, including myself, ever thought of a movement to broaden our knowledge of the English language. We soon learned a few words about the job, that was the preliminary creed; then came "bread", "shirt", "gloves". (not kid gloves), "milk". And that is all. We formed our own little world – one of many in this country. And the other people around us who spoke in strange languages might have been phantoms for all the influence that they had upon us or for all we cared about them. (68)

On the one hand, the narrator depicts a group of men from the Abruzzi capable of living in perfect harmony and solidarity. On the other hand, he also suggests an atmosphere of cultural closure within the humble dwellings of the laborers, a closure that might even be described as obscurantist. This element is crucial and must not be overlooked. Resistance to linguistic change is not merely a question of inertia but also the direct consequence of the type of work assigned to the group. It is hardly accidental that the narrator refrains from dramatizing his disappointment, instead offering only a laconic remark: "The foreman was showing one of them something. And I made my first acquaintance with the pick and shovel" (65) What follows is a detailed description of the earthwork that the team is required to carry out: "We were digging a way through a hillock" (65). From here comes a first analysis of this new beginning: "We were all very tired from our long hours, ten of labor and one of lunch, making eleven in all" (67). Here, gradually, the myth of America begins to crumble under the weight of a reality that proves harsher than that of the protagonist's native land. Life in Italy had indeed been difficult and marked by sacrifice, but it preserved a degree of autonomy: each farmer or shepherd could decide when and how to employ his labor. In stark contrast, on American soil every worker is compelled to submit to a tyrannical schedule, one that admits no exceptions and erases any trace of individual freedom.

After a series of wanderings across various counties on the East Coast, Pascal finally encounters New York, the city he had glimpsed only from afar since his arrival from Italy. From Ellis Island he had seen the skyline, but without being able to penetrate into the heart of the metropolis. The opening of Chapter VII offers a realistic representation of the city, framed by the continuing search for work on the part of the laborers' gang:

> My first real view of New York, the first time I actually realized the city, came in the summer of 1914 when I first visited Shady Side. Our job in Tuckahoe, New York, had stopped and I had come as a sort of advance agent for the gang in search of work. I came to the house of a couple of fellow townsmen. They boarded with some

> other Abruzzese in a shack perched on a high part of the Palisades." (74)

The negative experience continues in New York: the search for employment becomes even more frustrating as the narrator becomes aware – perhaps for the first time – of the stark social contrasts of a metropolis that seems to welcome everyone while at the same time disappointing everyone. In this respect, Pascal's itinerary amounts to a gradual formative acquisition of socio-cultural "knowledge", an experience that nourishes, almost daily, the poems interwoven into the texture of the autobiography:

> Gorge Road comes pouring like a stream from the cliffs and joins River Road. Dirty shacks and hovels are everywhere [...]. Men and women, dirty, speaking a mixed jargon of Italian, Polish, Hungarian, English, were hurrying all about. Two husky laborers were appearing from the gloom of a factory door. One old Italian with golden rings in his ears was prodding some goats upward toward the terraced shacks. Children played everywhere. (75)

Here, then, emerges another face of America. New York is equated with the slums of the suburbs, where sunlight never penetrates, and where human beings are abandoned to themselves. Nothing worthy of human dignity appears in these scenes dominated by filth, indifference, and neglect. The New York area, dotted with miserable villages devoid of identity, exudes an atmosphere of total decadence. As the writer observes, human life often seems to resemble that of animals: "Towns of filthy hovels, towns of congested quarters and unhealthy conditions, all of them, little miniature East Sides and Mulberry Bends, scattered among the green stretches and broad open spaces of America" (79). The discovery of this wasteland delivers yet another blow to the myth of America as a land of abundance and happiness:

> Walking up a street that I afterwards found out was called Manhattan Street, we finally came upon a brilliantly illuminated thoroughfare. I could hardly believe my eyes, it was so wonderful at first [...] We paused in front of another window. Again people edged away from us. And I heard some slurring remarks about 'those foreigners'. [...]

To me this thoroughfare was a magic vista. Men and women crowded continuously out of that dazzling distance. *Where did they all come from? And why their silence? Who had cast the spell over them all? How pale they all were, I thought. Weakly pale they all seemed, like sprouts of seeds washed up by the rain. Cars clanged and rumbled past, filled with rows of statue-like people who sat within, motionless, ignoring one another.*" (77-79, italics mine)

In these pages devoted to Manhattan, the prevailing atmosphere is one of systematic abandonment of the human dimension. Indifference, the pallor of death, spiritual impoverishment, and a deep-rooted inner gloom dominate the scene. Yet paradoxically, these are among the most beautiful and intense pages of the novel. The protagonist's acute sensitivity emerges before the anonymous crowd, as he evokes the spiritual aridity that seems to mark each individual life. As Pascal recalls: "We hovered outside a crowd, all looking at shoes" (79). The downward gaze of the masses signals a kind of death of the spirit; in contrast, Pascal's upward gaze seeks answers in the clear morning sky, or later among the constellations that illuminate the night. For this reason, he is all the more struck by the resigned and dysphoric attitude of the people in the crowd: "And I thought of how lovely and yet how repulsive this enchanted city was" (80). The apparent contradiction in the sentence closing Chapter VII must be interpreted in light of Pascal D'Angelo's love-hate relationship with the city – a relationship that, from his later position as a successful writer, he continued to acknowledge he had toward the metropolis that had given him so much, yet on the strictly human level had also taken so much away.

6. From a diegetic angle, Chapter X constitutes a decisive turning point. Within the team of workers from the Abruzzi, a sense of dejection emerges, culminating in the full awareness of the failure of what we might call the American "project". Day after day, among the group of laborers from Introdacqua, nostalgia grows, implicitly pointing toward a return to the homeland – a return that signifies the definite collapse of their American dream. At the same time, this chapter proves crucial for understanding Pascal's vehement opposition to the idea of returning to Italy. Here the narrative definitively abandons the

vision of America as a land of ease, where nothing prevents even the humblest immigrant from attaining wealth and prosperity. That landscape of abundance – an idealized construction of the imagination – gradually reveals itself to be nothing more than illusion. Over time, it becomes evident that America, far from embodying solidarity and humanity, presents a reality harsher and more inhumane than Italy itself. Not surprisingly, in these pages the great American nation appears as a land of despair, loneliness and death – a space that offers no redemption. Consequently, the team begins to dissolve as, one by one, the Italian workers find their way back to Italy, while Pascal remains behind alone. Paradoxically, America functions only as the catalyst for nostalgia, and in this sense, leads the young Pascal to re-evaluate, on a human level, the very village he had once sought to escape.

When the team reaches West Virginia, they realize that they are living not in a realm of light but under the domination of darkness and evil: "On reaching the West Virginia side we again plunged into the hilly darkness. After we had trudged on for heaven knows how long, we saw the faint glimmer of a lamplight through a small shanty window" (100). In this final attempt to secure decent work, the men once again find themselves subjected to conditions that strip them of their last vestiges of dignity – their lives reduced, in effect, to those of animals: "We were pigs in our sty" (103). Everything falls beneath the axe of extreme exploitation; everything is overshadowed by the presence of death: "We thought of our lost baggage and our vanished dreams of a sunny climate. *Sheeplike we followed our foreman where a large gang was already working*" (104-105, italics mine). The atmosphere of degradation reaches its climax when the workers witness a fatal accident in which two of their companions are killed: "Two men were pinned under the derrick. One of them was Theophile, the other our huge Andrea" (106). The tragedy leaves a profound mark on the small community from Introdacqua, forcing them to reflect bitterly on the futility of persisting in such conditions: "Within a few days after this fatal accident the gang broke up. We had lost all heart; work in that place was oppressive; we felt enslaved. And finally, discouraged and saddened by our loss, we decided to quit. Sadly we returned to New York" (106).

In short, all dreams vanish within a few hours. The failure touches everyone, including Pascal's father, who is particularly affected and falls prey to distrust and unrelenting depression: "[...] one night shortly after our return my father announced to me that he was thinking of leaving for Italy. "We are not better off than when we started", he said, and asked me if I wished to go back with him" (106). By contrast, Pascal – nourished quietly by the dream of literature – does not wish to abandon America, nor to relinquish the aspirations that seem to transcend both poverty and the misery of his daily life. For the father, the American dream has turned into a nightmare of suffering, in a social context defined by the struggle for survival. For the protagonist, however, the myth of a promised land still endures: he wants to believe that this new land, the language he is beginning to master, and the vibrant literary panorama will grant him the possibility of following his vocation – something inconceivable in the shadow of Mount Majella, where life remains motionless and primordial. Under this cultural impulse, Pascal D'Angelo transforms decline into ascent: economic poverty becomes inner wealth, and the slum through imagination is converted into the extraordinary backdrop of his writing.

The father's exit from the scene marks the moment in which the protagonist begins to assert himself with growing strength, animated by a desire to acquire a culture that is not merely linguistic but, above all, literary. Within him, vocation advances with urgency. It is in light of this new impulse that he starts to write in English, relying both on self-instruction and on his stubborn determination to carve out a place for himself within American literature: "I began to learn some Spanish from these two Mexicans. [...] Somehow, I found English more to my liking than Spanish. And about once a week even bought an English newspaper to look at" (129). The keyword that characterizes the beginning of this third phase is the adjective "alone". By 1916, at the age of twenty, Pascal D'Angelo no longer has his group of companions with whom he can share experience or solidarity. He stands alone, before the world, alone in a ruthless New York. Yet this same city becomes the main reservoir for his literary imagination which, as the final chapters reveal, increasingly asserts itself through incisive expression and imaginative force. Soon, however, the aspiring poet is compelled to measure himself against the harsh realities of New York publishing. Thus, following his initial enthusiasm, he is forced to confront the disappointments of his first unsuccessful attempts to gain recognition within the world of print.[5]

Observed from the standpoint of the plot, these disappointments appear as the inevitable consequence of repeated rejections by magazine editors who, apparently, recognized in him neither talent nor literary merit: "[...] I found my poems and a printed slip. It was elaborate and diplomatic, courteously thanking me for my kindness in allowing the editorial staff to consider my poems. I was flattered. [...] *Gradually I became skeptical about the honeyed phrases. I strongly suspected that there was some telepathic communication among the magazine editors to drive me and my poems from the thresholds of their temples*" (150-151, italics mine). A genuine breakthrough occurs only when Pascal resolves to write a long letter to the editor of *The Nation* – a letter in which he claims, above all, his right to be heard:

> *Oh! Please hear me! I am telling the truth. And yet who knows it? Only I. And who believes me?*
>
> *Then let my soul break out of the chrysalis of enforced ignorance and fly toward the flower of hope, like a rich butterfly winged with a thousand thoughts of beauty* (167).

And indeed, he will be heard. The "chrysalis" becomes a butterfly, free to soar in a country that, by contrast, had suffocated and constrained the group from Introdacqua. Thus, the closing scenes of the third part of *Son of Italy* do not linger on sadness and anguish, nor on the America of violence and subjugation. This is not the story D'Angelo intends to leave his readers. On the contrary, the final words are dedicated to his parents, whom he imagines proud to have a son who

[5] With regard to Pascal D'Angelo's reaction to the rejection letters, it should be noted that he comes to see himself as a tiny fragment in a vast and competitive literary landscape: "And now I realized that I was merely a small drop in the sad whirlpool of literary aspirants. In my cold stoveless, dingy room or in the Library, I was alone in my struggle to acquire a new language and a new world. But outside of that I was one, only one of the millions of literary beggars who clog the halls of literature, who stand like a sluggish crowd in the way of anyone wishing to forge ahead" (151).

has succeeded in conquering the literary world. Beyond this filial homage, however, the closing page celebrates the miracle of literature – "and the miracle happened" (167) – which is also the miracle of an autobiography that, as I have argued, manages to depict America with stark realism, yet without adopting the tones of defeat or resignation exemplified by his father. Rather, through his writing, Pascal D'Angelo affirms the possibility of transcendence, transforming individual hardship into creative triumph.

WORKS CITED

Barone, Dennis. 2023. "A Twilight of Memory: On the Life and Writing of Pascal D'Angelo. *Diasporic Italy: Journal of the Italian American Studies Association* 3 (October).

Bradbury, Malcolm. 1984. *The Modern American Novel.* Oxford and New York: Oxford UP.

Bradbury, Malcolm, and James McFarlane, eds. 1991. *Modernism: A Guide to European Literature 1890–1930.* London and New York: Penguin.

D'Angelo, Pascal. 2003. *Son of Italy.* With an afterword by Kenneth Scambray. Toronto and Lancaster (UK): Guernica.

Dostoevsky, Fyodor. 2008. *The Idiot.* Translated and edited by Alan Myers. Oxford and New York: Oxford UP.

Rideout, Walter B. 1970. *The Radical Novel in the United States 1900–1954: Some Interrelations of Literature and Society.* Cambridge, MA: Harvard UP.

Van Doren, Carl. 1924. "Introduction." In *Son of Italy*, by Pascal D'Angelo. New York: The Macmillan Company.

Villari, Lucio. 2011. *Notturno italiano: L'esordio inquieto del Novecento.* Bari and Roma: Laterza.

Translation as a Bridge to the Culture of Origin

Joseph Perricone
FORDHAM UNIVERSITY

Abstract: Translating offers a wide spectrum of gainful and useful possibilities both at the theoretical and practical levels. Pragmatically, it lends itself very effectively to the divulgation of text that for many would remain incomprehensible. Pedagogically it is a powerful tool to bridge the distance between cultures and promote the study and understanding of languages. In particular, in the area of Italian American experience, it has revitalized the memory of cultural heritage and has promoted the reappropriation of linguistic and cultural ownership among ethnic groups of Italian descent. The very limits of translation have fueled intellectual curiosity in seeking a deeper and more authentic awareness of the essence of the original text in its ineffable and incommensurate richness.

Translating lends itself to many uses and rewards, not least of them being the process itself with its demands of very attentive close reading of the original text and creative critical invention of ways to render it in a target language. Beyond this, there is the pedagogical approach to teaching a foreign language and literature using translation techniques, very gratifying and effective in the classroom. In the area of promoting and introducing a foreign literature to the wider public not well acquainted with its language, a bilingual side by side text is often very attractive and it proved very useful and most befitting especially with Italian American audiences as on many occasions I have had the enjoyable opportunity to experience over the years. Particularly gainful and fulfilling were the presentations of various literary figures that for many years I hosted at Fordham University for the Apulian Cultural Organizations of New York City, such as the United Pugliesi Organization based in Brooklyn, New York, in conjunction with the Department of Culture and Tourism of the Apulia Region. These events normally included the presentation of a book relevant for the occasion. Authors such as Joseph Tusiani often participated with readings from their works. Especially attractive to this public were the readings of poets who wrote in one of the vernaculars of the Region Apulia, among whom were, in addition to the already mentioned Joseph Tusiani, Francesco Granatiero, Lino Angiuli, Giuseppe De Donno, Pietro Gatti, Giacomo Strizzi, Cristanziano Serricchio, Arcangela Panulla, to mention only some of the better-known representatives. These readings stimulated the audience's curiosity and provoked many questions and commentaries. The choice of presenting mostly poets writing in dialect was not casual, rather it was dictated by the higher accessibility they offered to an audience that presented a great affinity with the social context and literary themes generally treated by these poets in a language that offered a certain psychological compatibility with the cultural background and milieu of the participants, whose sociocultural background had excluded them from a formative experience congenial with the italophone baggage typical of the dominant class. These poets, and Borazio in particular, exhibit those qualities in tune with that "popular progressive expression" theorized by Ernesto de Martino, as the conscious project of the people in response to their subaltern social condition (de Martino 2001, 122). The use of dialect as a vehicle of artistic expression, because of its greater consonance with the character of the audience, lessened any distance or barrier that might have been experienced in the presence of works in the national idiom. In general, the presence of vernacular culture elicited enthusiastic responses among those who had grown up with it or had any familiarity with it and learning that it was now used for elitist purposes such as writing poetry, awakened a certain sense of esteem and sparked a great deal of interest in the works and in their authors. Of course, in all this cultural transaction, translation played an important role as mediator, in its own way adding an aura of importance to the original work which was now showcased through the translation. Moreover, using dialect for artistic expression, raised its status to the level of the dominant idiom. When dialect takes on a form of protest with respect to a subaltern condition to which it had been confined, it gains dignity and makes a qualitative leap, as Prof. Michele Dell'Aquila states in the introduction to *La poesia dialettale pugliese* del Novecento (Dell'Aquila 1995, 19). This increased prestige of dialect feeds the self-esteem of those present in the audience facilitating and strengthening their ties with its culture of origin which was, by and large, of a subaltern dialect matrix.

For the purpose of this presentation, we will focus on the poet Francesco Paolo Borazio as he was one of those poets received with fertile enthusiasm by various audiences because of his biographical attributes and the content and style of his poetry. Borazio was born in 1918 in San Marco in Lamis, the same rural town in the Gargano Peninsula in which

Joseph Tusiani was born in 1924, six years later than Borazio. Although they both were from working class families, their lives took very different paths. Whereas Tusiani pursued a classical education at the University of Naples where he studied English literature and then migrated to New York where his father had gone to work nearly twenty years earlier, Borazio, on the other hand, after completing a fifth-grade education, went to work in the marble quarries near his town where his father worked as a stone cutter. In school he demonstrated an eagerness for learning and a creative inclination. Then, at the age of 21 he was drafted into the army and was sent to Croatia and the Alps where he became ill with tuberculosis and spent most of his life in sanatoriums in various cities in Italy until his death in 1953, at the age of 35. He dedicated much of his spare time to reading many of the Italian classics, especially the chivalric epics of Boiardo and Ariosto, and Pulci in particular. The study that he kept in his home in San Marco revealed a substantial library that included the works of major authors among whom are Dante, of course, and Ugo Foscolo, along with satirical authors, Parini and Giusti, and other canonical poets such as Carducci, Pascoli, and even D'Annunzio. He married and had a child and dedicated part of his time to painting scenes of his hometown. In the last years of his life, he designed posters for the Socialist Party. Many of the papers that Borazio left behind in his study contained poems in Italian that still await publication, while other notebooks were filled with poems written in the vernacular.

Borazio became known as an important poet in the vernacular posthumously thanks to critics like Sergio D'Amaro, Cosma Siani and Antonio Motta, who edited and published his works for the editor Quaderni del Sud. One book of his verse is a satirical mock-epic entitled *Lu Tajone*, published in 1977 and the other, a collection of poems under the title *La preta favedda*, also edited by D'Amaro, Siani and Motta, with an introduction by Tullio De Mauro, who compares Borazio to Pascarella, Buttitta and Carlo Porta, was published in 1982.

While his mock-epic poem *Lu Trajone*, is dominated by a satirical and ironical vein, in his collected poems *La preta favedda*, Borazio finds inspiration in a variety of situations that allow him to pluck various chords of the poetic lyre bending his vernacular to a variety of tonalities that range from the elegiac to farcical, ironic and satirical, bucolic and pastoral. His poems depict primarily scenes and characters from his town, scenes drawn with vivacious vividness and a *vis ludica* that always remains within the boundaries of good-hearted humor. His verse displays a range of tonalities and formal arrangements that testify to Borazio's well trained craft as a poet, by no means a spontaneous poet, but one highly conscious of his art, fitting Benedetto Croce's ideal of a "poesia dialettale riflessa" as he put it in *Uomini e cose della vecchia Italia* (Croce 1956, 223).

Borazio takes the cue from his profession as stone cutter for the title of his poetry collection, *La preta favedda*, an eloquent oxymoron that personifies the inanimate "preta" that speaks out denouncing the oppression, exploitation and injustice perpetrated by those who govern and abuse their power. Thus, Borazio's quick-witted and sometimes even harsh social criticism that characterizes some of his verse as poetry of protest drew the sympathies of many in the audience charmed by his satirical vein. Other qualities of Borazio's poetic style and themes resonated amiably with a captive audience. But let us now turn to some of the poems and draw directly from the text some examples of those salient characteristics of his poetry. Some members of the audiences attending our events responded with nostalgic fondness to the iconic monuments evoked in some of the sonnets, those churches and shrines typical of that area of Northern Apulia and empathized with the religious tone prevalent in some of Borazio's compositions. They responded sympathetically to some of the religious imagery that touched sensitive nerves in their unconscious memories of places that they might have heard mentioned in their childhood by parents and relatives; some even recalled visiting some of the places mentioned which, it is well to recall, mark the stations of the itinerary on the pilgrimage route known as the Via Sacra Longobardorum that leads all the way up to the cave of the Archangel Gabriel near Monte Sant'Angelo situated on the peak of the Gargano mountain. But Borazio is not a very pious person, and some of these places are at times treated with benign irony; rather what seeps through some of his verses is a genuine religious sentiment free from any conventional modes or dogmatic profession. But let us hear the poet's voice directly. This one is entitled is entitled "Santa Loja."

> Ne ne calava pe' la Cavulima
> nu jurne pedecagna pedecagna

e da nu belle cerre de castagna
lu patracchiolò cantava 'ncima

Dall'atu quarte culla stessa rima
pareva respunnesse alla sulagna
Santa Loja cu' tutta la muntagna
vestuta a festa e verda come a prima

Sci, come pprima, quanne 'ssi pentune
e 'ssi canale, mo tutte 'ndeserte,
jèvene vigne, mennele e perune.

A quiddu belle cante, come fosse
nu sonne a jocchi aperte, ei viste certe
quant'eva bella 'ntanne quistu fosse! (Borazio 1982, 21)

Walking down the Cavulima
one day along the mountain slope
an oriole was singing from the crest
of a tall and beautiful chestnut tree.

On the other side drenched in the sunlight
Santa Loja seemed to sing back
with the whole mountain, immersed
in the green and festive colors of yore.

Indeed, like long ago when these bare rocks
and these ditches, now a desert,
were vineyards, almond trees, and prunes.

In that wonderful chorus I swear
I really did see as in a daydream
how beautiful this ravine was then! (Translation mine.)

Nature occupies an important space on Borazio's visual palette and imagery related to it did not fail to draw the attention and the admiration of the audiences. And so did the theme of abandonment and desolation of the cultivated land caused by the migration of large numbers of workers seeking occupational opportunities in the industrialized cities within Italy or abroad where work was available in the postwar period. Borazio's melancholy nostalgia for the splendors of the rural past met with sympathetic solidarity with the public. The elegiac register also envelops several poems about the war, the suffering of those on the front lines, and especially, the suffering of those left behind at home, mothers, spouses and children.

The fable is a genre dear to Borazio who must have been fond of reading Aesop and La Fontaine and actually has little to envy these practitioners of that genre, except for the paucity of samples, given his short life. In *La preta favedda* there are several noteworthy examples applauded generously by the audience who related to them particularly well because of the social context and of the characters found in them with their sharp satirical wit and biting humor. Following are two examples.

"Nu cavadde e nu ciucce scalefone"

Nu cavadde e nu ciucce scalefone
tiravene na vota lu traine:
lu cavadde tirava pe' timone
e lu ciucce tirava a valanzine;
e pe' gghinte la Vadda di Stignane
cammenàvene 'nnanze a chiane e chiane.

Lu ciucce ch'eva ciucce appresentuse,
scuprennece a nu punte li varlese,
ha ditte: "E che vu' fa', i' so' fiamuse,
vide quanta medaglie porte apprese!
Ma pecché non me passano a ripose,
date che so' nu ciucce valorose?"

Ci vota lu cavvadde cu' rispette:
"Ce sa che si' fiamuse e si' deritte,
ma li medaglie che tu purti 'mpette
so' medgalie di ciucce… state citte!
Ma i' te dicirria, giuvenotte:
tuccame n'atu pochicche fa notte". (Borazio 1982, 45)

"A horse and a battered donkey"

A horse and a battered donkey
were pulling a cart together one day:
the horse was at the helm
and the donkey at his side;
through the valley of Stignano
they proceeded step by step.

The donkey, being a bit presumptious,
showing his sores at some point
said: "What can I tell you, I'm famous,
see all the medals on my breast!
Can't imagine why they don't retire me,
seeing I'm a donkey so valorous!"

The horse turned to him with respect:
"We know you're famous and even cunning
but the medals on your breast
are a donkey's medals… best you keep still!
My advice to you, young man, is this:
move a little quicker, it's getting late". (Translation mine.)

"Nu porce delli mamme"

Nu porce delli mamme, cu' na vota,
ha fatte decessette purcedduzze.
Ha ditte lu purcare: "Che recota!
Quist'anne avime voglia a dice juzze!"

E quanne l'allattava, ogni purcedde
teneva nu purpigne accaparrate;
ma ce ne steva une, puveredde,
che lenzava da fore sparecchiate.

Allora, pe' na quedda, lu purcare,
te conta li purcedde e li capcrchie,
e dice: "A come ve' lu pare e spare,
ce sta nu purcedduzze de superchie."

Responne lu purcedde: "E allu straccione!
li cunte li sa' fa' ma si' maligne:
e non te pare che cuntanne bone,
ce manca adderettura nu pupigne!" (Borazio 1982, 100)

"A Breeding-sow"

A breeding-sow in just one litter
gave birth to seventeen piglets.
The swineherd said: "what a harvest!
This year we can't say we're poor!"

At feeding time each piglet
had a nipple all his own,
but there was one, poor fellow,
that was left out all alone.

So, the swineherd to make sure
counts all the piglets and the nipples,
then exclaims: "I reckon by my tally
there is one piglet too many".

The piglet then replied: "you smelly wretch!
You're sure able to count but you're also wicked:
if you counted justly, you'd see
that what is really missing is an extra nipple!" (Tranlsation mine.)

Romantic love is a theme not often treated by Borazio, but when he does, it is usually narrated in the satirical ironical vein with comic tonalities typical of the best poetry of this bard who was not unschooled in the tradition of Cecco Angiolieri and the late thirteenth century poesia giocosa. One example is "Amore Sediticce" ("Stagnant Love").

'St'amore mia non mette chiù calima
e va' a capisci 'ncorpe che arracama,
'st'amore mia ci secca alla curima
e no' risponne manche a chi lu chiama.

La nenna mia non è chiù com'e prima,
Sta pensosa pensosa e chiù non m'ama:
quanne me vede, smesta e ci va a 'ncima
sope lu tavulate, quedda 'nfama.

Come pensasse: "Ne', che me ne fuma!"
Come dicesse: "A me che me ne prema!..."
Povere amore mia svanisce e sfuma.

Quistu core che tozzela e che trema,
mo preja alla Madonna che l'alluma,
se pe' disgrazia è diventata scema. (Borazio 1982, 25)

This love is not sprouting any buds
hard to figure what her mind is stitching up,
this love of mine has drooping boughs
doesn't respond to anyone calling.

My darling is not how she used to be,
she's deep in thoughts and loves me no more:
when she sees me, she turns and runs
atop her loft, the cruel woman.

As if she's thinking: "What do I care?"
As if she's saying: "What's it to me!"
My poor love is wasting and waning.

This heart that knocks and trembles,
now prays the Holy Mother to enlighten her,
since for some mishap she's lost her mind. (Translation mine)

Translation is a very versatile tool for teaching, for disseminating literary works across cultures, for critical interpretation of texts, and as a critical creative process. But in my personal experience, it works best as a pedagogical tool when the audience is made aware of the problems inherent to the translation process. Knowing that the translation cannot be a substitute for the original work raises the critical awareness of the formal literary and linguistic structures of the original text and underlines the uniqueness of its expressive language. This in turn serves as incentive toward the study and acquisition of the language. Drawing the attention of the audience on the original text through the reading of the translation increases their curiosity and interest placing once again the language of the original text at the center of their attention stimulating further their desire to study it. In this sense the translation works also as a tool for the critical exploration of the language of the original text showcasing the uniqueness of each language and the full value of their expressive properties. Ultimately languages are incommensurable as Umberto Eco points out in his book on translation entitled *Dire quasi la stessa cosa* where the adverb *quasi* reveals all the challenges that the translator faces who is confronted at every step of the way with having to negotiate, as Eco puts it, among numerous semantic and literary forms, and having to make choices that ultimately are dictated by the translator's literary tastes and creative inclinations (Eco 2003, 59).

In short, translating holds many rewards but it is also a protean task where the translator can never claim absolute victory since the original text cannot ever be identically duplicated in the translation. In this struggle to capture what is ultimately impossible to encompass completely and yet something of its essence and aura does flow into the translation, in this wrestling of meaning and form lies the agony and the ecstasy of the perennial task of the translator.

WORKS CITED

Borazio, Francesco, Paolo. 1982. *La preta fevedde.* Edizioni Quaderni del Sud / Lacaita.

Croce, Benedetto. 1956. *Uomini e cose della vecchia Italia.* Bari: Laterza.

de Martino, Ernesto. 2001. *Sud e magia.* Milano: Feltrinelli.

Dell'Aquila, Michele. 1995. *La poesia dialettale del Novecento.* Torino: Einaudi.

Eco, Umberto. 2003. *Dire quasi la stessa cosa.* Milano: Bompiani.

Salvatore Scarpitta: Beyond Painting

Lorenzo Canova
UNIVERSITÀ DEGLI STUDI DEL MOLISE

Abstract: The essay explores the work of Salvatore Scarpitta, an Italian-American artist who redefined the boundaries of painting through material experimentation. Bridging Italy and the U.S., Scarpitta evolved from expressionist and abstract influences to the radical use of "extroflexed" and "bandaged" canvases. His approach aligned with the Roman tradition of polimaterismo and was shaped by figures like Prampolini and Burri. Scarpitta's innovative techniques prefigured aspects of Minimalism and installation art, incorporating found objects and references to racing culture. His artistic journey—from Futurist-inspired chromaticism to a dynamic orchestration of matter—reveals a deep search for meaning and a new expressive reality. Through a transatlantic dialogue, Scarpitta emerges as a "bridge-artist," connecting avant-garde traditions and influencing both European and American art scenes.

Between Rome and the United States

Salvatore Scarpitta was pioneer of the visual arts during the second half of twentieth century, an exponent of a strand of the Italian avant-garde that would enjoy considerable international development, and an experimenter who blended techniques and expressive forms: He represents a special case and a bridge between Italy and the United States.

Firstly, let us recall the biographical events of Scarpitta's life: he was born in New York in 1919, to a Sicilian father and a mother of Russian-Polish heritage. After growing up in Los Angeles, he moved to Rome in 1936 to study at the *Accademia di Belle Arti.*

During the Second World War, having escaped imprisonment, he joined the Italian Resistance and became a liaison with the United States army. He later joined the US Navy and became a member of the 'Monuments Men'. [1] After leaving, he returned to Italy and settled back in Rome. Here, in the Italian capital, his artistic journey began. In 1948 he participated in the *Quadriennale* and the following year he held his first solo exhibition at the Tanino Chiurazzi Gallery. During the 1950s he took part in numerous exhibitions, including the editions of the

[1] See the biography in: https://www.mattiadeluca.com/artisti/salvatore-scarpitta/ (accessed 18 March 2025);
https://www.monumentsmenandwomenfnd.org/scarpitta-s2c-salvatore-c-jr?srsltid=AfmBOooPjZIG-ZnDiW1nBxV_P1byxNh1ic9uUqnh-SBgs--tMtrdLbOFy (accessed 28 February 2025)

Venice Biennale of 1952, 1956 and 1958. In 1958 he presented his 'extroflexed' and 'bandaged' or 'wrapped' canvasses in a further solo exhibition at *La Tartaruga* Gallery in Rome, attracting the attention of critics and influencing several Italian and American artists.

This exhibition in Rome led to Scarpitta being noticed by Leo Castelli, who subsequently invited him to exhibit his work at his New York gallery. Thus, in December 1958, Scarpitta returned to the United States and, the following January, presented his 'bandaged' paintings at the Leo Castelli Gallery. This exhibition marked the beginning of a long and fruitful professional relationship and friendship with Castelli, as evidenced by the numerous personal and collective exhibitions in which Scarpitta participated in the following years. After exhibiting in many Italian and international museums, Scarpitta died in New York in 2007.[2]

It is interesting to return to Scarpitta's training and artistic beginnings in Rome, which allow us to better understand the development of his work, from his painting to the use of 'extroflexed' canvases and extra-pictorial materials.

During a 1991 interview with Giacinto Di Pietrantonio, Scarpitta recalled the artistic figures that were important during his youth spent in Rome: "…the Cascellas, Andrea and Pietro, who then moved away due to the war. The only true friends at the time were some Futurists, including Sante Monachesi, Prampolini, Roberto Melli who, however, was from *Valori Plastici.* I also met Mafai [...]. If it hadn't been for these young artists of the time like Melli, Guttuso and Cagli, my life in Rome would have been impossible".

In the same interview he spoke about the formidable "figure of Scipione" and his closest friends after the Second World War: Mino Guerrini, Piero Dorazio, Giulio Turcato, Pietro Consagra and Mario Mafai (Scarpitta 1991).

Therefore, it is within this context that Scarpitta's Roman journey can be inserted; a period in which he developed his most mature style.

---

[2] For Scarpitta: Celant 1972; Sansone 1999; Sansone, Rinder, Russell 2011; Sansone 2005; Celant, Eccher 2012; Montrasio, Sansone 2016; Sansone 2024.

During this time, he progressed from figuration with Expressionist influences, to Abstraction, and from Informalism to the elaboration of his extroflexed canvasses and famous 'bandaged' or 'wrapped' works.

Through an analysis of the stages of his work, we initially notice the reflections of Chromaticism linked to the Roman School and its connection with the artists mentioned, from Melli, Cagli and Guttuso to Scipione and Mafai. These stages are then influenced by Roman multi-material techniques (*polimaterismo*). In particular, we will see their connections with the artistic experimentation of Enrico Prampolini and Alberto Burri.

The link between Scarpitta and Mario Mafai is of particular interest. Mafai was one of the masters of the Roman School. He opened Scarpitta's exhibition at Plinio De Martiis's *La Tartaruga* Gallery in Rome in 1955, where he spoke about his fellow artist's search for:

> a language that represented this new opening and that responded to the need for a different mentality. Indeed, Scarpitta has progressed from Expressionism and Abstractionism. Today, little by little, the formalist residues are left behind and he is not among those who still indulge in hedonistic gimmicks and vain poetic allusions. Thus, like the best, Scarpitta is in pursuit of meaning and, therefore, of the figure to which he wants to give a clear moral function. And it is, in my opinion, one of the right paths, if not the only one. (Mafai 1955)

Mafai continued:

> We see him passionately engraving on the canvas with reds that resemble somewhere between the red of blood and that of a seal of fire, against the grays and blues of the asphalts and the machines of the metropolis that represent, in all their brutal aridity, the anonymity of that civilization so dramatically rendered in the pages of the best American authors. (Mafai 1955)

In his engravings on the canvas and his evocation of asphalts and machines, Mafai seemed to pre-empt the subsequent direction of the artist's exploration: his journey from the materialism of painting to a break during which Scarpitta would remember having:

> literally torn the oil canvas. The oil canvas had become so hostile to me that to find a certain peace with myself I had to tear it up and I let these torn pieces become objects that I called paintings. This was in 1957 in Rome, later I started a job to clean up what had been a rather exasperated gesture [...] I took the canvas from an evil dimension to a more "surreal" almost abstract condition, whereby the rough and raw canvas was no longer torn, but stretched! (Scarpitta, quoted in Sansone 2024, 8-9)

Therefore, Scarpitta went 'beyond painting' by tearing his canvases. It is interesting to note, that in the same period, Mafai also made a choice to reset his artistic style. Firstly, this saw him make the transition from Abstraction to a form of Monochrome. For example, this can be perceived in his 1959 painting, *Graffiare come vivere* (here we recall the engraving on the canvas of his text dedicated to Scarpitta). Subsequently, there were his more extreme works, where he used strings pasted with color.[3]

This use of material fragments – rejected by critics with links to realism, but rated by some of the most important Italian critics and gallery owners connected to the avant-garde such as Lionello Venturi, Giulio Carlo Argan and Maurizio Calvesi, Plinio De Martiis and Bruno Sargentini, – place Mafai in an isolated and entirely personal position. His work is often thought to verge on Informalism but it may not be too far removed from the most radical experimentation carried out by Scarpitta. Indeed, the latter can be linked to a form of Roman *polimaterismo*, a parallel and sometimes intersecting line of artistic enquiry that developed in the Italian capital and will be discussed in the following section.[4]

"A form of greater reality"

In 1957 Scarpitta makes a definitive shift in his work. This is characterized by the monochrome of his extroflexed canvases and the weavings of 'bandages', which initially still display chromatic elements of his previous painting style.

---

[3] For Mafai: Appella, D'Amico, Terenzi, Vespignani 2004.
[4] For the late Mafai: D'Amico 2004; Rivosecchi 2004, 46-48.

This jointed path is one of the most significant results of the idea of "poetics of matter" that found a fertile ground in Rome for its development. Starting with the Futuristic *polimaterismo*, then through the intermediary work of Enrico Prampolini, it then developed through the work of Ettore Colla and, in particular, through Burri's *Sacchi* (sacks) and *Gobbi* (hunchbacks), works that Scarpitta was able to reflect on and transform, thus creating his own constructive code.[5]

However, in addition to the influence of Burri, it is likely that through his interaction with Prampolini, Scarpitta found new ideas for the direction of his experimentation. Moreover, not to be forgotten is his relationship with Sante Monachesi, who produced works with metallic embossing and multi-material compositions during this time.[6]

In comparison to Burri, Scarpitta's experimentation can be considered even more radical and interconnected with aspects of Prampolini's theorizations.

Burri and Scarpitta were also both involved in the activities of the 'Art Club', the Roman artistic circle open to innovations in concrete, abstract art that was headed by Enrico Prampolini during this time.[7]

Therefore, it would not be implausible to hypothesize a connection between Scarpitta and Futuristic *polimaterismo*. Indeed, not surprisingly, in 1991, Giorgio Franchetti, a great friend and collector of Scarpitta's work, wrote a text entitled *Il Futurismo nel vissuto e nell'arte di Salvatore Scarpitta*, which states:

> The great paintings of 1957 dedicated to that myth, the dearest from his youth, the *Via!:* in one show, these paintings bring the structure, form and suggestion of the first Futuristic decompositions. Successive works, also from 1957 and early 1958, with their broad, transverse brushstrokes suggest bundles of energy and foreshadow the great works with the crossed bands of canvas. The influence of Burri is legitimate and openly acknowledged but only in the use of materials, which are identified as necessary to emphasize with physically highlighted forms, the principle of tension and release, intrinsic to

[5] For Burri e new materials in art: Calvesi 2000a; Calvesi 2000b; Calvesi, Tomassoni 2005; Braun 2015; Corà, Iori, Olivieri 2016.
[6] For Monachesi: Franco 2011.
[7] For the Art Club: Simongini, Conte 1998; Benzi 2022, 39-40.

energy. Through form, this energy is freed from standard and technological models, and becomes myth. (Franchetti 1991, 50)

In this way, Scarpitta seemed to reconnect both with the exaltation of the machine and to Marinetti's manifestos and the futuristic theorizations that led to the new context of the aftermath of the Second World War. This was also a result of the 'tactile' *polimaterismo*, first theorized by Boccioni and then Balla, Depero and Marinetti (Calvesi 2000 a; Calvesi 2000 b).

This long journey then found a fundamental pivotal figure in Enrico Prampolini, theorist and creator of the term "*polimaterismo*."[8]

Indeed, Maurizio Calvesi remembers that it was precisely:

> Prampolini, to carry forward in the most systematic way the '*polimaterico*' experimentation (a term he coined himself) [...]. In 1944, for the *Le Edizioni del Secolo,* he published a small book entitled *Arte Polimaterica*, in which this new artistic approach was presented as a new genre, distinct from painting and sculpture – anticipating what now can be said about some of today's most widespread forms of expression, which are no longer identifiable with the traditional categories of "painting" or "sculpture" [...]. We are now approaching the early works of Alberto Burri, who, not surprisingly, was in close contact with Prampolini in his first years in Rome. At the beginning of the new decade, he embarked on his groundbreaking research. Of course, it is superfluous to point out the differences between the Futuristic "*polimaterismo* " and the attention paid by Burri to subjects such as the "wreckage of life", with an existential engagement that opened the way for Informalism and the implications of the sign – although he later oriented himself towards a more formally pure treatment of materials, including industrial ones. However, there is an undeniable line of continuity that, starting with Boccioni's premises, flows into the heart of the artistic transformations of the second half of the century. (Calvesi 2000 b, 90-92)

Calvesi, therefore, highlights Prampolini's relationship with Burri, but we also know of his bond of friendship with Scarpitta, which developed precisely in the years when the Futuristic artist was carrying out his research into multi-material or *polimateriche* techniques.

---

[8] For Prampolini: Crispolti, Siligati 1992; Pirani 2023.

Indeed, in the aforementioned book *Arte polimaterica* written by Prampolini in 1944 we can read about "the end of the feeling of color" and the birth of:

> a new feeling: that of the lyricism of matter. POLYMATERIAL ART IS NOT A TECHNIQUE BUT - LIKE PAINTING AND SCULPTURE - A RUDIMENTARY, ELEMENTARY MEANS OF ARTISTIC EXPRESSION, WHOSE EVOCATIVE POWER IS ENTRUSTED TO THE PLASTIC ORCHESTRATION OF MATTER. *Matter* understood in its biological immanence, as it is in its formal transcendence. The *subject-matter*, in its rudimentary poly-expressive aspects; from its most humble and heterogeneous (almost the wreckage of life) to its most - manually or mechanically - refined and elaborate. The *organism-matter*: a fundamental moment for the conception of *polimaterismo*, whose formative elements have an autonomous, dynamic and plastic value, whose associations and combinations determine the assumption of a new expressive state for the form of space and the form of time in the geology of matter itself. Finally, a concept that challenges the a priori and outdated concept of the beautiful and the eternal in art. "*L'ephémer est eternel*". (Prampolini 1994, 9-10)

It is precisely this "*subject-matter*", "almost wreckage of life" that may have led Scarpitta to change the direction of his work, which he described thus:

> In 1957, when I started, but didn't know what would come out of it, I only knew that my canvases were injured and so I had to bandage them [...]. Anyway, everything has been said about the bandages, even that they have connections with those of mummies, but honestly, I was struck by the 'bandaging' of the steering wheels of racing cars and bicycles: that's where they come from. (Scarpitta 1991)

The "wreckage of life", the poor material of car and bicycle 'bandages' thus becomes the new tool that leads the artist onto an innovative path, which is undoubtedly influenced by Burri. However, his ideas are expressed in an even more radical way: on the one hand, they are connected to Prampolini's theories, on the other, they are directed towards the Italian and international experimentation of Lucio Fontana, of

Piero Manzoni and American Minimalism all of which, in different ways, are indebted to Scarpitta (Sansone 2024b, 11-14).

Scarpitta, therefore, fulfills the main premise of Prampolini's theories, truly going "beyond painting" and "towards *polimaterismo*", the title of the 1934 Futurist manifesto by this artist (Prampolini 1934).

But it is Scarpitta himself who evoked Futuristic terms in his text in the catalogue of the 1958 exhibition at *La Tartaruga*:

> Speaking and expressing yourself, just like the material – which is only the canvas itself - reveals its weave and strength, its weaknesses and its lacerations. Even the bright color fades and the symbol decays. All this made me forget about beehives in which to insert the world [...]. There are tactile elements in these canvases, but they are not blind. And with these I leave the port of matter-painting. But above all, in the relief I desire a naked and modest contact [...]. I have removed the garment that covered my canvases [...]. After looking at the earth - its color and consistency, its organic weight, which I had inserted in my previous paintings - I realized the lightness of my eyelids. And I looked up. No dazzling glare. This is how I see. (Scarpitta 1958)

Scarpitta evoked the "subject-matter" of the canvas itself and the "tactile factors" of his canvases, likely linking himself to Marinetti's *polimetriche* tactile tables and his 1921 *Manifesto of Tactilism*, the predecessor to Prampolini's *polimaterismo*. In this manifesto the father of Futurism expressed his belief in the need for a state of induced blindness to better develop the sense of touch, ideas that are echoed in Scarpitta's writing: "there are factors in the tactile order in these canvases, but they are not blind" (Scarpitta 1958).

Marinetti himself links Tactilism to Boccioni, the original source of Futurist *polimaterismo*:

> There has also long existed an art of 'plastic tactility'. My great friend Boccioni, a Futuristic painter and sculptor, perceived things tactilely when, in 1911, he created his plastic ensemble:

Fusione di una testa a di una finestra, using materials that were absolutely opposite in terms of weight and tactile value: iron, porcelain and women's hair.[9] (Marinetti 1921)

The importance of this *polimaterico* line, which – through Marinetti – extends from Boccioni to Prampolini has already been noted in relation to Burri's work. However, in this regard, it is important to highlight how Scarpitta himself emphasized the difference between his work and that of Burri:

> Because Burri's job has a post-cubist structure, whereas mine doesn't. They have always called my work Expressionist, while I have fought an internal battle to contain this expressionism in my early work, which led to the crosses of St. Andrew. I come from a fairly classic background, like Fontana. If, in fact, you take some of my paintings and put them next to Fontana's, you realize that in him the cut is a gesture while for me, it is a conclusion. When oil paint dripped from my fingers, I felt that the canvas itself had to somehow open up, so that I could get to a greater form of reality with my work, because my story is not about aesthetics, it is a search for meaning. (Scarpitta 1991)

In his pursuits of reality, Scarpitta was not so much influenced by the Futurist fascination with speed, as by what Prampolini defined "a rudimentary, elementary means of artistic expression, whose evocative power relies on the plastic orchestration of matter" (Prampolini 1944). In this point, Marco Meneguzzo writes that:

> Sal Scarpitta's problem is not to completely reject every linguistic model, but rather to develop one that allows the artist to maintain that state and that stage of "innocence" of the work, which we can then call originality, primordiality, even primitivism, if we want to also add to the existential categories an aesthetic and historical-critical category. In this sense, his torn and recomposed canvases, the "X Frames", as well as the "sleds" must be understood. Unlike other artists - and especially Alberto Burri, who had nonetheless taught something with his "Sacks" - in Scarpitta's work the composition is

---

See also: Calvesi 2000a; Calvesi 2000b.

not as noticeable as the determined action required to build it. In other words, it is as if Scarpitta's work is constantly built before our eyes: what we see is, above all, is the artist tearing, pulling, weaving, stretching the X-frame, bending the straps, fastening and tightening the sled harnesses – preparing his mental equipment for the journey of exploration he is about to undertake. And yet, he does not reveal the territory, only the need to go forward. (Meneguzzo 1999)

Thus, for the artist, the experimentation with materials really had what Prampolini defined "an autonomous dynamic and plastic value, whose associations and combinations determine the assumption of a new expressive state" (Prampolini 1944).

Therefore, Scarpitta did not appear to be interested in the genuine multi-material work of the older Futurist artist. Rather, linked to his theoretical framework, was a search that, over the years, led to installation works in which the artist assembled materials and objects, often using his typical X-shaped structure. He also took inspiration from the world of motor racing, as Sansone - one of the greatest scholars of the artist – has argued:

Scarpitta's American phase, full of creative ideas, as well as further developing the bandaging theme is oriented in four main directions: the geometric realization of works with the significant 'X' structure; the vital grafting of materials from around the world of motor racing into his bandaged canvases (seat belts, exhaust pipes, car fragments); the construction of racing cars (some pretend like *Rajo Jack*, dedicated to a famous African-American drivers and others fully functional, participating in countless competitions on the clay circuits of Maryland and Pennsylvania); and the creation of sleds and towing structures inspired by the world of native Americans. (Sansone 2024b, 12)

Scarpitta's works of the 1960s continued his experimentation with recycled materials, which he repurposed with the patient strength of a constructive gesture that rescued the "wreckage of life" from rejection, creating a new existence for it.

Moreover, seeking further inspiration from Futurism, he may have wished to save the artwork and thus the efforts of the artist from the confinement of a gallery or a museum, thus encroaching on the space of life. This culminated in the building, for example, of racing cars, such as Sal's *Red Hauler Special* (1966–67), dedicated to Jean Christophe, the son of Leo Castelli, and in participating in races with his team. [10]

At the beginning of the 1970s, Scarpitta continued with his series of 'Sled' sculptures, moving onto totemic sculptures during the 1980s and the installation of the great *Hill Canoe* in 1990. These artworks pay homage to the culture of native Americans, using more recycled materials assembled, however, with a profound understanding of their sacredness. This crowned the journey of discovery and experimentation of a unique and extraordinary man, an artist whose history straddles Italy and America. We know how Scarpitta's work – often exhibited by the greatest gallery owners of his time such as Leo Castelli - inspired many American artists. Indeed, at the beginning of the 1960s, this happened with his "installations based on an X, true architectural structures in pictorial form", where "one can perceive an affinity and an anticipation of some of the themes of the American minimalists [...] who orient their research, with different materials, towards elementary forms and primary structures, accentuating the concept of seriality and multiple compositions" (Sansone 2024b, 13-14).

These artistic phases thus complete Scarpitta's circular journey, a man of Italian heritage, who was born and who died in New York but who was also capable of exporting the innovations of his complex Roman training. His work evolved from early chromaticism and pictorial density to extra-pictorial materials. His experimentation may have been influenced by the work of Enrico Prampolini, a friend from his youth and a key link between the history of the Italian and international avant-garde and the experimentations of younger generations. Scarpitta, therefore, represents a true bridge-artist, a link between countries and continents capable of weaving together and reinterpreting different influences. His journey uniquely gave rise to a personal and ex-

[10] For exhibitions of Scarpitta's *Racing cars* in American museums see, for example, Ho 2014; Melandri 2018.

traordinary fusion of chromaticism and *polimaterismo*, between Futurism and Minimalism, all within the coherence and rigor of an international vision.[11]

Works Cited

Appella, Giuseppe, Fabrizio D'Amico, Claudia Terenzi, e Netta Vespignani, eds. 2004. *Mario Mafai, una calma febbre di colori.* Catalogo della mostra, Roma, Palazzo Venezia. Milano: Skira.

Benzi, Fabio. 2022. "La Nuova Pesa di Alvaro Marchini." In *Una storia nell'arte. I Marchini tra impegno e passione.* Catalogo della mostra, Roma, Palazzo Carpegna-Accademia di San Luca; CIAC Foligno. Roma: Accademia di San Luca.

Braun, Emily. 2015. *Alberto Burri. The Trauma of Painting.* Catalogo della mostra, New York, Solomon R. Guggenheim Museum 2015–2016; Kunstsammlung Nordrhein-Westfalen, Düsseldorf K21 Ständehaus 2016. New York: The Solomon R. Guggenheim Foundation.

Calvesi, Maurizio. 2000a. "L'arte italiana nel Ventesimo secolo." In *Novecento. Arte e storia in Italia.* Catalogo della mostra, Roma, Scuderie Papali del Quirinale, Mercati di Traiano, 2000–2001, 19–39. Milano: Skira.

Calvesi, Maurizio. 2000b. "Dal Futurismo alle poetiche della materia." In *Novecento. Arte e storia in Italia.* Catalogo della mostra, Roma, Scuderie Papali del Quirinale, Mercati di Traiano, 2000–2001, 88–93. Milano: Skira.

Calvesi, Maurizio, e Italo Tomassoni, eds. 2005. *Burri, gli artisti e la materia. 1945–2004.* Catalogo della mostra, Roma, Scuderie del Quirinale. Cinisello Balsamo: Silvana Editoriale.

Celant, Germano, e Danilo Eccher, eds. 2012. *Salvatore Scarpitta.* Catalogo della mostra, Torino, GAM, 2012–2013. Cinisello Balsamo: Silvana Editoriale.

Corà, Bruno, Aldo Iori, e Rita Olivieri, eds. 2016. *Burri, lo spazio di materia tra Europa e USA.* Catalogo della mostra, Città di Castello, Fondazione Palazzo Albizzini, Ex Seccatoi del Tabacco, 2015–2016. Città di Castello: Fondazione Palazzo Albizzini.

Crispolti, Enrico, e Rosella Siligato, eds. 1992. *Prampolini. Dal Futurismo all'Informale.* Catalogo della mostra, Roma, Palazzo delle Esposizioni. Roma: Carte Segrete.

[11] I would like to thank Francesca D'Alfonso; Galleria Mattia De Luca, Rome; Daniela Fabrizi; Ruggero Montrasio- Montrasio Arte, Monza, Milan, Piacenza; Amy Muschamp; Fabio Sargentini, Galleria L'Attico, Rome.

D'Amico, Fabrizio. 2004. "L'ultimo Mafai." In Appella et al. 2004, 33–39.

Franchetti, Giorgio. 1991. "Il Futurismo nel vissuto e nell'arte di Salvatore Scarpitta." In *Scarpitta. Opere 1955–1964*, Catalogo della mostra, Roma, Studio Durante. Ristampato in Sansone 2024b, 49–50.

Franco, Francesco. 2011. "Monachesi Sante." *Dizionario Biografico degli Italiani*, vol. 75. https://www.treccani.it/enciclopedia/sante-monachesi_(Dizionario-Biografico)/ (consultato il 28 febbraio 2025).

Ho, Melissa. 2014. *Salvatore Scarpitta. Traveler.* Brochure della mostra, Washington DC, Hirshhorn Museum and Sculpture Garden, 2014–2015. Washington DC: Hirshhorn.

Mafai, Mario. 1955. "Salvatore Scarpitta." *Bollettino della Galleria La Tartaruga*, aprile. Roma.

Marinetti, Filippo Tommaso. 1921. *Il Tattilismo. Manifesto futurista.* Milano.

Melandri, Lisa, ed. 2018. *Salvatore Scarpitta. Racing Cars.* Brochure della mostra, St. Louis, Contemporary Art Museum. St. Louis: Contemporary Art Museum.

Meneguzzo, Marco. 1999. "Racing Sal." In Sansone 1999, 33–39.

Montrasio, Ruggero, e Luigi Sansone, eds. 2016. *Salvatore Scarpitta. Material X.* Catalogo della mostra, M&L Fine Art. Milano–Londra: Montrasio Arte, M&L Fine Art.

Pirani, Federica. 2023. "Una costellazione di elementi. Dal contesto archivistico alla filosofia dell'incertezza. La poetica di Prampolini dagli anni Trenta ai Cinquanta." In *Laboratorio Prampolini #2. Disegni, taccuini, e progetti inediti dal Futurismo all'Art Club*, Catalogo della mostra, Roma, Galleria d'Arte Moderna, 2023–2024, 11–23. Cinisello Balsamo: Silvana Editoriale.

Prampolini, Enrico. 1934. "Al di là della pittura verso i polimaterici." *Stile futurista* I(2): 8–10.

Prampolini, Enrico. 1944. *Arte polimaterica (verso un'arte collettiva?).* Roma: Edizioni del Secolo.

Rivosecchi, Valerio. 2004. "Mafai e la critica." In Appella et al. 2004, 41–49.

Sansone, Luigi, ed. 1999. *Salvatore Scarpitta.* Catalogo della mostra, Bagheria, Civica Galleria Renato Guttuso di Villa Cattolica. Milano: Mazzotta.

Sansone, Luigi, ed. 2005. *Salvatore Scarpitta. Catalogue Raisonné.* Milano: Mazzotta.

Sansone, Luigi, ed. 2024a. *Sal. Salvatore Scarpitta.* Catalogo della mostra, Roma, Galleria Mattia De Luca. Torino: Allemandi.

Sansone, Luigi. 2024b. "Salvatore Scarpitta, un americano a Roma." In Sansone 2024a, 8–17.

Sansone, Luigi, Lawrence Rinder, e Anne-Marie Russell, eds. 2001. *Salvatore Scarpitta. Trajectory*. Catalogo della mostra, New York, Marianne Boesky Gallery. Cinisello Balsamo: Silvana Editoriale.

Scarpitta, Salvatore. 1958. Testo in catalogo della mostra, Roma, Galleria La Tartaruga.

Scarpitta, Salvatore. 1991. Intervista a cura di Giacinto Di Pietrantonio. *Flash Art*, n. 161. https://flash---art.it/article/salvatore-scarpitta/ (consultato il 28 febbraio 2025).

Simongini, Gabriele, e Gisella Conte. 1998. *Art Club 1945–1964. La linea astratta.* Catalogo della mostra, Parma, Galleria D'Arte Niccoli. Parma: Galleria Niccoli.

Fig.1 Salvatore Scarpitta, Ammiraglio, *1958, bands and mixed media, cm 86 x 60, private collection.*

Fig.2 Salvatore Scarpitta, Untitled, Dedicated "To Cy" (Twombly), 1958, everted canvas, cm 35.5 x 30, Private Collection.

Fig. 3 Salvatore Scarpitta, Fasce (Bandages), 1958, bandages and painting, cm 68x58, courtesy Montrasio Arte Monza, Milano, Piacenza.

Fig. 4 Salvatore Scarpitta, Box Kite, 1961, bandages and mixed media on board, 164x135 cm, courtesy Montrasio Arte, Monza, Milano, Piacenza.

Fig.5 Salvatore Scarpitta, Gravity, 1963, bandages and painting on wooden armature, cm 55,5x52,5, courtesy Montrasio Arte, Monza, Milano, Piacenza.

Fig.6 Salvatore Scarpitta, Sal's Red Hauler Special, 1966-67, Dedicated to Jean Cristophe Castelli, racing car, 110 x 270 x 128 cm, courtesy Montrasio Arte, Monza, Milano, Piacenza.

La poesia dialettale in America

Luigi Bonaffini
BROOKLYN COLLEGE – NEW YORK

Abstract: It can be said that contemporary dialect poetry (or *neodialect poetry*, according to Brevini's definition) finally arrives in the United States with the publication of *Moliseide* (New York, Peter Lang Publishing, 1992) by Giose Rimanelli. This is no longer the Italian-American popular poetry centered on vignette-style storytelling and folkloric scenes, nor is it a matter of Italian dialect poetry included in anthologies. Rather, it is an Italian writer living in America who chooses to write a book of poems in his native Molisan dialect, freeing it from themes traditionally associated with dialect poetry – such as sentimental sketches, local color, and nostalgic sentimentality – with full awareness of all the expressive possibilities of the chosen medium, and entirely in tune with the formal and linguistic foundations and the most advanced techniques of contemporary dialect poetry. Luigi Reina calls it a "migrant" dialect, as it is rooted in the subjectivity of the emigrant/speaker, "committed to recovering a 'cultural' language that in some way reconciles him with contemporaneity and with 'nature' without succumbing to the risk of regression" (Reina 1990, 76).

La letteratura italiana, ci ha ricordato Gianfranco Contini, è l'unica grande letteratura nazionale per la quale il dialetto è una parte integrante ed ineliminabile. Questa profonda verità, troppo spesso dimenticata in passato, ed offuscata dal persistente pregiudizio del dialetto come strumento espressivo inadeguato ed "inferiore," si è venuta affermando in modo perentorio a cominciare dagli anni settanta del secolo scorso, grazie ad una inaspettata e quanto mai rigogliosa fioritura di poesia in dialetto, che rappresenta senza dubbio uno dei fenomeni più importanti e caratterizzanti della letteratura italiana del secondo Novecento, e che ha rimesso in discussione il concetto stesso di letteratura dialettale, poggiando anche su un proliferarsi senza precedenti di studi, di convegni, di libri, di dibattiti.

Negli Stati Uniti esiste da lungo tempo una tradizione di poesia dialettale di ascendenza popolare, quasi sempre legata ad un uso nostalgico della dialettalità volta al recupero di un'identità minacciata e di una realtà antropologica abbandonata ma mai dimenticata, e quindi ancorata alla tematica dell'emigrazione e ai problemi dell'acculturazione, compreso quello fondamentale della lingua. Le espressioni italo-americane[1] che spesso lardellano il testo sono le tracce visibili, testuali,

[1] Per uno studio del linguaggio degli Italo-Americani, vedi Haller 1993.

con remoti rimandi pascoliani, di questo arduo processo di acculturazione. I maggiori esponenti di questa poesia dialettale di emigrati sono i siciliani Vincenzo Ancona (1990) e Nino Provenzano (1994), il cui mondo poetico rientra per lo più nell'ambito della poesia dialettale tradizionale (ricordi, lavoro, quadri d'ambiente, affetti familiari), ma arricchito dal continuo confronto di due culture diverse, dal quale scaturiscono considerazioni sul mondo moderno e sulla condizione dell'emigrante. Una simile vena umoristico/moraleggiante percorre le poesie in dialetto napoletano di Nino Del Duca, una volta assiduo collaboratore del giornale italo-americano "America Oggi", che ogni domenica pubblicava un suo componimento mistilingue (dialetto, italiano e qualche anglicismo) in cui il poeta offriva i suoi commenti bonariamente ironici sugli aspetti più vari della vita di una grande città americana (Del Duca 2009).

La poesia dialettale in America

Miller Williams, *Sonnets of Giuseppe Belli.* 1981
"In alcuni ambienti c'è l'assunzione che, poiché il romanesco è considerato un dialetto da coloro che non lo parlano, le poesie di Belli non possano essere veramente tradotte a meno che non siano trasformate in una sorta di linguaggio regionale. La verità, naturalmente, è esattamente il contrario. Se traduciamo le poesie in qualsiasi tipo di dialetto, gergo o linguaggio slang, le sentiamo solo così come le avrebbero sentite e le sentono ora la classe media e alta romana. Se vogliamo avvicinarci a esse come facevano gli abitanti di Trastevere, allora dobbiamo sentirle come loro lo facevano, nel linguaggio semplice della nostra stessa conversazione. Il fatto semplice è che, per coloro che vivono a Trastevere, il linguaggio parlato a Trastevere è il modo in cui la gente parla." (Williams 1981)

John Duval, *Tales of Trilussa* (1990), *The Discovery of America* by Cesare Pascarella, 1992

Herman Haller, *The Hidden Italy: Bilingual Edition of Italian Dialect Poetry*, 1986.

Il libro di Herman Haller, "L'Italia nascosta: Edizione bilingue della poesia dialettale italiana", del 1986, è la prima edizione bilingue inglese di alcune delle migliori poesie dialettali italiane scritte negli ultimi due secoli. La selezione di più di quattrocento poesie in piemontese, veneto, milanese, romagnolo, romano, napoletano, siciliano e altri dialetti illustra per la prima volta l'impressionante varietà della civiltà letteraria e linguistica italiana.

The Other Italy: The Literary Canon in Dialect 1999.
"Un'altra Italia: Il canone letterario in dialetto" (Studi Italiani di Toronto) esplora i due canoni letterari italiani, uno nella lingua toscana e l'altro composto dai vari dialetti delle molte regioni italiane.
Il libro offre una panoramica dei dialetti letterari d'Italia in cinque secoli e attraverso le regioni del Paese, gettando luce su una civiltà profondamente plurilingue e policentrica. Come guida alla lettura e alla ricerca, fornisce un compendio di fonti letterarie in dialetto, ordinate per regione e accompagnate da sintesi delle tradizioni regionali con illustrazioni testuali selezionate.

Gaetano Cipolla.
Direttore della rivista bilingue (siciliano-inglese), *Arba Sicula: Journal of Sicilian Folklore And Literature,* specialista di poesia siciliana e traduttore. Edizioni Legas.

Giovanni Meli.
1.*L'origini di lu munni* (1985)
2 Don Chisciotti e Sanciu Panza (1986)
3. *Favuli murali* (1988)
4. *The Poetry of Giovanni Meli* 2015
5. *Philosophical tales about the origin of the world* 1985 di Giovanni Meli.
6. *The Poetry of Nino Martoglio,* 1993
7. Antonio Veneziano, *Ninety Love Octaves* 2008
8. Vincenzo Ancona, *Malidittu la Lingua/ Damned Language* 2010
9. Domenico Tempio: *Poems and Fables* 2010
10.*The Poetry* of *Nino De Vita* 2014
11. Nino Provenzano *Vinissi (I Would Love to Come)* 1999, and

12. *Tornu* (The Return), 2009;
13.*The Poetry of Ignazio Buttitta*, 2023

John Welle and Ruth Feldman *Peasants Wake for Fellini's *Casanova* and Other Poems* 1997.
Zanzotto: "Nelle traduzioni, quindi, se il passaggio dall'italiano all'inglese (o in un'altra lingua) è già incerto, il passaggio dal dialetto a una lingua straniera diventa quasi impossibile. Il dialetto non può essere reso in Inglese Standard. Sarebbe necessario trovare qualche patois o gergo che fosse comunque piuttosto ampiamente conosciuto nell'area anglofona."
L'introduzione di Welle cita i successi di altri traduttori come Williams, Haller, DuVal e Cipolla come un fattore contributivo nella decisione di "non seguire il percorso suggerito da Zanzotto".

Joseph Tusiani
POESIA DIALETTALE
1. *Làcreme e sciure*, 1955;
2. Il primo canto dell'Inferno in vernacolo garganico, 1977;
3. Tìreca tàreca. Poesie in vernacolo garganico, 1978;
4. Annemale parlante, 1994;
*4.La poceide. Poemetto in dieci canti in dialetto garganico*1996;
5. Na vota è 'mpise Cola. Favola in dieci canti in dialetto garganico, 1997;
6. Li quatte staggione e poesie ritrovate, 1998;
7. Lu deddù. Poemetto in ottava rima in dialetto garganico, a c. 1999;
8. Maste Peppe cantarine. Favola in sette canti in dialetto garganico, 2000;
9. Làcreme e sciure, 2000;
10. Lu ponte de sòla. Melodramma in dieci canti in dialetto garganico, 2001;
11. L'ore de Gesù Bambine. Favola natalizia in dialetto garganico, 2001;
12. La prima cumpagnia, 2002;
13. Lu frustere, 2002;
14. La tomba de Padre Pi', 2003;
15. Lu cunte de Pasqua. Atto unico in tre scene in dialetto garganico, 2003;
16. La padula. Poesie in dialetto garganico, 2004;
17. Lu scazzamuredde, 2005.
18. Storie dal Gargano. Poesie e narrazioni in versi (1955-2005), 2006;
19. Sciusce de vente, 2009.

Maurizio Godorecci, *Tra li fijeume/ Between Rivers*, Legas 2010 (abruzzese)

Raffaello Baldini, *Small Talk* (romagnolo, translation by Adria Bernardi), Gradiva 2009.

Raffaello Baldini, *Page Proof* (theatrical monologue, romagnolo, translated by Adria Bernardi), Bordighiera Press, 2001.

Tonino Guerra. *Abandoned Places*, (romagnolo, translated by Adria Bernardi), Guernica 1999.

Salvatore Di Giacomo: *Love Poems: A Selection, Guernica* 1999 (napoletano, translated by Frank Palescandolo).

Amedeo Giacomini, *Presumut Unviar/ It Looks Like Winter/ Presunto Inverno* (friulano, translated by Dino Fabris) Legas 2016.

Mariano Bàino *Yellow Fax and Other Poems*, translated by Gianluca Rizzo and Dominic Siracusa, napoletano, Agincourt Press 2019

Ma credo si possa dire che la poesia neodialettale approda finalmente negli Stati Uniti con la pubblicazione di *Moliseide* in edizione trilingue (dialetto-italiano-inglese) dello scrittore molisano Giose Rimanelli nel 1992. Non si tratta più di poesia popolare italo-americana imperniata sul bozzettismo ed i quadri di costume o di poesia dialettale italiana riportata in antologie, ma di uno scrittore italiano che vive in America e decide di scrivere un libro di poesie nel suo dialetto molisano, svincolandolo dai temi tradizionalmente legati alla poesia dialettale, come il bozzettismo e il colore locale, con piena coscienza di tutte le possibilità espressive dello strumento prescelto, e completamente in sintonia con le tecniche più avanzate della poesia dialettale contemporanea. Il poeta dialettale contemporaneo non è più legato al municipio, alle tradizioni locali, alla cultura regionale, alla cultura del folklore espressa dall'antica civiltà contadina ormai scomparsa, ma è una persona colta, che ha fatto le stesse esperienze letterarie e culturali del poeta in lingua, che conosce altre lingue e altre letterature, s'interessa ad altre forme d'arte e di comunicazione come la musica o il giornalismo.[2] Spesso vive lontano dal luogo natio, e rimane quindi estraneo

[2] Queste osservazioni provengono da *La maschera del dialetto*, a cura di A. Foschi e E. Pezzi, Longo,

alla cultura letteraria regionale, riscoprendo la lingua materna dopo notevoli esperienze letterarie ed esistenziali, ormai purificata da condizioni e implicazioni psicologicamente e culturalmente subalterne. Questo decentramento culturale gli permette di inserire esperienze culturali eccentriche nel corpo della poesia dialettale, ed è proprio la tensione che si crea tra l'ampiezza delle esperienze culturali ed il mezzo linguistico periferico e locale che caratterizza la poesia del neodialettale. I riferimenti culturali non sono più le letterature regionali, ma le letterature straniere (francese, inglese, americana) in un orizzonte culturale ormai illimitato, che è poi l'*habitat* naturale in cui si muove l'opera di Rimanelli. Seguendo le indicazioni di Brevini, che distingue tre gruppi di poeti dialettali – quelli che scrivono solo in dialetto, quelli che approdano al dialetto dopo un'esperienza in lingua e quelli che alternano i due codici – Rimanelli si colloca senz'altro nel terzo, gli "autori in cui l'esercizio della poesia avviene all'interno di un orizzonte di tipo sperimentale, sfruttando tutte le risorse legata alla variazione alessandrina dei codici".[3]

La traduzione della poesia dialettale in inglese presenta problemi particolari, relativi soprattutto alla premessa molto discutibile che vede il dialetto come deviazione rispetto ad un linguaggio standard.[4] Infatti, la maggior parte dei traduttori non solo rifiuta il concetto di dialetto come linguaggio deviante ed eccentrico, ma lo considera invece il luogo della naturalezza e della spontaneità, la norma linguistica di una determinata comunità e quindi (secondo un criterio metodologico solo in apparenza paradossale) l'esatto contrario di deviazione. Nelle poesie in dialetto molisano di *Moliseide,* che recano a fronte la mia traduzione inglese, il problema del dialetto è complicato dalla estrema letterarietà del testo, sistematicamente contaminato da riferimenti alla poesia trovadorica, alla poesia latina medioevale, alla poesia americana e francese, al jazz e ai blues. È un testo caratterizzato dal plurilinguismo e pluristilismo e da una ricca varietà di soluzioni metriche, dal verso libero alla ballata, dall'endecasillabo al doppio settenario, con abbondanza di rime

---

Ravenna, 1988, p.64.

[3] Brevini, *Le parole perdute*, Torino, Einaudi, 1990, pp. 125-126.

[4] Per la problematica della traduzione dal dialetto, rimando al mio saggio *Traditori in provincia. Appunti sulla traduzione dal dialetto,* in "Italica" 72.3 (estate 1995), pp. 209-227.

ed assonanze. Il dialetto è quindi il tronco su cui si innestano le più svariate esperienze linguistiche e letterarie ed il traduttore è costretto a seguire gli intricati percorsi testuali della parola poetica, nella consapevolezza che la difficoltà maggiore risiede più nella stratificazione culturale e letteraria del testo e nella ricerca di un risultato anche ritmicamente adeguato, che rispetti il movimento interno del verso, che nello specifico dialettale. L'intraducibilità del dialetto, cioè la sua opacità semantica, è proporzionale all'uso gergale, fortemente idiomatico della parola, circoscritta al colore locale, municipalistico. D'altra parte, la traducibilità del dialetto dipende appunto dall'eliminazione degli elementi più strettamente gergali, delle punte idiomatiche troppo accentuate, come accade in Giotti, in Marin ed in Noventa (Cfr. Brevini 1990, 236-243). Ma anche in *Moliseide* il dialetto evita uno spessore troppo marcatamente idiomatico, anche perché vi predomina la componente musicale, la rima e l'assonanza, a cui male si adatterebbero un linguaggio volutamente disarmonico ed una sintassi frantumata e concitata. Prendiamo ad esempio la prima strofa della prima poesia di *Moliseide*:

Quanne t'èzzíccche a i vríte du pènziére
e fóre chiagne u sole, ze fa' nòtte,
u sanghe te ze chiátre, sie' strèniére:
a vije da terre tíje dónde sta'? (Rimanelli 1992)

Quando t`avvicini ai vetri del pensiero / e fuori piange il sole, si fa notte, / il sangue ti si gela, sei straniero: / la via della tua terra dove sta?

Da notare, oltre alla sapiente orchestrazione melodica ed alla forte evocatività delle immagini, la prima in particolare, che in questa strofa non c'è nessuna parola o espressione dialettale che presenti particolari difficoltà per il traduttore, proprio perché mancano gli idiomatismi troppo accesi; è invece nel tono che esse si annidano, nella modulazione ritmica e nella struttura metrica, per cui nella traduzione è stata per necessità scartata la rima, che avrebbe inciso notevolmente sulla possibilità di seguire la sottile linea melodica del testo:

When you get near the glasspanes of your thoughts
and outside the sun weeps, and darkness falls,
your blood turns into ice, you are a stranger:
the road back to your land, where can it be?

WORKS CITED

Ancona, Vincenzo. 1990. *Malidittu la lingua / Damned Language.* New York: Legas.

Bàino, Mariano. 2019. *Yellow Fax and Other Poems.* Trans. by Gianluca Rizzo and Dominic Siracusa. Napoletano. Agincourt P.

Baldini, Raffaello. 2001. *Page Proof.* Theatrical monologue in Romagnolo, trans. by Adria Bernardi. Bordighera P.

________. 2009. *Small Talk.* Romagnolo, trans. by Adria Bernardi. Gradiva.

Belli, Giuseppe Gioachino. 1981. *Sonetti.* Bilingual edition, translated by Miller Williams. Baton Rouge: Louisiana State UP.

Bonaffini, Luigi. 1995. "Traditori in provincia. Appunti sulla traduzione dal dialetto." *Italica* 72 (3): 209–227.

Brevini, Franco. 1990. *Le parole perdute.* Torino: Einaudi.

Capobianco, Michael F., trans. 2009. *Io stongo 'e casa 'America / I Live in America: Neapolitan Poems by Nino Del Duca.* New York: Legas.

Del Duca, Nino. 2009. *Io stongo 'e casa 'America / I Live in America: Neapolitan Poems.* Trans. by Michael F. Capobianco. New York: Legas.

Di Giacomo, Salvatore. 1999. *Love Poems: A Selection.* Napoletano, translated by Frank Palescandolo. Guernica.

DuVal, John, trans. 1990. *Tales of Trilussa.* Fayetteville: University of Arkansas Press.

________. 1992. *The Discovery of America.* By Cesare Pascarella. Translated from Romanesco. Fayetteville: U of Arkansas P.

Giacomini, Amedeo. 2016. *Presumut Unviar / It Looks Like Winter / Presunto Inverno.* Friulano, trans. by Dino Fabris. New York: Legas.

Godorecci, Maurizio. 2010. *Tra li fijeume / Between Rivers.* Abruzzese. New York: Legas.

Guerra, Tonino. 1999. *Abandoned Places.* Romagnolo, trans. by Adria Bernardi. Guernica.

Haller, Hermann W. 1986. *The Hidden Italy: A Bilingual Edition of Italian Dialect Poetry.* Detroit: Wayne State UP.

________. 1993. *Una lingua perduta e ritrovata: L'italiano degli italo-americani.* Firenze: La Nuova Italia.

________. 1999. *The Other Italy: The Literary Canon in Dialect.* Toronto: U of Toronto P.

Provenzano, Nino. 1994. *Vinissi / I'd Love to Come.* New York: Legas.

Rimanelli, Giose. 1992. *Moliseide.* Trilingual edition (dialect-Italian-English). New York: Peter Lang.

________. 1998. *Moliseide and Other Poems.* Ottawa: Legas.

For further reading, see also:

Bonaffini, Luigi. *Italian dialect poetry* (website): http://userhome.brooklyn.cuny.edu/bonaffini/dp/aboutme.htm

A Global Photographer Returns to His Roots: Frank Monaco (1917-2007)[1]

Norberto Lombardi
INDEPENDENT SCHOLAR

Abstract: Upon returning to his family's homeland—Molise—young American Frank Monaco reconnects with the deepest roots of his identity. This experience leads him to shift from his artistic studies to photography—a pursuit that would define his life and establish him as an internationally acclaimed photographer worldwide. Dating back to the early 1950s, his early photographs document the anthropological transformation of Southern Italy's rural society. They portray its gradual disintegration, brought on by a new wave of emigration, and the evolving role of women in work and social life. After relocating to London in the mid-1950s, Monaco created a body of work still appreciated by experts and scholars today. His photos capture the places of suffering and pain, as well as the houses of interiority and prayer that he visits. They depict cloistered monasteries and dwell on forms of spirituality and harsh life in India. Critics have praised Monaco's work for his "rare ability to see" and the "gentle realism" of his photographic eye. His pictures are described as "consistently rich in human content, always well-structured, and—despite evident luminist exploration—anchored in psychological and realistic depth". Frank Monaco wished for his ashes to be returned to Molise.

The 'Return'

On September 11, 2007, ninety years after his birth (Brooklyn, December 27, 1917), Frank Monaco makes his definitive return to Italy. More precisely, he 'returns' to Molise, to the locations of his childhood imagination, where he sought his family and cultural roots, and where his calling as a photographer first emerged.

On this day, Molise is bathed in dazzling sunshine. In the morning, a hall in the castle of Macchiagodena hosts a conference dedicated to commemorating the Twin Towers attack—where a descendant of emigrants originally from the village also lost his life—and to honoring Monaco, who had passed away in London just over two months prior (June 26, 2007). This unusual pairing is due to the intricate family ties that Frank's parents had with Macchiagodena. During the meeting, a London-based nephew of Frank's wife Lavinia—who herself had died a few years earlier—unexpectedly appears in the conference hall. Without explaining the reason, he discreetly invites a select few of those

[1] Translated from Italian by Barbara Quaranta.

present to join him in the late morning at the Taverna, the old inn nestled on the *tratturo*, the ancient sheep track, at the crossroads of Cantalupo del Sannio.

As the sun reaches its zenith, a dozen cars descend upon the open space facing the Taverna. Judging from the occupants' exchange of warm greetings, primarily in English, they seem to be acquainted with one another. Soon, the London-born nephew and some Italian relatives led the group towards a bridge over a nearby stream, the Rio, a tributary of the River Biferno. A young woman, smiling, offers a flower to each of those present. Shortly after, the nephew reveals Frank's heartfelt wish for his ashes to be scattered in the river. Then, in a hush of absolute participatory silence, he recites a few verses in English. Following this secular prayer, from a small bridge, he empties the ashes from the urn into the stream. The attendees join in, casting their flowers into the water. Silence lingers for a few minutes, filled with emotion and memories, before the group returns to the Taverna. The voices have now grown louder. At last, the attendees weave their way to a restaurant in Cantalupo, where an abundant and welcoming reception awaits.

Family Background

Born in the United States and residing in London, a photographer who was constantly on the move across various continents to work and expand his knowledge, at the end of his intense life, makes a symbolic gesture: having his remains returned to the place his parents had left about a century earlier, when they moved overseas. What meaning lies behind such a decision? What existential and ethical forces drive an internationally renowned professional and artist to choose an unexpected, remote, and intimate location for his final resting place?

Frank Monaco's story is inextricably linked to his biography. It is essential not only to understand his human and psychological traits, but also, as we shall see, to outline the stages of his professional and artistic origins as well as his distinctive features. It is thus worthwhile to reflect on his family and youth.

For Frank's family, America first materializes during the Great Emigration, when his maternal grandfather, Francesco Compagnucci, makes his decision to leave the Carabinieri Corps and join the vast wave of emigration that led millions of Italians and tens of thousands of *Molisani*[2] to experience life and work in the United States. Unfortunately, a hunting accident leaves him permanently disabled, plunging his small family into a precarious situation. Francesco decides to report his case to the authorities and seek help from none other than the supreme commander of the Carabinieri Corps, the king of Italy, who provides him with financial assistance after some time. This allows Francesco to return to Italy with his wife Cristina and their daughter Bianca, born in America, and purchase the old tavern on Cantalupo's tratturo. In addition to becoming their family home, the Taverna also serves as the new source of income for the Compagnucci family, which grows rapidly. Six more daughters are born, including Chiarina, Frank's mother, and finally Vincenzo, the long-awaited son.

Chiarina grows up caring for little Vincenzo and lending a hand in the Taverna, until she strikes up a friendship with her cousin, Giacomo Monaco, from Santa Maria del Molise, a nearby village. This is not well regarded by her parents, particularly her mother—herself a Monaco—who, wishing to steer her daughter away from this unwelcome relationship, sends her to New York to stay with relatives. It is now 1915 and amidst the bustling community of southern immigrants where her relatives are settled, Chiarina meets a young Italian, Antonio Rispoli, from Pietrelcina, a village in Benevento, now known as the birthplace of Padre Pio. The two young emigrants get married, and Frank is born, taking on his father's surname: Frank Rispoli. However, the situation takes a sudden turn when Antonio falls victim to the raging Spanish flu epidemic in early 1919.

Meanwhile, Giacomo Monaco, Chiarina's cousin from whom she had been taken away, also arrives in New York. Thanks to his *compaesani,*[3] he learns of Chiarina's new circumstances and reconnects with her. They finally find their way back to each other, and from their newfound love, three more children are born: Daniel, Anthony, and John. Frank can once again enjoy a father's presence and affection, but for Chiarina, it is not enough: she wants him to be just like his siblings,

[2] Translator's note: *people from Molise.*

[3] Translator's note: *fellow villagepeople.*

even in name, and to embrace the new surname. Frank Rispoli thus becomes Frank Monaco.

Unlike his younger siblings, however, Frank still speaks primarily in his native Italian dialect with his parents. After all, the stories, especially those his mother told him, are a constant reminder of their relatives back home and the life they lead. They evoke characters, idioms, traditions, and social and religious customs that had taken root in a society that is structurally and culturally rural. Typically, on special occasions, the menu offers traditional foods, dishes, and flavors that taste like family. This is not a one-dimensional experience: Frank's work, the streets, the school, the neighborhood, his network of acquaintances, and the inescapable social rules increasingly feed the traits of his new life context into the traditions of his origins. Frank's childhood imagination harbors duplicity of feelings and ways of thinking that are typical of second-generation immigrants, which will later ignite his everlasting desire to weave together the rediscovery of his roots and the exploration of the new world in which his existence unfolds. It is through this quest that he seeks to understand his mother in a more authentic and intimate way; he is deeply connected to her and, through her, to himself.

His Arrival in Rome

Frank's childhood and early youth unfold in a context typical of Italian immigration context: a family with deep-rooted ethnic ties, a neighborhood where old and new regional elements blend in an environment that is both original and traditional, yet one where strong and widespread assimilation dynamics are at play. In his words: "Back then, my relatives, like most immigrants, had one goal in mind: to become *'Mericani*[4] as quickly as possible."[5] He attends school until the age of 16. Then, to escape the inertia and the risks of dubious company within the neighborhood, he swaps his paperwork in order bring forward his military service, serving in Panama for two years. When he returns, he is more mature and ready for work. Yet, an inclination begins to surface, that, even as a child would lead him to transform everything he

[4] Translator's note: *Americans* in the local dialect.

[5] Frank Monaco, *Obiettivo sull'anima*, edited by N. Lombardi, Cosmo Iannone, Isernia, 2002, p. 22.

saw and felt into images, into drawings everything he sees and feels into images and drawings since his childhood. He begins attending evening classes for drawing at various universities. This first artistic training allows him to find work more suited to him and more enjoyable—that of a designer of advertising posters—which he refines while continuing with the evening classes.

In 1942, the echoes of war grow louder and more urgent. Frank is drafted into the military and is sent to England as a sapper. As D-Day draws near, he is reassigned to his unit. As he is instructing recruits on how to defuse one particular bomb, the device explodes in his hands, severing several fingers of his right hand, the hand he uses for drawing. Following the arrival of the wave of wounded from the Normandy landings, the hospitals are cleared, and Frank is discharged with a permanent disability pension.

The impact of war on Frank's life leaves an indelible sign, marking a series of existential turning points and opening new horizons to be pursued under the impulse of an increasingly explicit calling for artistic expression. The injury to his right hand causes him significant distress, particularly regarding his potential to continue the artistic training he had embarked on prior to his departure for the European front. On the other hand, the disability pension provided by the United States government spares him any practical hardships and, within certain limits, grants him the freedom to pursue a career that comes closer to matching his expectations. He divorces the woman he had married before leaving—their marriage had not withstood the long separation. However, from this relationship is born a son, Clifford, who will give Frank four grandchildren: a lasting source of affection over the years.

Unable to continue his work as an artist, he joins an advertising agency, where he works tirelessly for several years until he rises to the position of manager. Just when he seems to have successfully launched onto this new path, he leaves it, much to the dismay of his relatives and He focuses on his university courses in art and journalism, which until then had been confined to evening hours. He takes another step forward by seizing the opportunity to benefit from the scholarships offered by the government to war veterans to facilitate their reintegration into the workforce. He thus decides to refine his skills in Rome, where he takes art classes at Studio Hina in Villa Borghese. It is now 1950. With him, is his brother David, who is studying aeronautics and who stays until he is drafted for the Korean War.

The Rome in which the two young men find themselves is a feverish yet contradictory city, still reeling from the frictions of a challenging transition from the Fascist regime. A constant and tense confrontation unfolds between the religious traditionalism surrounding the pontificate of Pius XII and the secular drive of the political-cultural forces that have emerged in the new democratic climate. Rome's civil life is burdened by the ingrained behavioral and social problems of its citizens. Yet it is animated by a quest for novelty and freedom that ignites many consciences and sparks a wave of people seeking new opportunities and experiences. Particularly, writers, journalists, artists, aspiring actors and directors flock to the 'capital', as they see it as a place to test their mettle and establish themselves. These are the years when neorealist cinema catapults the name and allure of a modern, restless, and unrefined Rome onto the international scene. Meanwhile, the revived myth of a vibrant, energetic, and powerful America is rapidly spreading across Italy. This is especially true in Rome, particularly in the realm of cinema.

In that bustling hub of encounters, connections, and exchanges, Frank cultivates friendships with various artists, notably Pericle Fazzini[6] and Afro Basaldella.[7] While the Hina courses seem to follow the school

---

[6] When Frank Monaco begins seeing Pericle Fazzini in the renowned Via Margutta studio, the Marche sculptor was already a well-established artist on both the national and international scene. He has already exhibited in Paris and Rome, received an award at the 1935 Rome Quadriennale, and participated in the Venice Biennale with several works, including the renowned *Portrait of Ungaretti*, who named him 'the sculptor of the wind'. In the late 1930s, Fazzini joins the ranks of the leading Italian artists in the 'Corrente' group, all of whom are united by their anti-fascist leanings. In 1947, he exhibits at MoMa in New York, showcasing the Italian art of the 20th century. He returns in 1952, while Frank is still in Italy, following his anthological exhibition in Rome (1951) and before his second participation in the Venice Biennale (1954). During his regular visits to his friend, Monaco captures the lengthy creation of the *Transfiguration* on celluloid, the grand bas-relief that can be seen during papal audiences behind the Pontiff.

[7] Precisely during the years of contact with Frank, Afro Basaldella, a native of Friuli, makes his entry in the American art scene. This experience provides him with crucial inspiration for his evolution toward abstract art, leading to a lasting style that garners significant and generally widespread recognition. After his initial encounter with the Roman School and the subsequent period of maturation in Milan, he participates in the *Quadriennale* of Rome (1935) and the Venice *Biennale* multiple times during the 1930s. In 1950, with the help of Corrado Cagli, he embarks on his first journey to the United States, where he discovers motifs and inspiration that lead him to transition from a 'neocubist' figuration to an abstract style. In New York, he entertains a long-lasting relationship with the Catherine Viviano Gallery, where many of his works are showcased. He is one of the artists featured in the exhibition *'The New Decade: 22 European Painters and Sculptors,'* which tours the major US cities.

routine, his interactions and contact with his fellow artists open doors and windows, allowing him to breathe fresh, invigorating air.

The People of Molise

Thanks to their stay in Rome, Frank and his brother Daniel are also brought incredibly close to the places of their mother's stories and family memories: Molise, Cantalupo, and the Taverna. All the more so, since a coach from Rome to Campobasso departs daily, despite the ongoing challenges of post-war transportation. The bus also calls at Isernia, where Zio[8] Vincenzo Compagnucci's popular gas station is located.

The two young men board the coach, winding their way through the ruins of Cassino, where Frank will return many times, moved by a sense of compassion and camaraderie for the thousands of soldiers from all nations who had died in the battle of Monte Cassino. Then they venture through the Tre Torri pass, still plagued by muggers lurking in the woods, and reach Isernia, where Zio Vincenzo's family welcome them with open arms and warm hearts. After a few days, their uncle drives them to Cantalupo and the Taverna, where strong-willed and dynamic Zia Vincenza[9] embraces them with her boisterous courtesy.

Their return to their family roots is not just a reunion with evocative and symbolic places, but a journey into memory, into the tales that his mother told him, and the image that the young boy had woven around them. The entrance to the rooms, his grandfather's rifle hanging on the wall, the portraits, the grand fireplace, the washbowl, and the mirror are all emotional threads that form a tapestry of emotions, a mosaic hidden by time that Frank had already pieced together in his imagination, and in that moment, is brought back to life. He joyfully entertains conversations with his uncles and acquaintances, who come to visit their 'American relatives', but deep down, Frank is profoundly moved. When at last, they are alone in the room that once belonged to his grandparents, he envisions his entire family, both near and far, dead and alive, as if they have been reunited to live together in the grand house.

---

[8] Translator's note: *Zio* is the Italian for Uncle.

[9] Translator's note: *Zia* is the Italian for Aunt.

The following day, Zia Vincenza introduces him to a small world that he has never seen before and yet has always been present in his imagination. She shows him the places from his mother's stories and the people he has heard about. Frank's ears start to pick up the sounds of the workers and the animals roaming around the Taverna. In the subsequent days, he immerses himself in the social life of the village: the square, the market, and the church. A community profoundly shaped by emigration, not only in the distant past when Frank's family had been torn apart, but also in the aftermath of the fall of fascism, when departures have once again become frequent[10]. He witnesses the pivotal role women play in managing family life, tending to the fields, caring for the elderly and children, upholding religious practices, and preserving traditions[11]. He begins to realize that these humble people, deeply rooted in their land and family, may seem crude and even primitive to the metropolitan visitor's eyes. However, they possess a tenacity, willingness to sacrifice, and an inclination to form open and supportive relationships. These qualities stem from deep-rooted convictions and ingrained traditions.

Frank begins to develop a feeling of affection for this environment, not only because of the familiar cues he recognizes and takes, but also because of the authentic values he breathes, despite their being different from those of the city where he grew up. After his initial visit, he frequently returns to the Taverna and Cantalupo, always armed with pencils and paper, to capture the discoveries and impressions of his visits and encounters in the form of drawings. Even though figurative drawing remains his main concern, he also brings a camera with him

---

[10] From the time the official statistics of Italian emigration began, in 1876 and until 1915, the *Molisani*, who were 395,000 in the 1901 census, crossed borders approximately 315,000 times. In the first 25 years of the second half of the 1900s, nearly 150,000 *Molisani* out of a population of 406,000 in 1951 permanently left their homeland. The district of Campobasso [translator's note: *district* translates here the typically Italian *provincia*] has one of the highest emigration rates among the Italian districts, both in the first and second waves. Source: Italian General Commission for Emigration; ISTAT.

[11] For a deeper understanding of the complex dynamics of feminization in exodus areas and women's participation in emigration flows, please refer to Franco Ramella, *Reti sociali, famiglie e strategie migratorie* (pp. 143-160), and Bruna Bianchi, *Lavoro ed emigrazione femminile* (pp. 257-264), both in P. Bevilacqua, A. De Clementi., E. Franzina (eds.), *Storia dell'emigrazione italiana - Partenze*, Donzelli, Roma 2001. To understand the condition of Molise women during the Great Emigration and the feminization phenomenon in rural Molise during the second half of the twentieth century, see Adele Rodogna's *La solitudine delle donne molisane ai tempi della prima grande emigrazione*, Meltemi, Milano, 2018, and Ricciarda Simoncelli's, *La femminizzazione dell'agricoltura. Il caso del Molise*, USPI, Roma, 1972.

to capture the essence of places, figures, and forms, perhaps with the intention of transferring them onto his drawing sheets.

During a meeting with the artist Afro Basaldella, Frank shows him the drawings. Afro is impressed.

> "Where did you do them? Where are these people?"
> "They're country folk, people of Molise."

Eager to satisfy his friend's curiosity, Frank also shows him the photographs he has taken. Afro gazes at them for a long time, over and over again.

> "Frank, everything you're trying to capture in your drawings is already in these photos. Why bother looking any further?"

'Your honest hands'

Frank senses that a new, unexpected path is waiting to be explored. He makes a sacrifice and buys a Rolleiflex, which becomes his inseparable travel companion on his excursions. In Cantalupo, he captures the essence of the village through his lens, immortalizing the people, places, and animals that are part of its daily life, such as women at the market, processions, festivals, and everyday routines. With Zia Vincenza as their intermediary, women often request that he photograph their families to send the photos to relatives overseas. The photographs he is requested chiefly to take are those of children born after their fathers' departure or who have recovered from long illnesses: a sort of certificate of survival and good health. Thus, Frank gains access to people's homes. In the interplay of light and shadow, he captures the plainness, the restraint, the simplicity of those who live there, and the pervading warm atmosphere. One day, however, while walking along a trail, he encounters a young woman tending to a small flock. He greets her, but she simply looks through him and remains silent. On another occasion, he is called to the home of a young mother to take a photo of her baby, born after the father's departure. When he enters, the young woman covers her head with a black scarf out of modesty in front of a stranger. Then, she spontaneously reveals her breast and begins to feed the baby, while posing for the camera. (Fig.1. Frank Monaco is summoned to a farmer's house to take some photos of a child born after his father's emigration, so that he can get to know his baby. Upon the stranger's entrance, the woman respectfully covers her head with a black scarf. Then, with such natural ease, she uncovers a breast and offers herself to the camera while breastfeeding. Thus, restraint and decorum pertain to social relations, not to natural functions. The light falls on the child and the woman's breast, a figurative reference that seems to highlight the idea of motherhood in the rural world.

Frank realizes that despite feeling he belongs to these people in some way, to them he is still a stranger; as much as they are fond of him; he is still ‘the American’. He thus realizes that he needs to take a step forward. Observing with sympathy and openness, capturing the images of their busy day or their jovial social lives is not enough. He has to strive to connect with their life principles, the dignity they display in facing separation, poverty, and marginalization. He has to reach out for the courage they show while trying to redeem themselves from their impoverished condition and sufferings. As evidenced by his best photographs taken in what has become 'his' farming community, Frank eventually manages to take such a step further. He gradually reduces the level of randomness and externality in the images, highlighting the most intimate and authentic dimension of the situations he captures in his images. He also feels the need to share this evolution with his mother, as in a letter he sends her during those years, he writes:

> I tried to approach your paesani as close as I could, wherever I met [translator’s note: *them*]. At times, I was on a margin, like the straniero; then there were moments when their land and their folkways were as native to me as your voice, your laughter and your prayers. From a distance, and then, near enough to feel the friendly clasp of their honest hands, I tried to show their dignity, strength and integrity. (Monaco 2002, 33)

This emotional and ethical journey also marks a significant shift in his style and critical approach. It helps him evolve from representing the human and social reality in a southern village to committing to interpreting their codes and rules. Such norms inspire individual behavior and foster collective relations in a community that has its own internal cohesive force. The transformation does not only involve a more introspective interpretation of figures and environmental contexts, but also a more meticulous pursuit of the images' formal quality, particularly in terms of compositional care (Fig.2. Frank is asked to capture the special moments of a baptism. A woman is holding the baby, already dressed in ceremonial attire, while two girls are entertaining him. The play of light does not focus on the child, who remains in the shadow of his mother, but rather highlights the cheerful gestures of the young women reaching out to him, creating a dynamic continuum of figures and a sense of movement. By reversing the light exposure of the group members, the image does not just capture the baby who is being celebrated, but the joyful atmosphere that gathers around the entire family. Although, as we shall see, Monaco would later describe his photography as an immediate and dynamic way to connect with people and things, his artistic training and attention to spatial organization are evident from his very first shots, particularly in his skillful use of light shafts to define the image's background (Fig.3. A scene of everyday life, such as women collecting water for domestic use, becomes an opportunity to bring together multiple aspects of community life in a refined stylistic synthesis: the routine of everyday life, women's work and customs, the solidity and beauty of their bodies, and the female sociability, a trait that was best displayed at the fountains. A white background highlights the figures that are framed by the windows through an angle of light that accentuates such themes. The diagonal shadow cast by the axis conclusively arranges and connects the spaces). A polarity of interests, thus, begins to emerge - art and the 'real' people in their daily lives—as mentioned by Tarquinio Maiorino.[12] This journalist, who knew Frank well, describes such duality as a combination that would follow him throughout his career as a photographer.

---

[12] T. Maiorino, *Il giramondo col Molise nell'anima*, in F. Monaco, *Obiettivo sull'anima*, cit., p. 17. In 1950, Monaco meets the *Molisano* journalist in Isernia through a mutual friend. They would meet again several times in Rome, eventually forming a genuine friendship. A former director of widely popular Italian magazines

The occasional and intentional photographs taken in Cantalupo and its surroundings in the early 1950s will prove to be a significant and valuable record of the condition of a southern community at a time when a profound transition was taking place: that from a persistent state of rurality[13] to a slow and belated 'modernization'. This transition would undoubtedly lead to improved living conditions and a spread of the so-called '*opere di civiltà*'[14]. However, it would also erode a wealth of anthropological traits, traditions, and social patterns. These images capture the essence of such a way of life and environmental situation just before they vanish in a process of profound change. It is for this reason that their value transcends immediate representation, rightly placing them in a historical and documentary dimension (Fig.4. This image is one of the most 'profound' and representative of Molise and the people who inhabited it. After World War II, it also became a symbol of a historical era with its hilly landscape barren in autumn and winter, its stone villages resting on the hillside, its settlements in scattered houses, its few winding, unpaved roads, isolation, and rocky paths. The farmers are dressed in their traditional dark attire and have 'cioce' on their legs [translator's note: traditional leather footwear with large soles, tied to the leg by straps]. The women are wearing black headscarves and shawls.

This collection of visual records, which, as we have seen, also captivated some of Frank's artist friends, not only outlines the rural community he frequents and the entire Molise region, but also, to a large extent, reflects the essence of Southern Italy and its inland areas. In fact, beyond the occasional circumstances in which they are taken, the images about work bring us back to the fundamental paradigm of activities aimed at ensuring survival and a life of hardship at the cost of extreme daily struggles. Yet at the same time, those related to festivals and religious rites renew the complex debate concerning the existence

---

such as '*Sorrisi e Canzoni*', '*Donna*', and '*Tutto Turismo*', Maiorino commissions Monaco several photo shoots to be published in his magazines.

13 According to the 1946 Agricultural Census, Molise's rurality rate was still 80.1%, with only a slight decrease from the previous decade's 80.3%. This is the highest percentage among the Italian provinces, which in 1936 leads the fascist regime to publicly label Molise as an 'extremely rural province'.

14 Translator's note: in English 'works of civilization', which refer to governmental projects and interventions aiming to modernize the country.

of an underlying persistent 'peasant civilization' in the historical events of the community. This is consistent with the situation described in other parts of Southern Italy during the same period, as confirmed by the statistical indices[15] and the so-called 'peasant literature'[16].

The Women of Molise

A key to understanding the crumbling reality captured in Monaco's 'peasant' images lies in the prevalence of women not only in the domestic sphere but also in work, religious rites, and community festivals[17]. Perhaps the intertwining of maternal memories and Zia Vincenza's effusive chatter inspires Frank to delve into the heart of village life.

---

[15] The 'Southern question' [translator's note: the Italian *questione meridionale*] has been a recurring theme since the late 19th century, raised by leading southernists from the liberal school (Villari, Sonnino, Franchetti, Fortunato, Nitti, De Viti De Marco), the radical democratic school (Dorso), and the socialist one (Salvemini, Ciccotti, Gramsci). However, it is only after World War II that it becomes a genuine economic and social dualism, with the indices of regional areas showing a different trend depending on whether they refer to areas located in the Center-North or in the South of the country.: 'In 1951, the distinction between the Center-North and the South was clear: Italy was a dualistic economy. Apart from Marche and Umbria, in all regions of Central-Northern Italy, the per capita income is higher than the national average. However, in Campania, the richest southern region, it barely reaches 68%. In Calabria, Abruzzo, Molise, and Basilicata, the per capita income is about half of Italy's average'. This is according to Vittorio Daniele and Paolo Malanima's work, 'The Product of the Regions and the North-South Divide in Italy 1861-2004,' published in the *Journal of Economic Policy* in March-April 2007, pp. 280-81. Translated.

[16] The recent centenary of Rocco Scotellaro's birth (1923-2023) has led to a re-edition of his works (Rocco Scotellaro, *Tutte le opere*, edited by Franco Vitelli, Giulia Dell'Aquila, Sebastiano Martelli, Oscar Mondadori, Milano 2019). This anniversary has also sparked a broader critical re-examination of the tense debate that arose in the first decade after World War II. This involved on the one hand intellectuals who affirmed the originality and autonomy of a 'peasant civilization' in the Southern folk culture (Levi, De Martino, Rossi Doria, Scotellaro) in various ways. On the other hand, other scholars (Alicata, Manacorda, Sereni, etc) took part who were in line with the guidelines provided by the PCI's cultural committee [translator's note: the acronym stands for the *Italian Communist Party*]. Such intellectuals considered these cultural traits as a factor of political-cultural backwardness and an obstacle to the democratic renewal of both the country and the South itself. This debate gradually fades away in the mid-1950s, partly due to the structural changes occurring in the South and following extraordinary interventions and emigration. The only two interludes in this process are the publication of *Inchiesta a Palermo* by Danilo Dolci and *La chiesa di Canneto* by Felice Del Vecchio (relaunched in 2023 in a critical edition by Cosmo Iannone), both of which were awarded at Viareggio in 1957. Today, the 'peasant literature' is being revisited due to its relevance in addressing the need for repopulation and revitalization of rural areas, as well as its connections to ecological issues.
For a comprehensive anthropological perspective, refer to Giovanni Battista Bronzini's *Cultura contadina e idea meridionalistica*, published by Dedalo, Bari, 1882; for an account of the literary debate on the phase mentioned above, see S. Martelli, *Il crepuscolo dell'identità. Letteratura e dibattito culturale degli anni cinquanta*, Ed. Laveglia & Carlone, Agropoli (SA), 1988; F. Vitelli, *Perché abbiamo bisogno di Rocco Scotellaro*, in R. S., *Tutte le opere*, cit. pp. V-XVI.

[17] For further readings on the role of festivals in reflecting the structure of a community's social relations and providing opportunities for social cohesion, see Gino Massullo, *Francesco Jovine tra letteratura, antropologia, storiografia e politica*, in F. Jovine, *L'impero in provincia*, Cosmo Iannone, Isernia, 2024, pp. 134-35.

However, it is equally plausible that he seeks to capture a genuine process of change that had been brewing in the rural world during the early 1950s. The men are resuming the path that the Molisani had been taking for at least seventy years, along with millions of other southern Italians. Fascism tried in vain to disrupt this outflow, only managing to put it on hold temporarily. This time, it is not just '*Merica*[18] that draws them in, but also Italian cities and beyond the border to Belgium, France, the United Kingdom, and, subsequently, Switzerland and West Germany.

As a result, the role of women, which in the rural world has never been confined to traditional reproductive and domestic functions, becomes increasingly pervasive and extends to the structural functions of the community. Monaco's work is a significant testament, particularly in the areas of harvesting, as well as breeding and tending to animals. The image of a woman pausing her work to observe a stranger with a steady, inquisitive gaze is now considered a symbol of the deep-rooted rurality of the Molise people, reaffirmed at the time of its passing. Yet, it is also emblematic of the dignity and autonomy of a world that has been hastily labeled as backward and vestigial (Fig. 5). While going from Isernia to Cantalupo del Sannio, Monaco spots a woman who is working in a field on her own. He asks the person who is driving to stop, gets closer and takes a photo of her. The woman turns to him and gives him a questioning yet dauntless look. Then, she casually resumes her work. The woman's solitary work, her firm and reserved demeanor, the rugged landscape, and the barren soil make it one of the most expressive and indicative photographs of the post-war condition in the region, as it also evokes Molise's historical rurality.

Still unaware of his professional calling, the American photographer captures moments of social life with the same attentiveness and insight as he does during festivities and religious practices (Fig.6. The vibrancy, strength, and beauty of Frank Monaco's rural women shine through this photo, taken during one of the village's festivals. The protagonists' play of hands forms a spiraling upward movement, giving the scene a sense of dynamism and joviality. Smiling at the stalls while

[18] Translator's note: *America* in the regional dialect.

choosing clips for their hair, covered with the customary black head-scarf, the young women exude femininity, joy, vitality, and firm beauty. They do not consider those moments as mere interludes in a closed and resigned existence, but they adopt a distinct viewpoint on a world that is not lacking internal complexity.

The images capturing women's participation in the festive mass and the procession of the patron saint echo a conventional type of religiosity that is crucial for preserving community traditions. Similarly, the photographs taken by Monaco during a long devotional journey along the Adriatic to the sanctuaries of Loreto, Assisi, and Padua, up to Venice, transcend the boundaries of the sociological document. They somewhat resemble a travelogue where the environmental diversity and the radiance of the sea spark psychological reflections, igniting the peasant women's wonder at discovery and excitement for newness (Fig.7. "I was captivated by their enchanting encounter with the sea, their wonder at things never seen before, their curiosity for the new, and their awe towards the unknown", Monaco 2002, 32. Translated.

For Frank, this journey becomes a chance to delve deeper into the world he has rediscovered, inspired by his mother's memories.

> Throughout the long journey, [the women] interspersed joy and friendly jokes with moments of prayer, singing together the hymn of *Santa Maria Madre di Dio.*[19] They would then grab their baskets, unfold their large, colorful napkins, and eat the bread and cheese they had brought from home. They offered me some, demonstrating their warmth and decency.[20] I listened to the heartfelt confessions, the resounding joy, the prayers, and the anguish of those women dressed in black, yet as fresh and lively as lush, green plants. I was captivated by their enchanting encounter with the sea, their wonder at things never seen before, their curiosity for the new, and their awe towards the unknown. (Monaco 2002, 32)[21]

It is thus through his encounter with the feminine that Monaco senses this rural world as the bearer of values, skills, and work ethics,

---

[19] Translator's note: *Saint Mary, Mother of God.*

[20] Translator's note: in Italian *creanza*

[21] Translated.

bonds of solidarity, decency,[22] traditions and a strong fertile connection with nature. When intertwined, these elements can weave the fabric of a 'civilization' that should not be overlooked or allowed to wither because it is backward and distant from a presumed model of 'modernity'. Instead, it should be understood and appreciated for its 'otherness' and its ability to embody the essence of humanity and a spirit of solidarity. All the more so as the feminine interpretation of the rules and practices of that world is revolutionizing the ancient gender hierarchy, fostering more flexible and respectful relationships within it.

Frank knows that the greatest threat to the world he now feels connected to lies within it, as the new wave of emigration leads to social disintegration. He has grasped its profound and venomous nature, and he seeks to expand his family experience with moments of direct knowledge and insights into potential remedies. He ventures to the port of Naples, where he witnesses the poignant departure of a ship brimming with emigrants, as their farewells and tears fill the air. Still, he does not dwell on this heart-wrenching pain. Drawing on his previous evening courses in journalism, he crafts a lengthy story, which unfortunately will never be published. In this narration, Monaco envisions the return of an emigrant who, having amassed a great fortune, decides to share it with those who remained, in a bid to keep them from leaving. However, to keep the beneficiaries' existential impulses and their drive toward newness alive, he lays down a condition: each of them must set a goal to strive for. In essence, they would follow in the footsteps of those who had left, albeit in different circumstances.

In another iconic image, this time of the exodus, he once again turns to women to highlight the enduring bonds that persist even during and after the abandonment, and the unwavering strength of female *restanza*.[23] In the village square, Frank captures the luggage, which

---

[22] Translator's note: the Italian *creanza*.

[23] Translator's note: this could be defined as the act or fact of remaining or being left over which is complementary to the act of leaving or departing. The term is a neologism that was initially coined by Jacques Derrida and introduced in English as *restance* through Barbara Johnson's translation of Derrida's work *Dissemination*, The Athlone Press with University of Chicago, London, 1981. In Italy, however, this term was reinterpreted and reintroduced by Italian anthropologist Vito Teti in his 2011 book *Pietre di pane: un'antropologia del restare*, edited by Quodlibet. The book was subsequently translated in English as *Stones into Bread. Trans. by Francesco Loriggio and Damiano Pietropaolo*, Guernica Editions, Toronto, 2018. In this case, *restanza* specifically refers to the condition of the people from the South of Italy who deliberately choose

stands out in the foreground as a symbol of departure. Then, surrounding the departing man, a 'crown' of women emerges before him, as if to block his path (Fig. 8. To different extents, all the southern villages' squares were estuaries of emigration currents: transoceanic first and, in the decades following World War II, also European. The Matesina area [translator's note: Italian for the area of Matese], where this photo was taken, was historically one of the most significant contributors to the entire Molise exodus. This image reveals two dimensions. One is the crown of women surrounding the departing man, making him the focal point of the scene, with a cut of light that outlines his profile. A sense of a non-temporary detachment is conveyed by the other dimension, which emphasizes the luggage, placed in the foreground and bathed in a clear, radiant light. Once again, the focus is on the concept of departure and parting, rather than on the individual narrative. In another image, the farewell embraces, which involve not only a man but also a woman, probably the man's wife, suggest that the female presence in the village, albeit in a less traumatic way, is starting to disintegrate.

Monaco recognizes the profound roots of his personal and family life in these photographs, but he also appreciates the documentary value and artistic quality of the images, which he holds as a significant part of the foundation of his professional career. In early 1955, a specialized magazine 'Montaggio' partially publishes these images for the first time, with a meridionalist stance. A critical note accompanies the publication, highlighting the images' representative power, as well as their human and social density. Indeed, according to the magazine's editorial team, the images narrate

> the humanity of customs, the serene dedication to work, the hospitality to the poor, the ancient dignity of women, and the intimate decision to stand firm to stand still in a barren land. From here a unique reconstruction of the image stems that is always rich in human content and, despite the evident luminist pursuit, is structured

---

to remain in their place of origin. Unwilling to break their bonds with it, they keep a proactive and constructive attitude towards remaining and inhabiting it. For a deeper understanding of *restanza*, please refer to V. Teti, *La Restanza*, Einaudi, Torino, 2022. For more information on the meaning of the term *restanza* in Italian, see Raffaella Setti, *Restanza*, "Italiano digitale", XXIV, 2023/1(gennaio-marzo), Accademia della Crusca, 2023.

around a core of psychological and realistic interest. (Monaco 2002, 37)[24]

However, after his first stay in Italy, Monaco merges them with the others, gathered in the narrow alleys of Naples and in the meeting places of ordinary people, squares and streets[25], and carries them with him when he moves to London. In 1955, they will be relaunched in England and America[26], and nearly 50 years later, they will be collected in a London publication entitled 'The Women of Molise / An Italian Village'.[27]

The Global Photographer

As his previous interests in drawing have now been entirely eclipsed by photography, Frank knows that London holds a wealth of opportunities to transform his newly discovered passion into a professional career. The American pension provides him with financial stability, freeing him from the daily struggles and the pressure to sell his photographs at any cost, even if it means compromising the quality of the product. The consistent quality of his images and the homogeneity of his production will be a constant in his work, a fact that nearly all critics will notice.

---

[24] Translated.

[25] In Naples, Monaco captures the votive shrines scattered throughout the historic center's streets. These photos will be on display in the sacristy of Cantalupo del Sannio's *Chiesa Madre* for a long time. Critic Vladimiro Settimelli acknowledges these works for a certain degree of formal quality. In the photos taken on special occasions, the focus on women and everyday life returns and is a constant in Monaco's poetics.

[26] In the years following World War II, the underdeveloped areas in the Italian Mezzogiorno enjoy a remarkable interest also internationally. This is owing to the knowledge gained through the British interventions in the *special areas*, and the significant experience of the Marshall Plan, which enabled interventions worth 1.2 billion dollars carried out in Italy from 1948 to 1951. For many sociologists, anthropologists, economists, social workers, and others from the United States, southern Italy becomes a field of study and research. Among others, it is worth noting the presence of the historical anthropologist George Peck in Tricarico, Lucania, the town where mayor, poet, and writer Rocco Scotellaro operates. The philosopher Friedrich G. Friedmann, committed to study Levi's 'peasant civilization', is also worth mentioning. In Bagnoli del Trigno, Molise, anthropologists Stephen C. Cappannari and Leonard W. Moss conduct their research, later published in prominent American anthropology journals and now available in G. Massullo (ed.), *Studi in Molise 1951-1969 di S. C. Cappannari e L. W. Moss*, EdM, 2021. This trend continues into the subsequent decades. In the early 1970s, for instance, the sociologist and anthropologist W.A. Douglas visits Agnone to conduct a remarkable study on the local society and emigration, published in Italy a decade later by *Centro Studi Alto Molise*: William A. Douglas, *L'emigrazione in un paese dell'Italia meridionale. Agnone tra storia e antropologia*, Giardini, Firenze, 1984 (reappeared in an updated critical edition and retranslation by publisher Cosmo Iannone, Isernia, 2018).

[27] F. Monaco, *The Women of Molise, An Italian Village, 1950*, Four Seasons Publishing, London, 2000.

Monaco's images begin to grace prestigious magazines and newspapers, including 'The Observer' and 'The Times'. However, his existential and professional breakthrough comes within a few years, following three significant events. The first event is a personal encounter with a young woman, Lavinia Jones. She too, has some publishing experience in New York and marries Monaco a year after his arrival there. Lavinia stands by Monaco's side throughout his life, even joining him on long business trips, to assist him with networking and research. The other two events are of a professional nature: his collaboration with the Catholic-inspired magazine 'Jubilee' and, from the early 1960s, his relations with the Rex agency. Over the decades, Rex will manage to feature his photographs in over 450 newspapers, magazines, and books worldwide.

Spanning over a decade, his collaboration with 'Jubilee' is particularly fruitful in terms of content and style. With its cultural characterization and strong social inspiration, the magazine prompts him to delve into religious spirituality and human suffering. Frank gets to access the ancient convent of Serra San Bruno, where a pilot from the bomber who had dropped the atomic bomb on Hiroshima was said to have sought refuge in penance. He also ventures into the Benedictine Abbey of Monte Cassino, the Roman Trappist convent of *Tre Fontane*, the Carthusian monastery of Subiaco, and several convents. His photographs capture moments of prayer, study, and industriousness that blend into a serene spiritual atmosphere. They embody the inner harmony of those who choose to dedicate their lives to witnessing faith (Fig.9. One of the most structured images of monasteries that Monaco has left us. From a thematic perspective, it highlights the three key elements that the artist emphasizes in the spiritual atmosphere emanating from these environments: contemplation and prayer, the study and transmission of wisdom, and the inner balance achieved through dialogue with oneself and God. Stylistically, the soft lighting effects and overlapping planes create depth in the image. The geometry of the lines frames the human figure in the background, as if to express that the entire system remains centered around the human being).

At the same time, he visits Nomadelfia, where war orphans are sheltered, and the Cottolengo Institute in Turin, where he witnesses scenes of unspeakable loneliness and extreme suffering. Through his lens, Frank seeks to capture the spirituality and inner peace that permeates these sacred spaces. However, his gaze also turns to the interiors of convents, in search of a more universal balance between people and objects. Stylistically, his deep compositional wisdom and his equally established ability to select the perfect light cuts resurface, creating effects that are on the verge of formal complacency.[28] However, the outcomes are particularly stunning and evocative, and are duly collected and published in two volumes, which will be released nearly two decades apart.[29]

Monaco rediscovers his inclination towards ordinary people during his frequent excursions among the fishermen of Bagnara Calabra, where he witnesses the grueling work of tuna fishing. He also forms a deep bond with a family of fishermen, later dispersed due to emigration to Australia. Years later, he is the guest of honor at the celebration for the return of the head of the family (the 'Commander'). After the man's death, Monaco immortalizes him in a portrait that will become a cherished memory for his faraway children.

His production in India, however, is the most comprehensive collection of his aesthetics, the natural and logical culmination of his cultural and human journey, and the pinnacle of his artistic evolution. Frank first travels to India in 1965 and returns there after a period of 14 years, during which he tours Italy and America. He will travel to India seventeen times, staying for months every time, driven by an unquenchable thirst for knowledge, a desire to uncover the people's spirituality and immerse himself in the poverty and hardship of the marginalized. In this context, what becomes increasingly attractive is the force generated by the poles of his aesthetics: the testimony of spiritual forms (Fig.10. Among the numerous images that Monaco dedicates to Hindu temples [*the Houses of God*, as Gandhi once called them], typically characterized by intense *chiaroscuro*, this stands out for its light exposure. The statue of the deity is illuminated, revealing its dynamic forms

[28] 'The photos taken in sanctuaries and convents hold a certain charm, even if they occasionally veer towards mannerism. However, a discerning eye can easily spot the professionalism and meticulous care taken in the framing': W. Settimelli, *Il realismo gentile di Frank Monaco*, in *Obiettivo sull'anima*, cit., p. 10. Translated.

[29] F. Monaco, *They Dwell in Monasteries*, Seabury Press, New York and London, 1982; F. Monaco, *Brothers and Sisters*, Darton, Longman and Todd, London, 2001.

and power. At the same time, the elderly figures emphasize devotion, fragility, need, and the symbol of social contradiction. A duality and a dialectic that permeates the photographer's entire work on India) and the evocation of human suffering (Fig.11. India).

> Through the lens of my camera, I strived to capture the expressions of spirituality that channeled through the paintings, the social connections that emerged through religious practice, and the paths that seemingly anyone follows in their personal dialog with God. I did this without overlooking the poverty and social decay that enclose those forms of spirituality. (Monaco 2002, 38)[30]

While in India, Frank plans a journey to Tibet, to capture the Springs of life, scattered across a rugged and hostile territory. Due to health issues, his wish to celebrate life has to be deferred and will remain unfulfilled. Neither his wish to publish a collection of 120 black-and-white and 80 color photographs on the spirituality of the Indian people, which he would have entitled *The House of God*, as a reference to Gandhi's principles, will ever come true. What remains, however, is the legacy of this serene and composed protagonist of world photography who sought to rekindle the value of human intimacy and solidarity in a time of irreversible secularization of culture and customs and a gradually fading commitment to the marginalized.

His Stylistic Profile

Those who, like me, have discussed with Frank Monaco about his style and the meaning of his photography have received a straightforward, almost minimalist response:

> Every day, just like many people do with their dogs, I take my camera out for a walk. In India, they crafted a lightweight, agile case for my Leica, which is silent, always ready, and never hindered by low light thanks to its excellent lenses. I don't bother creating images. Things exist and talk to you. All you need to do is answer. (Monaco 2002, 40)[31]

---

[30] Translated.
[31] Translated.

Beyond expressing his composure and human measure, these words embody a principle of realism that critics have unanimously acknowledged in the American photographer's work[32], albeit with varying connotations. However, this should not be interpreted in a literal and simplistic way. Frank himself seems to soften his realism, blending it with a subjective element that makes it more relevant to his work: 'Of course, we too are in the world. Indeed, each of us is, with our own unique sensitivity and cultural background. Everyone establishes their own unique dialogue with things, yet it remains a dialogue between realities that truly exist.[33]

Here, the first factor that personalizes and elevates Monaco's production is his unique sensitivity.[34] Even in the photographs of "a rigorous and painful realism [...], everything is rendered with kindness, discretion, and due regard to those being photographed"[35]. This is essentially "gentle realism", as Settimelli himself has put it. Such sensitivity transcends mere character and, of course, much could be said about its roots. For the purposes of this essay, it may suffice to mention his story, his upbringing and his special bond with his mother who embodied a supportive and patient peasant culture. It may also have been the result of a religiousness that was not eschatological, but rather a richness of human values and respect. His choice to delve back into the hospitable environment of his origins must have also played an essential part, as well as his effort to acquire status and identity as a boy and young man in an environment that was certainly not easy for a child of immigrants. Some or all of these factors together may have contributed to developing his sensitivity.

A second defining factor in his photography is, as already mentioned, his background in art studies and graphic design practice in an advertising agency, where the demands for clarity and communicative

---

[32] 'For him, the camera has always been a tool for capturing [...], a means to an end. From this perspective, Monaco has a lot in common with the earliest photographers. His photos are simple, straightforward statements that he never manipulated using optical tricks or technical extravagance. Monaco possesses a rare ability to 'see' and the camera allows him to capture what he sees': Norman Hall, picture editor "The Times", in F. Monaco, *Obiettivo sull'anima,* cit., p. 44. Translated.

[33] *Ibid.* Translated.

[34] 'What makes Frank Monaco's work stand out from other photographers is his unique sensitivity. This has always been a constant in his work…': Norman Hall, cit., p. 44. Translated.

[35] W. Settimelli, *Il realismo gentile di Frank Monaco*, cit., p. 10. Translated.

fluidity are closely linked to the instantaneous nature of an image. Frank carries his Leica everywhere, and as soon as his eye catches a subject, he uncovers his lens. However, his eye is prompted to spot subjects that spark his interest thanks to a built-in interpretive framework. Even though he is not aware of it at times, when he photographs, he does so based on compositional codes of spaces and elements acquired and perfected through the study and vision of art. This approach allows him to capture the moment without sacrificing the immediacy of the shot and is evident in his effortless selection and adoption of lighting solutions, which bring high quality and originality to his work. His vision and creativity are undeniable, yet they draw nourishment and strength from the cultural and experiential settlings that have occurred.

On a comparative level, his images, particularly the ones in black and white, have been likened to those of Henry Cartier Bresson's journey in Abruzzo and Ferdinando Scianna's work on Bagheria, Sicily, and folk festivals. They have also been analogized to Salgado's 'humanitarian' photos and those on the *Sem Terra*. I would like to add reference to Franco Pinna's journeys to the Southern 'lands of silence'.[36] This should be considered not only in the context of Ernesto De Martino's ethno-anthropological expeditions in Basilicata and Calabria, but also in response to the desire to witness a condition that is 'constantly undermined by the Enlightenment and the moralistic desire for progress, as well as the equally motivated aspiration to preserve one's roots and nativist identity'.[37]

The critical comparisons I am proposing here are particularly intriguing and fascinating, as they involve the work of some of the most renowned photographers of the 20th century. However, it has to be acknowledged that, despite seeking out similarities in content and style, Monaco was not directly influenced by these photographers. Widely

[36] Translator's note: in Italian *'terre del silenzio'*.

[37] Diego Carpitella, *Franco Pinna e la fotografia etnografica in Italia*, in Id., *Viaggio nelle terre del silenzio*, Idea, Milano 1980, p. 9. For a broader reflection on the use of photography as a tool for historical and ethnographic documentation in Southern Italy, please refer to Giuseppe Giarrizzo and Fosco Maraini, *Civiltà contadina. Immagini del Mezzogiorno degli anni Cinquanta*, edited by Enzo Persichella, De Donato, Bari, 1980. Translated.

considered 'foundational' and of the highest quality[38], the photographs of what we have termed the 'return to his roots' are in fact coeval with the production of Cartier Bresson and the initial work of the 'Bressonian' Pinna. They were taken many years before those of the other artists that I have mentioned.[39]

To conclude, a significant and suggestive fact is worth mentioning. Having exhibited in various American cities and academies, in London galleries and universities, in Canterbury, Tallin, and Bombay, this artist found his ultimate and most convincing recognition in 'his own' Molise. Upon departing this life, he chose Molise as his final resting place: the land that had welcomed him as a 'son' returned from a distant continent and time.

WORKS CITED

Bevilacqua, Piero, Andrea De Clementi, and Enzo Franzina, eds. 2001. *Storia dell'emigrazione italiana. Partenze*. Rome: Donzelli.

Bianchi, Bruna. 2001. "Lavoro ed emigrazione femminile." In *Storia dell'emigrazione italiana. Partenze*, edited by P. Bevilacqua, A. De Clementi, and E. Franzina, 257–64. Rome: Donzelli.

Bronzini, Giovanni Battista. 1882. *Cultura contadina e idea meridionalistica*. Bari: Dedalo.

Carpitella, Diego. 1980. "Franco Pinna e la fotografia etnografica in Italia." In *Viaggio nelle terre del silenzio*, 9. Milan: Idea.

38'His history of Molise is one of the finest photographic productions in the past decade, comparable to W. Eugene Smith's Spanish village. The reason for its limited recognition lies in the fact that Frank Monaco is one of the most overlooked photographers': Norman Hall, cit., p. 45. Translated.

39 During the Second World War and its aftermath, Molise was the backdrop for the work of other renowned photographers, who left their mark on the region. As they did not have direct contact with F. Monaco, we will just mention them in this case. I refer to Robert Capa (1913-1954), an authorized war photographer for 'Life' magazine. He captured images of troops stationed among the olive trees of the Venafro area, near Cassino, as the Allied forces prepared for their final assault on the strategic Monte Cassino. William Congdon (1912-1998), who worked along the Gustav line, left behind images, paintings, and writings about his experience. In Molise, an exhibition was dedicated to him, titled *La pace non è anch'essa un'emergenza? William Congdon e l'American Field Service in Molise 1943-1946* [translator's note: 'Isn't Peace Also an Emergency?' William Congdon and the American Field Service in Molise, 1943-1946], September-October 2024, and a seminar at the University of Molise in January 2025. Despite having been born in the USA, Tony Vaccaro (1922-2022) spent his childhood and adolescence in his parents' hometown of Bonefro, Campobasso, due to severe family circumstances. He later became a reporter in Rome for major newspapers, frequently returning to Molise, like Monaco, during the 1950s and 1960s, and in the decades around the turn of the century. His extensive work has been broadly showcased in a number of catalogs and exhibitions in Molise.

Daniele, Vittorio, and Paolo Malanima. 2007. "The Product of the Regions and the North-South Divide in Italy 1861–2004." *Journal of Economic Policy*, March–April 2007.

Derrida, Jacques. 1981. *Dissemination.* London: The Athlone Press with University of Chicago.

Douglas, William A. 1984. *L'emigrazione in un paese dell'Italia meridionale. Agnone tra storia e antropologia.* Florence: Giardini.

Giarrizzo, Giuseppe, and Fosco Maraini. 1980. *Civiltà contadina. Immagini del Mezzogiorno degli anni Cinquanta.* Edited by Enzo Persichella. Bari: De Donato.

Maiorino, T. 2002. "Il giramondo col Molise nell'anima." In *Obiettivo sull'anima*, edited by N. Lombardi, 17. Isernia: Cosmo Iannone.

Martelli, Sebastiano. 1988. *Il crepuscolo dell'identità. Letteratura e dibattito culturale degli anni cinquanta.* Agropoli (SA): Ed. Laveglia & Carlone.

Massullo, Gino. 2021. *Studi in Molise 1951–1969 di S. C. Cappannari e L. W. Moss.* Edited by G. Massullo. EdM.

———. 2024. "Francesco Jovine tra letteratura, antropologia, storiografia e politica." In Francesco Jovine, *L'impero in provincia*, 134–35. Isernia: Cosmo Iannone.

Monaco, Frank. 1950. *The Women of Molise: An Italian Village.* London: Four Seasons Publishing.

———. 1982. *They Dwell in Monasteries.* New York and London: Seabury Press.

———. 2000. *Brothers and Sisters.* London: Darton, Longman and Todd.

———. 2002. *Obiettivo sull'anima.* Edited by N. Lombardi. Isernia: Cosmo Iannone.

Ramella, Franco. 2001. "Reti sociali, famiglie e strategie migratorie." In *Storia dell'emigrazione italiana. Partenze*, edited by P. Bevilacqua, A. De Clementi, and E. Franzina, 143–60. Rome: Donzelli.

Rodogna, Adele. 2018. *La solitudine delle donne molisane ai tempi della prima grande emigrazione.* Milan: Meltemi.

Scotellaro, Rocco. 2019. *Tutte le opere.* Edited by Franco Vitelli, Giulia Dell'Aquila, and Sebastiano Martelli. Milan: Oscar Mondadori.

Setti, Raffaella. 2023. "Restanza." *Italiano digitale* XXIV (1, January–March). Florence: Accademia della Crusca.

Settimelli, W. 2002. "Il realismo gentile di Frank Monaco." In *Obiettivo sull'anima*, edited by N. Lombardi, 10. Isernia: Cosmo Iannone. (Translated.)

Teti, Vito. 2011. *Pietre di pane: un'antropologia del restare*. Macerata: Quodlibet.

———. 2022. *La Restanza*. Turin: Einaudi.

———. 2018. *Stones into Bread*. Translated by Francesco Loriggio and Damiano Pietropaolo. Toronto: Guernica Editions.

Vitelli, Franco. 2019. "Perché abbiamo bisogno di Rocco Scotellaro." In Rocco Scotellaro, *Tutte le opere*, edited by Franco Vitelli, Giulia Dell'Aquila, and Sebastiano Martelli, V–XVI. Milan: Oscar Mondadori.

Visual Appendix

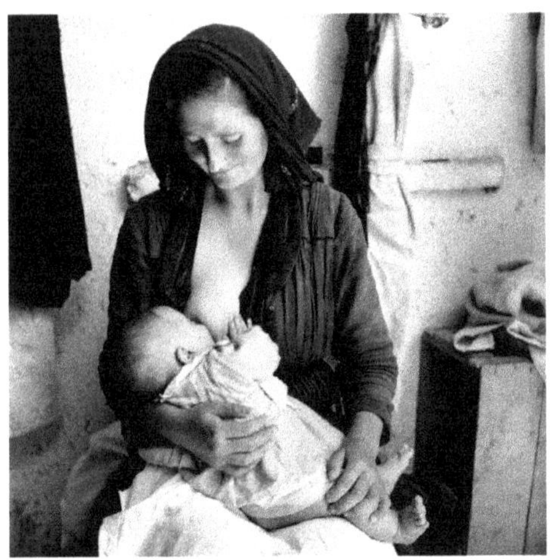

Fig. 1

Fig. 2

Fig. 3

Fig. 4

Fig. 5

Fig. 6

Fig. 7

Fig. 8

Fig. 9

Fig. 10

Fig. 11

From Stereotype to Post-Stereotypical Discourse: Ethnic Identity and Linguistic Performance in The Sopranos *and* The Bear

Alessandra Olga Grazia Serra
UNIVERSITÀ DEGLI STUDI DELLA TUSCIA

1. INTRODUCTION

In the landscape of American television, Italian American identity has long occupied a paradoxical space – obvious in public discourse, yet often represented in reductive ways, emotionally resonant, yet burdened with rigid and oversimplified meanings. From *The Godfather* to *Goodfellas*, from *Taxi Driver* to *Everybody Loves Raymond*, Italian American characters have served as vehicles for a set of symbolic codes: familial loyalty, performative masculinity, and emotional volatility. At the same time, stereotypical markers as Catholic guilt and food as a vehicle of ethnic memory have evolved into a repertoire of easily recognizable traits, functioning simultaneously as indexical cues and ideological constructs. While television and cinema have historically embraced excess – criminal, affective, and culinary – to frame the semiotic economy of Italian American identity, recent serial narratives have complicated this picture. They evolved into what may be called *post-stereotypical forms of representation*[1] that no longer *parade* ethnicity but *hint* at it, no longer declaring it but nudging it through complex stylistic and pragmatic strategies.

This analysis examines how such a transformation unfolds through language, and more specifically through the linguistic and discursive choices displayed in *The Sopranos* and *The Bear* (FX/Hulu, 2022 –). While radically different in tone, format, and historical location, both series offer productive ground for investigating how Italian American identity is textually constructed, negotiated, and contested at the same time. The point of departure is not simply thematic, but methodologically structured: how does language participate in the production of

---

[1] See Serra 2024.

ethnic identity on screen? And how does the shift from a performative stereotype to a post-stereotypical register manifest itself linguistically?

To address these questions, this study focuses on one of the most culturally saturated narrative sites in the Italian American media imaginary: the family meal. As both a symbolic ritual and discursive battleground, the family dinner scene has long been the locus for staging affective density, generational conflict, and ethnic belonging. It is here that identity is most performative and most precarious, where hierarchy and intimacy collide. By comparing the linguistic texture of episodes with relevant family meal scenes in *The Sopranos* – specifically season 1, episode 9 ("Boca") and season 2, episode 10 ("Bust Out") – and from *The Bear* – particularly season 2, episode 6 ("Fishes")[2] – this article explores how stereotypes, emotions, and ethnicity are encoded, as well as simultaneously affirmed and contested, through speech.

Methodologically, this article draws on a corpus-informed approach to discourse analysis, integrating qualitative reading and frequency-based evidence from these selected episodes. This limited corpus was compiled from the transcripts of the episodes mentioned above and then processed using the *Sketch Engine* tool for text analysis, focusing on lexical frequency, intensifiers, taboo language, and semantic structures, in conjunction with close discursive reading.

2. Theoretical Framework

The corpus-linguistic component of this study is informed by Paul Baker's methodological approach to stereotype analysis through corpus tools (in his case, focused on Gender representation), particularly in relation to discourse construction and the use of *Sketch Engine* (Baker 2015, esp. introduction 1-28). Rather than relying on anecdotal impressions or thematic readings, Baker advocates for the use of keyword analysis and frequency lists as entry points into the ideological patterns embedded in language. In our case, this led to searching for clusters of words, such as taboo expressions, ethnic tags, or food-related items,

[2] All the quotes and examples from *The Sopranos* cited in this article are drawn from the two episodes under examination: season 1, episode 9 ("Boca") and season 2, episode 10 ("Bust Out"), while the examples from *The Bear* are taken from episode 6 ("Fishes") of season 2.

that may recur in the transcripts of *The Sopranos* and *The Bear*[3]. However, following Baker's lead, the analysis never treats the quantitative patterns as conclusive on their own: it uses them as *signals* to be contextualized within broader discursive practices.

In *The Sopranos*, for example, language serves as an ethnic marker, but it is also a means of exchange and intimacy within the inner circle of mobsters. Expressions such as "Say a *Hail Mary* for your grandfather" exemplify how dialogue embeds both ritualistic and ethnic meanings: the implication is that of a definite *belonging* to a definite cultural context. On the other hand, in *The Bear*, the speech of characters such as Carmy and Richie is often stiff, full of ellipsis, and marked by affective compression. A typical outburst like "Mike, just / Don't throw fuckin' forks / at people," occurs during a peak of emotional intensity in "Fishes" and dramatizes a dysfunctional relational dynamic. His brother Michael hurls a fork at their stepfather, and Carmy responds with a single, curt admonition. The understated reaction highlights not only the power of restraint as a stylistic device but also marks emotional tension and attempted self-control.

Such discursive performances call for a sociolinguistic perspective that moves beyond lexical content, aligning with Nikolas Coupland's view of *style as performance*[4] – that is, speech as a sequence of stylized acts informed by social positioning and interactional goals. In particular, he highlights how in media discourse linguistic identity is often designed and performed within scripted and institutionally mediated contexts, where style becomes a tool for narrative and ideological effect. This concern with stylized performance is particularly resonant when viewed through the lens of Italian American cultural studies: scholars such as Jennifer Guglielmo, Fred Gardaphé, and Anthony Tamburri[5] have long emphasized the paradoxical nature of Italian American representation in U.S. media: extreme visibility through stereotypes, yet invisibility in cultural complexity. Guglielmo, for instance, discusses

[3] Transcripts of *The Sopranos* were retrieved from "The Sopranos (1999–2007) – Full Transcript," Subs Like Script, https://subslikescript.com/series/The_Sopranos-141842 (accessed July 26, 2025); transcripts of *The Bear* were retrieved from "The Bear (2022–) – Full Transcript," Subs Like Script, https://subslikescript.com/series/The_Bear-14452776 (accessed July 26, 2025).

[4] See Coupland 2007, esp. 146–156.

[5] See Guglielmo 2003; Gardaphé 2006; Tamburri 2002.

how Italian American racial identity has often been shaped by a politics of (paradoxical) containment: ethnic traits exaggerated to the point of caricature, rendering the subject both readable and 'safely' marginal. The linguistic performances in *The Sopranos*, with their overcoded "mama's boy" anxieties, aggressive diminutives, and fragmented interjections, fit within this logic of exaggerated legibility.[6]

By contrast, *The Bear* seems to displace this control strategy. Ethnicity is not openly stated, yet its echo resounds in food references, in the prosodic features of dialogue, and the affective echoes of Italianness. If *The Sopranos* speaks in the loud voice of the ethnic patriarch, *The Bear* just hints at its Italian background, staging a form of *post-stereotypical visibility* that deconstructs and refracts ethnicity through trauma, work ethic, and emotional volatility. This movement from stereotype to post-stereotype is not merely a shift in content but in discursive strategy: where earlier texts deployed ethnicity as performance and identitarian backbone, newer ones often withhold or fragment it, asking viewers to piece together a dispersed identity from affective cues rather than explicit markers.

Such dynamics can also be read through what Anthony Tamburri (1991)[7], identifies as the Italian/American *split* – an unresolved tension between ethnic legacy and national assimilation, between narrative emphasizing and strategic erasure. As Tamburri argues, the formulation *Italian/American* – with a slash instead of a hyphen – should not be read as a neutral label. It functions as a semiotic marker of the cultural rift between the "Italian" of origin and the assimilated "American," with the slash emphasizing discontinuity and tension rather than synthesis. In *The Bear*, that slash becomes patent: the unspoken trauma, the suppressed anger, the interrupted family rituals, all point to an identity no longer glued by the grammar of stereotype but still shaped by its syntax.

In light of these considerations, the following section opens with a brief overview of the evolution of the Italian American stereotype in U.S. cinema and television, tracing its journey from the iconic gangster tropes of *The Godfather* and *The Sopranos* to the fragmented and affective-

[6] See Trotta 2003.
[7] See also Tamburri 1998.

ly flawed representations in *The Bear*. Far from suggesting a mere transition from negative to positive imagery, the analysis aims to demonstrate how contemporary media have *reconfigured* the stereotype, sometimes amplifying it, sometimes dismantling it, in response to changing cultural climates, genre conventions, and expectations of authenticity.

3. Evolution of the Italian American Stereotype

To approach the discursive shift toward post-stereotypical Italian American identities in contemporary television, a valuable point of departure is the phase in which the stereotype was at its peak of stability and narratively codification. *The Godfather* is perhaps the most emblematic instance of a mythic and solemn vision of Italian American masculinity – made up of silence, duty, and ritualized violence – while, decades later, *The Sopranos* introduced a version of the male protagonist that was flawed from the inside: neurotic, hyper-verbal, and striving to reach self-awareness and psychological balance.

The transition between these two models is not just fictional or generational, but mainly *linguistic*. Vito Corleone speaks rarely, and when he does, it is in a hoarse, deep, dramatic cadence, a voice no one dares respond to, resonating with the awe of the listeners – and thus communicating power and undisputable authority. Tony Soprano, on the other hand, fills the screen with visual and vocal excesses: curses, food terms, interjections, ethnic insults, and routine commands, repeated with mechanical insistence, somehow devoid of symbolic resonance because of their repetitiveness and unpretentiousness. His speech is not just expressive, it is compulsive, a code through which his leadership is both asserted and destabilized. Italian American identity is here performed through linguistic overload.

This reorientation is particularly evident in domestic settings. In *The Sopranos*, home is not a space of familial cohesion but a conflicting arena where power is negotiated and contested. His wife Carmela's stern retorts, his daughter Meadow's interruptions, and Tony's escalating tone all signal how language functions as a site for generational conflict and gendered resistance. Far from being authentic, this plausible but highly stylized dialogic pattern reanimates the stereotype even as it forces its boundaries. With *The Sopranos*, the language of the Italian

Americans is no longer just symbolic: it becomes vernacular, bodily, and fierce. David Chase's series updates the gangster archetype for the postmodern age: Tony Soprano is not only a mobster but also a man undergoing psychoanalytic therapy, a father, and a man in constant linguistic engagement. His speech, laden with interruptions, threats, diminutives, ethnic taboo terms, and intensifiers, renders Italian American masculinity a mix of declarative authority and emotional derailment. While words like "madone," "gabagool," no longer function solely as ethnic colors – they become *lexical performances of a cultural identitarian background*, acting as signs of group belonging and, at the same time, indicators of emotional turmoil.

During family meals, this linguistic stylization becomes most recognizable. Language, in these scenes, is never neutral: it reaffirms patriarchal authority, signals allegiance, or reveals fracture. A telling example occurs when Tony remarks (in the "Boca" episode), "I thought you were a baccala man, Uncle Jun'." The line, framed as a teasing comment about food preferences, actually encodes a complex interplay of masculinity, family loyalty, and a mocking tone. Food here becomes a discursive tool through which identities are negotiated and power dynamics asserted. In this sense, the show exemplifies what Gardaphé (2006) identifies with the stereotypical representation of Italian American ethnic characterization: "Of the many ways in which Italians have been stereotyped, the two most prominent, besides the gangster, are as lovers of food and sex" (140). In this sense, *The Sopranos*' basic structure remains bound to rigid stereotypes: the world it presents is male-dominated, violence-prone, and inherently conservative. Although the series adds psychological depth and self-reflexivity to the gangster figure, it grants narrative complexity to Italian American identity only within the inherited framework of the mafia archetype.

In contrast to the expressive excess of *The Sopranos*, *The Bear* stages a quieter, more fractured, and emotionally overfilled version of Italian American identity. Here, the markers of ethnicity are not foregrounded as performance but folded into affective residual traces of cultural memory embedded in verbal restriction and relational disconnection. Carmen "Carmy" Berzatto does not speak "Italian American" in any recognizable or stylized way: his identity emerges through what is *not said*, through linguistic hesitations, ellipses, and a vocabulary that privileges exhaustion over bravado.

Thus, if *The Sopranos* locates identity in the codified (and stylized) buzz of family exchanges (even if conflictual), *The Bear* reveals identity through their collapse. The episode "Fishes" focuses on a chaotic Christmas dinner, disrupting the performative cohesion of earlier Italian American narratives: the meal is not a celebration of family reunion – it is a stage for trauma, dysfunction, and emotional breakdown. Overlapping dialogue, shouting, incomplete utterances, retreat into silence, and barely restrained aggression do not convey performative authority but instead a desperate attempt to survive the weight of familial and ethnic legacy.

Carmy, in this sense, represents a new phase in the representation of Italian American masculinity: he is no longer the portrait of machismo or aggressive ethnicity, but a man marred by fragility, emotional repression, and psychological instability. His speech is characterized by hesitations, repetitions, and a lack of overt cultural markers, suggesting a form of *linguistic subtraction* that replaces stereotype with interiority. His identity is shaped not through declarative tropes, but through absences: the missing father, the unexpressed grief, the relational unavailability. The Italian American protagonist in *The Bear* is no longer a gangster, a lover, or a mama's boy: he is a man burdened by PTSD, struggling to inhabit the debris of cultural patterns.

Framing this evolution through the lens of the post-stereotype proves helpful: it does not imply the erasure of ethnic tropes, but rather their re-mediation and partial dismantling. *The Bear*'s vocabulary of the kitchen ("yes chef," "fire," "behind," "corner") functions as a new grammar of hierarchy and discipline, supplanting the old codes of mafia loyalty. If Tony Soprano barked orders with patriarchal determination, Carmy mutters commands with professional urgency and emotional fragility. The pragmatic register has changed: from threat to stress, from criminal code to kitchen protocol, but the underlying structures of pressure and identity remain.

Notably, *The Bear* never entirely abandons the ethnic frame: in moments of tension, it comes back: a nostalgic reference to Italian beef, a visual motif of the family shrine, the worship of a specific recipe for spaghetti tomato sauce. These are not identity anchors but *dislocated remnants*, echoes of a cultural identity that cannot be stabilized. In this sense, *The Bear* is profoundly post-stereotypical: it doesn't simply invert or satirize the old tropes, but filters them through silence, repetition, and burnout. The stereotype lingers, but just in the background of a more complex, emotionally disjointed representation.

Moreover, what distinguishes *The Bear* from its predecessors and positions it firmly within a post-stereotypical mode is not simply its aesthetic restraint or emotional fragmentation, but this reconfiguration of Italian American masculinity through vulnerability and repressed grief. Carmy carries the burden of his brother's suicide, the instability in his family, and the toxic legacy of cultural and familial traditions. Yet, all the pressure he endures does not lead to violence or authoritative stances. Instead, it manifests itself through micro-gestures and the almost pathological pursuit of control within general chaos.

The distinction is not only psychological but deeply discursive. In *The Bear*, language often collapses under emotional weight. Carmy's conversations are brief, hesitant, and frequently interrupted; sentences remain unfinished or are left unspoken. As mentioned above, his authority in the kitchen proceeds through commands. Still, even these are inflected with determination rather than dominance, while the emotional life of the character is constantly on the verge of rupture, but never allowed full expression.

4. Family Meals under Scrutiny

To better clarify the methodology of the corpus analysis, beyond what has been previously discussed, the transcripts of the selected episodes were pre-processed to remove irrelevant metadata, such as speaker tags and stage directions, to focus exclusively on verbal interactions. The cleaned texts were then uploaded to *Sketch Engine*, with *enTenTen21* used as the reference corpus. At the micro-level, the analysis focused on lexical items (e.g., intensifiers, interjections, taboo words, ethnic markers, and Italianisms) and pragmatic features such as speech acts related to emotional escalation (including interrupted or incomplete utterances). At the macro-level, attention was paid to how these linguistic elements contribute to discursive patterns of family dynamics, emotional instability, performative masculinity, and ethnic identity. Although the number of selected scenes is limited, their representativeness allows for the identification of linguistic and discursive strategies through which the ethnic stereotype is both reproduced and, paradoxically, challenged and reconfigured.

4.1 Lexical Intensity and Verbal Volatility

In televisual storytelling, especially in genres such as the ethnic family drama, verbal style carries much of the emotional and ideological charge. Specific lexical items – ranging from taboo words to culture-specific interjections – function not only as *semantic markers* of affective involvement or cultural identity, but also as *pragmatic devices.* Far from being casual or ornamental, these expressions serve to perform affect, negotiate status, and position characters within encoded frameworks. These elements, to be clear, are not to be considered immune to stereotypization: they are in line with cultural expectations of Italian Americans. In this regard, Labov's theory of narrative evaluation[8] offers key interpretative tools, as it emphasizes the emotional and social importance of "evaluative" language and specifically the function that intensifiers play in revealing emotional stance through language that extends beyond pure factual meaning. More recently, Monica Bednarek (2010, 126) has examined how television dialogue strategically employs intensifiers and affective adverbs to convey emotional stances, particularly in family dramas where the level of relational conflict is often high. From his perspective, Jason Mittell (2015) noted that "moving-image media convey subjective interior states through the accumulation of exterior markers of what we see and hear about characters: appearance, actions, dialogue, and other sorts of evidence explicitly presented within the narrative discourse" (130).

In narratives such as those examined here, these (semantic and pragmatic) patterns contribute to a complex portrait of different individu-

---

[8] William Labov introduces the concept of evaluation as a fundamental component of oral narrative, noting how narrators (in his case, African American adolescents from Harlem) use implicit linguistic cues to "indicate the point of the narrative". See Labov 1972, 366. This pragmatic use of language to signal conflict, emotion, or social hierarchy mirrors the discursive traits found in the brief dialogue excerpt discussed above. For a description of intensifiers see esp. 378-379.

alities, dramatize the character's personal traumas, and function as sites of both resistance to and submission to inherited social roles, including those shaped by gender norms. The use of lexical intensifiers like "freakin," "fuckin," "madone," or "whoa," for instance, does not merely give an ethnic nuance to the script – instead, it underlines significant micro-performances indexing cultural identity and emotional relevance.

The following dinner scene from *The Sopranos'* "Bust Out" episode is one of the many examples among various occurrences in the series:

> *Tony*: You think this is a fuckin' game? You got no fuckin' idea what it takes!
> *Carmela*: Don't you dare raise your voice like that in front of our son!
> *Tony*: Oh, Jesus Christ, here we go again.

The verbal exchange above represents an everyday Italian American family quarrel – culturally specific in tone – where authority is challenged, toxic masculinity is restrained, and emotions are voiced but promptly dismissed. The lexical intensifier "fuckin" adds emotional tone to Tony's outburst, functioning not only as an expletive but as a performative index of patriarchal arrogance and frustration as well. At the same time, the interjection "Oh Jesus Christ" in the last sentence signals what could be defined as an emotional deflection strategy as it removes the immediate conflict and reframes Tony's loss of control as exasperation. As Felix Ameka (1992) argues, interjections "are all produced in reaction to a linguistic or extra-linguistic context and can only be interpreted relative to the context in which they are produced" (108). In this light, the dialogue's lexical choices are designed not only to sound spontaneous and emotionally charged, but they also serve to construct a culturally recognizable mode of family interaction, especially within ethnicized contexts.

Food, in this sense, is not only consumed but talked over, fought around, and used as a social anchor, even if it happens in an artificially re-constructed ethnic context. As Jonathan Cavallero (2021) notes, this kind of 'narrative ethnicity,' as in cinema and television, "disconnects ethnic identity from lived experience, allowing it to be attained through consumption (of food, popular culture, fashion, or something else) and/or performance" (52). The linguistic analysis confirms that this performance is as much about *how* things are said – through raised voices, clipped sentences, or emphatic interjections – as it is about *what* is said.

4.2 Quantitative Insights and Discursive Patterns

The analysis focused on three primary areas: 1) Lexical Intensifiers and Interjections; 2) Lexical Markers of Verbal Conflict; 3) Ethnic Markers and Italianisms. While the first two categories were examined through a quantitative approach, the third, as will be discussed below in 4.3, is addressed from a more discursive and qualitative perspective.

Below is an overview of the most salient findings and their relation to broader discursive dynamics. For the first category, I explored the emotional dimension of spoken interaction by querying the corpus for common single-word interjections and intensifiers frequently used in this genre of television series. While their frequency might suggest a mimetic function – reproducing the cadence of natural speech – items like "oh," "yeah," or "so" instead reveal systematic patterns of affective positioning. They act as *discursive indicators* within specific interactional environments, enhancing the emotional tone and often anticipating or overlapping with more explicit forms of verbal conflict.

Examples: Lexical Markers of Emotional Intensification

Episode	*Term*	*Concordance Line*
FISHES	yeah	Yeah. Yeah? Hmm. Yeah. I love you, bear
FISHES	yeah	That's good. Yeah. Yeah. Carm, will you handle Mom?
FISHES	yeah	Yeah. Hey, Carmen. Yeah. Stop giving mc shit!
FISHES	yeah	Ma, are you good? Yeah, yeah, we're good.
FISHES	oh	That's sweet of you. Oh, okay. Thank you.

SOPRANO-BOCA	so	He's a kid. So he should neglect his elders?
SOPRANO-BOCA	so	I'm goin'. So, you fuckin son of bitch, get off the field
SOPRANO-BOCA	oh	You're not excused! Oh, let her go. Go.
SOPRANO-Bust Out	yeah	Tony. Yeah. It's good you could meet
SOPRANO-Bust Out	oh	Today? Oh, jeez! What's the matter

The second category of analysis addresses lexical markers such as insults, threats, and expletives – terms that frequently characterize confrontational exchanges and articulate power relations. Their recurring collocation with vocatives and imperatives points to a discursive pattern in which tension is dramatized through direct, emotionally charged language. Together, these lexical choices shape the verbal texture of conflict-driven scenes, contributing to the emotional realism and cultural specificity of each series. The computational analysis confirms the centrality of lexical intensifiers and interjections as pragmatic resources in *The Sopranos* and *The Bear*: the frequency data extracted from *Sketch Engine* highlights a set of recurring terms:

- *Fuck/fucking* (288 occurrences),
- *shit* (45),
- *Jesus* (20),
- *Christ* (13),
- *God* (36),
- *whoa* (16),
- *Jeez* (2),
- *Goddamned*, *crap* (1 each).

Moreover, as Bednarek (2010) points out, the frequency and intensity of taboo words in series such as *The Sopranos* is qualitatively different from their use in more family-oriented television: "The use of strong expletives and taboo words (such as *fuck*, *shit*, etc.) in *Gilmore Girls*, *Friends*, *Dawson's Creek* and *Golden Girls* differs greatly from their use in programmes that do not aim to be 'family friendly,' and that do feature a high frequency of such language (e.g. *The Wire* […], *The Sopranos* […], *Sex and the City* […])" (87). Even items like "Jesus," "Christ," and "God" are pragmatically refunctionalized in these dialogues: they seldom serve as religious interjections, but rather as spontaneous expressions of disbelief, frustration, or confrontation, often aligning with what Ameka (1992, 105) terms *primary interjections*, i.e. non-sentential elements whose meaning is entirely dependent on context and strongly associated with emotional expression. To support this observation, an illustrative table is provided below, showing specific uses of this kind of lexical markers of verbal conflict. The examples highlight their pragmatic function across different episodes.

Examples: Lexical Markers of Verbal Confrontation and Power Dynamics

Keyword	*Concordance Line*	*Episode*	*Function*
ckin	I'm not fuckin' doing that again.	Bust Out	Intensifier + Refusal
ck	You little fuck, shut up!	Boca	Insult
Jesus	Oh Jesus Christ, here we go.	Bust Out	Interjection + Exasperation
freakin	It's freakin chaos in here.	Fishes	Intensifier + Frustration
whoa	Whoa, calm down, everyone!	Fishes	Interjection + Surprise
Christ	Christ, can we just eat?	Fishes	Interjection + tension

4.3 Ethnic Markers and Italianisms: From Explicit Codes to Embodied Discourse

While earlier portrayals of Italian American fictional identity often relied on a distinct ethnic lexicon (especially related to food), including terms such as *gabagool*, *ziti*, *goomba*, and *cannoli*, such explicit markers are progressively less employed in more recent quality TV series like *The Sopranos* and *The Bear*.

This transition resonates with theories of discursive ethnicity, as outlined by Alim and Reyes[9], according to which belonging is *enacted* rather than explicitly declared, and silence or ambiguity may substantiate cultural membership as powerfully as speech. The departure from overt to latent ethnic coding is manifested across these two series with different strategies. While in David Chase's *Sopranos,* traditional Italian American slang, often related to food, still recurs, in *The Bear* it functions more as an *echo* of an earlier, overtly ethnic register, one that relied heavily on marked culinary and explicit linguistic identity. Thus, as lexical markers of Italian American identity have receded into the background, they have done so not in the service of dismissal but of *transformation.* What emerges in their place is a *grammar of ethnicity* grounded in affective exchange, embodied ritual, and discursive rhythm.

This dynamic is particularly evident in "Fishes": although explicit Italianisms are rare, the episode draws on familiar cultural elements that collectively evoke a recognizably Italian American atmosphere. One of the clearest examples is the emotionally charged exchange about the meaning of the "Feast of the Seven Fishes" – the tradition behind the Berzatto's Christmas dinner – which Donna, Carmy's mother, passionately attempts to explain:

> Why the seven fishes? Oh, my God. What is up with everyone today? I'm just trying to make a nice fuckin' thing. I just mean why the fuck do people even do it? Because it's based on people who left Italy to find new dreams and homes with new people. And they brought their seven best things from their sea to their new homes…

[9] "[A] group orientation need not comply with the dialect orientation (i.e. it allows for ethnic identity to be produced without an ethnic dialect)," in Alim and Reyes 2011, 380.

Here, the tradition is neither exoticized nor adapted for a general audience; instead, it is *defended* and *recontextualized* within a moment of familial tension. The ethnic dimension lies not in the use of Italian words, but in the *symbolic density* of the ritual – its invocation of heritage, migration, and intergenerational responsibility.

Throughout the dinner sequence, family members interrupt, shout, and accuse one another with a mixture of rage and affection that carries cultural resonance. Exchanges such as "She's gonna ruin the sauce," "You're being disrespectful in front of your uncle," and "I'm not mad, I'm just saying" (the latter in response to being accused of speaking too loudly), exemplify the emotional tension embedded in everyday family discourse and are filled with *cultural specificity*. The sauce becomes a metonym for maternal authority and culinary tradition, while respect for elders emerges as a non-negotiable social norm within the Italian American familial code. The recurrent justification of emotional outbursts, such as "I'm not mad," recalls the widely circulated meme "I'm not yelling, I'm Italian," widely popular on merchandise and social media, where it serves as a humorous assertion of identity. What emerges is a "family grammar" that is less a matter of traditional ethnicity and more an articulation of *cultural territory*.

Conclusion

This final consideration points to what is perhaps the most critical aspect of this analysis: the progressive disappearance of ethnic markers is not incidental – it reflects a broader process of *discursive assimilation*. *The Sopranos* reworks Italian American stereotype through irony and ambiguity, while still relying on linguistic and cultural clichés, and by contrast, *The Bear* erodes these surface elements, opting for more implicit codes of performance and affective style.

Drawing on Bourdieu's notion of *habitus*[10] as a system of internalized dispositions shaped by one's position within specific social fields, ethnicity can be reconfigured as a *dispositional field* – a repertoire of embodied practices, such as arguing, cooking, breaking down, which makes explicit ethnic labeling unnecessary. It is not a "look" or a "sound" but a lived,

[10] See Bourdieu 1977, 78.

performative grammar of everyday interaction. Fred Gardaphé (2006) calls for a critical mode that moves "from wiseguys to wise men," suggesting that Italian American ethnicity in fiction is being reimagined as identitarian *complexity*. Post-stereotypical discourse has shifted from *signaling difference* to *inhabiting (and coping with) inherited structures*. It is not the negation of ethnicity, but rather its naturalization, its domestication, its sedimentation into the linguistic practices of the present.

WORKS CITED

Alim, H. Samy, and Angela Reyes. 2011. "Complicating Race: Articulating Race across Multiple Social Dimensions." *Discourse & Society* 22 (4): 379–84.

Ameka, Felix K. 1992. "Interjections: The Universal Yet Neglected Part of Speech." *Journal of Pragmatics* 18 (2–3): 101–18.

Baker, Paul. 2015. *Using Corpora to Analyze Gender*. London: Bloomsbury.

Barreca, Regina, ed. 2002. *A Sitdown with The Sopranos: Watching Italian American Culture on TV's Most Talked-about Series*. New York: Palgrave Macmillan.

The Bear. 2022–. Created by Christopher Storer. Produced by FX Productions. Distributed by Hulu.

Bednarek, Monika. 2010. *The Language of Fictional Television: Drama and Identity*. London: Continuum.

Bourdieu, Pierre. 1977. *Outline of a Theory of Practice*. Cambridge: Cambridge UP.

Cavallero, Jonathan J. 2021. "Gangsters, Cannoli, and Marginal Ventriloquism: Ethnic Voices in *The Sopranos*." *Italian American Review* 11 (1): 33–50.

Coupland, Nikolas. 2007. *Style: Language Variation and Identity*. Cambridge: Cambridge UP.

Gardaphé, Fred L. 2004. *Leaving Little Italy: Essaying Italian American Culture*. Albany: SUNY Press.

_______ . 2006. *From Wiseguys to Wise Men: The Gangster and Italian American Masculinities*. New York: Routledge.

Guglielmo, Jennifer. 2003. "White Lies, Dark Truths." In *Are Italians White?*, edited by Jennifer Guglielmo and Salvatore Salerno, 91–107. New York: Routledge.

Labov, William. 1972. *Language in the Inner City: Studies in the Black English Vernacular*. Philadelphia: U of Pennsylvania P.

Mittell, Jason. 2015. *Complex TV: The Poetics of Contemporary Television Storytelling*. New York: NYU Press.

Parla, John. 2016. "How Capicola Became Gabagool: The Italian New Jersey Accent, Explained." *Atlas Obscura*, April 6, 2016. https://www.atlasobscura.com/articles/how-capicola-became-gabagool-the-italian-new-jersey-accent-explained

Scarpino, Cinzia. 2010. "Sopranos-Speak: Neapolitan Dialect, Mafia Jargon, and Silence: Or, Feeling All Agita All the Time." In *Translating America: Importing, Translating, Misrepresenting, Mythicizing, Communicating America: Proceedings of the 20th AISNA Biennial Conference, Torino, September 24–26, 2009*, edited by Marina Camboni, Alessandro Carosso, and Serena Di Loreto, 203–13. Torino: Otto.

Serra, Alessandra. 2024. "*The Bear*: New (Stereotypical) Representations of Italian Americans in Contemporary Television Series." *Forum Italicum* 58 (1): 126–47. https://doi.org/10.1177/00145858231223974

The Sopranos. 1999–2007. Created by David Chase. New York: Home Box Office.

Tamburri, Anthony Julian. 1991. *To Hyphenate or Not to Hyphenate? The Italian/American Writer: Or, An Other American?* Montreal: Guernica Editions.

_______ . 1998. *A Semiotic of Ethnicity: In (Re)cognition of the Italian/American Writer*. Albany: SUNY Press.

_______ . 2002. *Italian/American Short Films and Videos: A Semiotic Reading*. West Lafayette: Purdue UP.

Trotta, Joe. 2003. "Bada-Bing! Looking at Language in *The Sopranos*." *Moderna Språk* 97: 17–36.

One of the Sun's Lost Words: The Growth of a Pick and Shovel Poet's Mind in Pascal D'Angelo's Son of Italy

Renzo D'Agnillo
UNIVERSITÀ DEGLI STUDI G. D'ANNUNZIO CHIETI-PESCARA

Abstract: Pascal D'Angelo's *Son of Italy* is not only an autobiographical account of the hardships endured by an Italian immigrant in 1920s America but also a description of the development of its author as a poet. D'Angelo included ten poems relating to different moments of his life which reveal an extraordinary linguistic sensitivity and diversity, even beyond the fact that they are the product of a man with little or no education. The following proposes to redress the almost unanimous critical neglect of D'Angelo's verse by taking into close consideration a selection of the poems in *Son of Italy* to reveal a keen poetic sensibility equally responsive to the quasi-magical mountainous landscape of his childhood and the squalid urban world of his life as an immigrant. Central to his poetic vision is the process of recollection in which temporal dimensions are fused and complicated in an intensely lyrical self-dialogue.

Pascal D'Angelo's autobiography, *Son of Italy*, may testify to "one of the most thrilling episodes in American literature" (D'Angelo 1924, xi) but the author's eventual poetic fortune came at a heavy price. Indeed, that the recognition of his poetry was marred by the "psychological wounds of rejection that further impacted the author's wretched physical state" (xi) is a factor that leaves the reader wondering how a poetical temperament could flourish at all in the ruthless day-to-day survival described in his self-narration. If only for this reason, it is inexplicable (if not inexcusable) that his poetry has drawn such scant attention. The few exceptions have gone only a little way to compensate for this critical neglect. In his 1998 survey of Italian immigrant poets, Luigi Fontanella cites the case of D'Angelo only to stop short at a general lament of the conspiratorial silence surrounding his verse which he ascribes to an apparent attempt to eradicate the memory of the squalor and suffering endured by Italian immigrants. In 2003, however, an article by Robert Viscusi, albeit concerned with Italian immigration and American culture in general, includes a consideration of D'Angelo's verse with an exploration of its connections with Walt Whitman and Percy Shelley. However, the remaining bulk of his discussion concentrates on the influence of Verdi's opera *Aida* in political nationalistic, rather than poetical terms. More recently, *Voices in Italian Americana* dedicated a special issue to D'Angelo. Unfortunately, the articles focus almost exclusively on his autobiography, although the issue opens auspiciously by reprinting eleven of his poems. It is the present writer's hope that the following discussion will generate a livelier critical interest in a poet of undoubted originality.

Far from "turning aside" (XI) from his poetry merely to tell his story, as Carl Van Doren suggests, D'Angelo saw *Son of Italy* as an opportunity to promote himself as a poet as much as to denounce the hardship and injustice of living as an Italian immigrant in 1920s America. His attention to language and phraseology, surprising in a man with next to no formal education, is apparent from the very opening sentences which describe the nebulous tabula rasa stage prior to memory:

> As I glance back over the time-shadowed sky of my infancy, I seem to see a vast expanse of mist that gives no light to any early events. But here and there looms a faint pyramid of recollection that can apparently never fade. (D'Angelo 1924, 1)

The extent to which D'Angelo's prose reveals a confident assimilation of the English language is a moot point, however, since it is difficult to surmise how much external editing was involved in the compositional process. D'Angelo's describes his earliest attempts at writing as grounded on the memorising of vocabulary. This mental exercise expanded to such a point that he became capable of using "the most unheard-of English words" (144), which explains not only the surprising variety of his diction but also his almost child-like feel for words. On a structural level, all ten poems in *Son of Italy* (and indeed all of D'Angelo's poems) adopt the free unrhymed verse form that had become common with American poets at the turn of the century. Walt Whitman is an obvious influence, particularly in terms of D'Angelo's propensity for long, nonmetrical unrhymed lines. Yet, from the point of view of tone and feeling D'Angelo's verse contains none of Whitman's grand, incantatory resonance. Quite contrary to the invocation, chant and ceremony typical of Whitman's mode, D'Angelo's poetic voice is more in debt to the intimate lyricism of romantic poets like Shelley and Keats. His discovery of these poets would have confirmed the validity of his sensitive response to the quasi-magical world of mountains, mystery, witches and wizards of his early childhood, as evidenced in the opening chapters of *Son of Italy* – which was not only "a bucolic place where time did not seem to pass" (Cacco 2022, 13). but also, an important imaginative source of D'Angelo's development as a poet.

Autobiographies are inevitably selective. But D'Angelo's self-narration excludes important circumstantial details and proceeds episodically, often blurring the temporal sequence of events. This method of narration, in which incidents drawn from memory become the inspiration for his verse (similar to Wordsworth's notion of 'spots of time') – is what makes *Son of Italy* more than just an autobiographical account. The process is already at work in the first poem included in the text which follows a strange incident during his childhood involving the death of a man known to the local community as the wizard. D'Angelo recalls how he and his mother, caught in a violent storm sought refuge at the old man's house:

> He lived alone and had little to do with the world. He seemed to hate all who came near him. He cried in a harsh voice, "What do you want?"
> "Shelter."
> He laughed and called back his dogs. Just then the two trees alongside the hut became tipped with flame and something like a great star appeared in the doorway over the man's head. And a terrific thunder broke upon us. The man fell. The lightning had blinded us all for an instant. Then my mother, who still gripped me in her arms, shrieked and began to run down the road. Down, toward the town, through the rain, dashing through pools of water she fled. At the first houses some of the people came out and helped her in. I was wondering.
> (D'Angelo 1924, 16)

From the bewildered point of view of the child ("I was wondering"), the death of the wizard is imaginatively revised in terms of the transfiguration of the scene through powerful, destructive natural forces. As D'Angelo notes, "it made a profound impression upon me, not so much at that time as later in my memory" (17). The poem, tagged onto this section, almost as an afterthought, belongs to the dreaming period of his childhood and replicates the same process of recollection and mythical representation of the natural world as the prose description. As has been noted, the title "Midday," as translated to "Mezzogiorno," plays on a double meaning, being the temporal setting of the poem, but also the antonomasia for the forgotten and downtrodden southern part of Italy (Diraviam 2021, 38), though this derogatory connotation is contradicted by its general atmosphere of fun and excitement:

> The road is like a little child running ahead of me and then
> hiding behind a curve –
> Perhaps to surprise me when I reach there.
> The sun has built a nest of light under the eaves of noon;
> A lark drops down from the cloudless sky
> Like a singing arrow, wet with blue, sped from the
> bow of space.
> But my eyes pierce the soft azure, far, far beyond,
> To where roam eternal lovers
> Along the broad blue ways
> Of silence. (D'Angelo 1924, 18-19)

The twenty-two long syllable opening line is striking in its suggestion of teasing expectancy stretched out in time. But it is also hauntingly suggestive of the poet's imminent encounter with his own childhood self. Although described in a series of stock images and clichés, the natural landscape, which becomes the central feature in the rest of the poem, represents a timeless world of magic and mystery appropriate to a child's worldview. The energy of the natural landscape is suggestively rendered in the movement of the Shelleyan lark that drops dynamically down "from the cloudless sky / Like a singing arrow" countered by the vertical gaze enwrapped in a reverie of "eternal lovers". The transition from child to adult lover with which the poem concludes signals the temporal lapse between the scene recalled and the moment of recollection and poetic composition which, as noted, is a common feature of D'Angelo's verse, together with the loose, natural rhythms of his versification and effective use of alliteration.

D'Angelo includes two other poems which refer to his childhood and youth in Introdacqua. The first, *Monte Majella*, again shows a similar sense of spatial and temporal dislocation between natural and human world:

> The mountain in a prayer of questioning heights gazes upward at
> [the dumb heavens,
> And its inner anger is forever bursting forth
> In twisting torrents.
> Like little drops of dew trickling along the crevices
> Of this giant questioner
> I and my goats were returning toward the town below.
> But my thoughts were of a little glen where wild roses grow
> And cool springs bubble up into blue pools.
> And the mountain was insisting for an answer from the still
> [heaven.
>
> (D'Angelo 1924, 23)

The extraordinary opening line runs for twenty syllables, not only to signal the predominance of the mountain in the poem on a rhetorical and graphical level, but also to underline the magnitude of an existential angst which is further reinforced by the emotional turmoil of an "inner anger bursting forth / in twisting torrents". Within this landscape of all-pervading suffering the boy is seen as a tiny presence "trickling along the crevices / Of this giant questioner" in an intimate daydream. The two-parts of the poem are marked by the shift in tense from present indicative (lines 1-5) to past tense (lines 6-9) where the child in the first part becomes the adult recollecting the moment in which his younger self was absorbed in a reverie oblivious to the external world of suffering and confusion. It appears all the more evident in this poem how, the fact that he D'Angelo has chosen to compose in a language that is not his native tongue, creates an inevitable dissociation between his present self in America and past self in Italy to the extent that the poem revolves around the double focus of the adult's mature perception at the moment of composing the poem and the interplay between the abstract musings of the child remembered and the emotional turmoil objectified in the natural world around him. The contrast is phonically reinforced in the intricate alliterative patterning of the following lines:

> A lark drops down from the cloudless sky
> Like a singing arrow, wet with blue, sped from the bow of space.

Whilst the visual imagery is clearly reminiscent of Shelley, the oral sensuousness of the language derives from Keats. Yet far from the ecstatic romanticism of these poets D'Angelo's vision of nature here hinges on an unresolved existential condition. Against this sensuous participation in the landscape, is an implicit sense of the interrogating mountain as the objective embodiment of an unconscious unease already stirring within the child.

In this respect, the final poem relating specifically to his adolescence in Italy, "Fantasio," represents a progression in terms of the dramatic participation of the poetical voice. The poem describes a night-time scene of strangeness and intrigue after the child has learnt of the death of the local witch, a figure that had always filled him with terror:

> As Night like a black flower shuts the sun within its
>   petals of gloom,
> The silent road crosses the sleeping valley like a
>   winding dream –
> While the whole region has succumbed under the
>   weight of a primeval silence.
> The mountains like mighty giants lift themselves
>   with a regal haughtiness out of the ruling gloom.
> Across the dim jagged distances are pearl-gray wings flitting
> Flitting –
>
> The moonlight is a hailstorm of splendour
> Pattering on the velvet floor of gloom –
> The moon!
> The moon is a faint memory of a lost sun –
> The moon is a footprint that the Sun has left on
>   pathless Heaven!

Pearl-gray wings are whirling distantly
Whirling!
A fever of youth streams through my being
Trembling under the incantation of Beauty,
Like a turmoil of purple butterfly caught in a web of light.
(D'Angelo 1924, 43)

Thematically, the incident recalls the death of the wizard, and a similar gothic-like atmosphere of menace and mystery is established in the opening lines with the eerie simile of the black flower shutting out the sun. This deathly atmosphere is sustained by the dreamy, oppressive silence of the second and third lines. However, the dramatic centre point of the poem, concerns the gigantic mountains which no longer embody the existential suffering of the previous poem but disengage themselves in superior antagonism from the world upon which the moon pours its distant light to create a nightscape of suggestive forms whose flitting motions resonate with the passionate reveries of the poetic voice. This is further heightened by the accelerated rhythm of the erratic line lengths in the second part of the poem and their contrast with the long resonant lines of the first stanza. With respect to the previous poems, the relationship between poetic voice and immediate world now moves from unconscious infantile daydream to a mounting eroticism, particularly rendered in the insistent use of anaphora ("The moon / The moon is a faint memory of the lost sun / The moon [...]") and lexical repetition with variation (petals of gloom ... ruling gloom ... velvet floor of gloom ..."). Despite its stock gothic imagery, the poem is artfully constructed in terms of the way its lineation emulates the sense of oppressive weight on the one hand and rapid, fleeting emotions on the other and concludes with an unexpectedly striking simile ("like a turmoil of purple butterfly caught in a web of night") which is simultaneously suggestive of the ephemeral nature of passion and its entrapment.

"Night Scene" is the first poem of D'Angelo's that refers to his period in America as a pick-and-shovel worker. It is prefaced by an ingenious observation on the difference between his physical and poetical labour and his allegiance to the latter:

> All my works are lost, lost forever. But if I write a good line of poetry, then, when the night comes and I cease writing, my work is not lost. My line is still there. It can be read by you today and by another tomorrow. But my pick and shovel works cannot be read either by you today or by anyone else tomorrow
>
> (D'Angelo 1924, 74-75).

These words recall Seamus Heaney's poem "Digging" in which there is a similar ideological association between working with a spade and poetic composition. The difference, besides the ethical and political implications of Heaney's poem, is that whilst the latter had no spade with which to follow his father and grandfather before him, D'Angelo is fated to his pick and shovel whilst his poetry is written in defiance of the temporal and finite nature of his pick and shovel works to affirm his own immortality through his verse:

> An unshaped blackness is massed on the broken rim of night.
> A mountain of clouds rises like a Mammoth out of the walls of
> [darkness
> With its lofty tusks battering the breast of heaven.
> And the horn of the moon glimmers distantly over the glares and
> [clustered
> stacks of the foundry.
>
> Uninterruptedly, a form is advancing
> On the road that shows in tatters.
>
> The unshaped blackness is rolling larger above the thronged
> [flames that
> branch upward from the stacks with an interwreathed fury.
> The form strolling on the solitary road
> Begins to assume the size of a human being.
> It may be some worker that returns from next town,
> Where it has been earning its day's wages.
> Slowly, tediously it flags past me –
> It is a tired man muttering angrily.

He mutters.
The blackness of his form now expands its hungry chaos
Spreading over half of heaven, like a storm,
Ready to swallow the moon, the puffing stacks, the wild foundry.
The very earth in its dark, furious maw,
The man mutters, shambling on –
The storm! The storm! (75-76)

Once again, the mountain is the central presence. But in this case, it is depicted as a savage beast attacking the heavens while the flames of the iron foundry engulf the nighttime skyline. D'Angelo's surprisingly sensitive ear for phonic effects is apparent in his use of soft nasals and harsh consonant clusters to convey the sense of compression and suffocation of the industrial landscape. In the second part of the poem there is a surprising turn where the "unshaped blackness" against the sky blurs into the form of an angry worker returning home from another town. The image of the man is then expanded, like something out of an expressionistic painting, into a monstrous form in the poet's imagination, his anger echoing that of the nighttime landscape, to dwindle back to "the size of a human being" as he "slowly, tediously" passes him by only to enlarge once again leaving behind an expansion of "hungry chaos/Spreading over half of heaven, like a storm, ready to swallow the moon". In no other poem does D'Angelo render the idea of the hunger that constantly tormented him in such a powerfully hyperbolic manner. The poem undoubtedly marks a central moment of maturity revealing the rhetorical force of D'Angelo's diction, the rhythmic intensity and semantic density of his verbal repetitions and shifts of register in a vision of eternal suffering that fuses into the final image of universal discord represented by the storm.

"Accident in the Coal Dump" is another poem which alludes to an incident narrated in *Son of Italy*. It was inspired by a fatal accident during which a friend of the poet was crushed to death in the workplace. This tragedy seems to have triggered D'Angelo's father's decision to ultimately abandon all attempts at trying to make a living in America. D'Angelo, on the other hand, has decided to remain, refusing to accept the idea of failure and continuing to doggedly pursue his ambition to become a famous poet. Although the prose account of the incident reveals the extent to which it obviously made a deep impression on him, the poem was written at a much later date and, as a result, its superimposition over the tragedy creates an effect of emotional restraint and even lack of sentimentality that gives the tragedy even more pathos:

> Like a dream that dies in crushed splendour under
>   the weight of awakening
> He lay, limbs spread in abandon, at the bottom of
>   a smooth hollow of glistening coal.
> We were leaning about on our shovels and sweating,
> Red-faced in the lantern light,
> Still warm from our frenzied digging and hardly
>   feeling the cold midnight wind.
> He had been a handsome, quiet fellow, a family man
>   with whom I had often talked
> Of the petty joys and troubles of our little dark world;
> In the saloon on Saturday night.
> And there he was now, huge man, an extinguished
>   sun still followed by unseen faithful planets,
> Dawning on dead worlds in an eclipse across
>   myriad stars –
> Vanished like a bubble down the stream of eternity,
> Heedlessly shattered on the majestic falls of some
>   unknown shores.
> And we turned slowly toward home, shivering,
>   straggling, sombre –
> Save one youngster who was trying to fool himself
>   and his insistent thoughts,
> With a carefree joke about the dead man.
> Snow began to fall like a white dream through the
>   rude sleep of the winter night,
> And a wild eyed woman came running out of the
>   darkness.
>
> (D'Angelo 1924,117- 118)

The metaphorical representation of the first line directly alludes to the tragic accident. Yet by qualifying the noun splendour with the adjective *crushed* D'Angelo establishes an ambivalent connection between the friend's sudden death and his beauty. The continual tension between life and death in the juxtaposition of *weight* and *awakening* (which are also interconnected through alliteration) seems to be resolved by the idea of a spiritual resurrection suggested by the verb. On the human plane, the emotional understatement, so characteristic of D'Angelo's verse in general, is poignantly rendered in the touching image of the men who, in spite of their toil and suffering, still cling to life, dazed, red-faced and sweating from their "frenzied digging" and "turn slowly toward home, shivering, straggling, sombre." In another of his characteristic reversals of temporal perspective, D'Angelo recalls the man when alive as "a handsome, quiet fellow, a family man". Yet death has now transformed him into a "huge man [...] an extinguished sun [...] dawning on dead worlds." The finale is reminiscent of the end of Gerard Manley Hopkins' "Felix Randal the Farrier" in which the strength and power of the man is also reaffirmed after the description of his death. Besides this metaphorical representation of the man's death the cruel contrast between the young man's attempts to make light of the situation and the powerful final image of the anonymous wild-eyed woman running out into the darkness adds a psychologically realistic effect to the poem which (in the absence of circumstantial reference to the original incident) suggests the tragedy of a universal suffering. This sombre atmosphere is taken up in "Omnis Sum" which follows immediately after:

> On the Calvary of thought, I knelt, in torment of
> silence.
> The stars were like sparks struck from the busy forge
> of vengeful night.
> The sky was like a woman in fury
> Dishevelling her tresses of darkness over me.
> It seemed as if the whole universe were accusing me
> Of the anguish of Deity.
>
> (D'Angelo 1924, 119)

The poem reveals a series of significant intratextual analogies. In a revisitation of "Monte Majella," the preying mountain now becomes the adult poet kneeling "[O]n the Calvary of thought". This transition from unconscious reverie to a self-conscious "torment of silence" is echoed in the transformation of the romantic youth of "Fantasio" into a figure of universal guilt against a background of natural forces merging with the flames of an industrial landscape. Finally, the vision of the sorrowful woman running aimlessly out into the darkness at the end of "Accident in the Coal Dump," is countered by the personification of "the vengeful night" as a woman who unleashes all her fury at the poet. The religious connotation suggested by the title in Latin should not go unnoticed since its meaning (I am everything) reinforces the dramatic representation in the poem of the self's sense of total responsibility.

The heavily religious connotations in *Omnis Sum* are resumed in the short poem which concludes this brief survey "Song of Light":

> The sun robed with noons stands on the pulpit of heaven
> Like an anchorite preaching his faith of light to
>   listening space.
> And I am one of the sun's lost words,
> A ray that pierces through endless emptiness on emptiness
> Seeking in vain to be freed of its burden of splendor.
>
> (D'Angelo 1924, 155-156)

The somewhat contrived metaphors of the opening two lines in no way prepare the reader for the complex change that occurs at the extraordinary phrase: "And I am one of the sun's lost words." The negative representation of the landscapes that dominate the previous poems is now resolved in the image of the poet as mediator between the sun (God?) and the listening space around him as he acknowledges the spiritual and divine origin of his poetic inspiration. However, this embodiment comes with the equal realisation that he is also only one of other lost words scattered through the universe after a sun storm. The splendour of being only one of its disciples carries a responsibility which he cannot renounce. Just as Coleridge's Ancient Mariner is doomed to retell his tale to passers-by, D'Angelo feels fated to pierce "through endless emptiness on emptiness" in what appears to be a frustrated attempt at poetic self-expression. In this sense he ultimately shows the extent to which he realises the limitations and the insufficiency of language to fully liberate him from the divine, poetic source that holds him in its grasp.[1]

WORKS CITED

Cacco, Michele. 2022. "The Italian Immigrants and the American Dream in Pascal D'Angelo's *Son of Italy*." *International Journal of Linguistics, Literature and Culture* 9 (2002): 10-21.

D'Angelo, Pascal. 1924. *Son of Italy*. New York: MacMillan.

Diraviam, D. S. 2021. "Translations and Transmutations: Examining the Repatriated *Son of Italy*." *VIA (Voices in Italian Americana)* 32 (1) (2021): 27-41.

Fontanella, Luigi. 1998. "Poeti emigrati ed emigranti poeti negli Stati Uniti." *Italica* 75 (2) (Summer 1998): 210-225.

Viscusi, Robert. 2003. "*Son of Italy*: Immigrant Ambitions and American Literature." *MELUS* 28 (3) (Fall 2003): 41-54.

---

[1] Yet even the one example he provides of an early attempt at writing English contains, for all its errors of grammar, spelling and syntax, rhetorical turns of phrase and a literary lexicon similar to what one finds in his autobiography. (D'Angelo, 1924: 142-3).

"...two words that they had never heard of": Pascal D'Angelo's struggle with a new language

Michela Marroni
UNIVERSITÀ DEGLI STUDI DI TERAMO

Abstract: Viewed from the perspective of the appropriation of the English language, *Son of Italy* (1924) can be regarded as a very original autobiography and extremely important for understanding the literary formation of Pascal D'Angelo. This article argues that the key to reading *Son of Italy* should not be sought in the narrated events concerning the various adversities encountered by the gang of immigrant workers from Abruzzo, but in the protagonist's gradual awareness of his literary vocation. Indeed, Pascal D'Angelo recounts how he felt totally committed to following his vocation as a poet in the English language. In this sense, this article analyzes the autobiography from the perspective of language, trying to demonstrate how Pascal D'Angelo's journey is unique not only on the cultural level but, even more, on the linguistic level. Moreover, this journey sheds light on a personality that, overcoming obstacles and prejudices of all kinds, ultimately manages to affirm the value of his poetic production.

1. In his autobiography, *Son of Italy* (1924), Pascal D'Angelo recounts the various stages of his sociocultural encounter with American reality, which gradually instills in him the desire to become a poet. Due to the exceptional nature of his character, the autobiographical text can also be read as a *Bildungsroman* with its hero confronting a sequence of ordeals that he must overcome. In this sense, *Son of Italy* stimulates a series of reflections of a linguistic and traductological order. Indeed, his formation, as it emerges from the pages of *Son of Italy*, is undoubtedly an important testimony that, while confirming the uniqueness of Pascal D'Angelo's journey, also shows how he delineates the image of himself as a poet. In light of his particular position as a young Italian immigrant, it is worth highlighting the peculiarity of his linguistic choice in terms of poetic invention. Indeed, the protagonist possesses a poetic vocation whose diction aspires to be totally immersed in the English language, having nothing to do with the language of origin. The book thus narrates how the young Pascal, with determination and perseverance, strives to achieve his transition from the Italian language to the English language, of which – it should be noted – he had no knowledge upon arriving in New York. Paradoxically, we could assume that, in his restless imagination, the will to learn English and the desire

to be a poet are the same thing. The English language and poetry occupy the same territory without any apparent connection with the culture of origin from a linguistic point of view. Significantly, the small village at the foot of the Maiella, the rural lore, and its various dialects constitute something that D'Angelo loves to remember with a vague nostalgic tone but does not want to acquire as an integral part of his creative imagination.

In this sense, his transition reveals that he is endowed with an intralinguistic mind, which a few decades ago Giampaolo Sasso defined in these terms:

> *The intralinguistic mind* [...] *is that particular part of the mind that appears specialized in coordinating in a semantic and structural sense the intralinguistic phenomena due to the instability of the sign, and with an amplitude of such functions as to suggest an appropriate definition.* (Sasso 1993, 9)[1]

It is not out of place to argue that D'Angelo, in the face of the instability of the sign, constructs each verse of his poems with the conscious reflection of an author who already has a very clear understanding of the linguistic dynamics of the poetic text, basing its structure on a very solid aesthetic method. For example, if we consider the composition "Fantasio," reported in full at the end of the third chapter of *Son of Italy*, it is evident that both the principle of repetition and the double suggestion of a lexeme such as "like," which, while meaning "similar to" in the context of various occurrences, also manages to convey the concept of "pleasure". And it is the pleasure experienced by the poet in contemplating the night and its suggestive mutability: "Trembling under the incantation of Beauty, / Like a turmoil of purple butterfly caught in a web of light, / A black foam of darkness overflows from the rim of night, / And floods away the pearl-gray wings!" (D'Angelo 2003, 43-44).[2] These are the last four lines in which the insistent repetition of the voiceless labiodental "f" conveys the idea of time inexorably fleeing, and in fleeing, it carries with it the many evoked images.

---

[1] The original reads as follow: "*La mente intralinguistica* [...] *è quella particolare parte della mente che appare specializzata nel coordinare in senso semantico e strutturale i fenomeni intralinguistici dovuti all'instabilità del segno, e con un'ampiezza di tali funzioni da suggerirne una definizione appropriata*" (Italics in original).
[2] All quotations are from this edition, with page numbers in parentheses.

D'Angelo, however, remains a talent in which the English language (with its tradition starting from the great romantics) and a distinctly Italian sensitivity, warm and sanguine like the nations overlooking the Mediterranean, converge: "Although he found inspiration in Shelley and Keats and chose English as the language for his art, he did indeed, in his poems, remain a son of Italy" (Barone 2023, 4). Upon closer inspection, the semiotic considerations that apply to his poems can also be, albeit only in part, referred to his narrative text. The extreme awareness in the use of words is evident from the first chapter when the narrator recalls his childhood, making that distant season the first stage of his memory:

> As I glance back over the time-shadowed sky of my *infancy*, I seem to see a vast expanse of mist that gives no light to any early events. But here and there looms a faint pyramid of recollection that can apparently never fade. Toward them I grope, almost in a twilight of memory, seeking to bring out what really happened to me while I passed through the little world of *childhood* and poverty. (7, my italics)

The narration begins with Pascal D'Angelo's childhood in a remote village in Abruzzi in 1898. The incipit is characterized by circularity with two synonyms – *infancy* and *childhood* – that seem to linguistically envelop the dominant social element: *poverty*. In these isolated areas, far from the great currents of thought, high culture is unknown; everything is primordial, and men live in the same spaces where domestic animals are raised. It goes without saying that in such a rudimentary world where human existence is reduced to its essentials (work, fatigue, rest, hunger, and sleep), life is degraded also on the level of feelings and values typical of small communities. In these villages, the possibility of an education corresponding to the aspirations of its most sensitive and aware inhabitants is denied. Not only is there no space for culture, but the language itself is reduced to a superfluous element, something that has no relation to daily life, which for most means a Darwinian struggle for survival. But here the narrator's voice grafts something magical onto this representation of a rough and primitive universe. In many ways, Pascal transforms that space into an extraordinary world that goes beyond the banality and immobility of the small community – a community that knows only the meaning of the daily struggle against poverty, which is also a struggle against death:

> We of the uplands of Abruzzi are a different race. The inhabitants of the soft plains of Latium and Apulia where in winter we pasture our sheep consider us *a people of seers and poets. We believe in dreams.* There are strange beings walking through our towns whose existence, we know, are phantasies. We have men who can tell the future and ageless hags who know the secrets of the mountains and can cure all illness save witchcraft with *a few words*. (14, my italics)

Language, which is absent as a manifestation of knowledge and high culture or as an elevated and bureaucratic and institutional expression of power, returns to the scene in a popular form. Indeed, what D'Angelo remembers is the ritual expression of knowledge that, in a diachronic sense, has its roots in an archaic world where, in many ways, everything was word, every gesture was associated with a linguistic textuality: from prayers to magical formulas, from dialectal forms of incantations against the evil eye to many other manifestations of popular culture where formulas intended as certainties of the community ritual dominated. All this was possible because the archaic rituality was based on an interpretable reality since the distinction between good and evil knew no intermediate spaces. From this conception of the world – a world where black opposed white and vice versa – the possibility of understanding events arose.

In 1957, Richard Hoggart in *The Uses of Literacy* (1957) emphasized this aspect by speaking of "the hold of superstition and myth" in early twentieth-century England: "The world of experience is mapped in every point, particularly closely at the great nodes, in two colors, into those things which 'mean good luck' and those which 'mean bad luck'. These divisions are invoked daily and automatically" (Hoggart 1976, 29). Therefore, in societies where the mythical framework of the past persisted, reality was interpreted in the simplest possible way, that is, the dichotomy of black and white prevailed. Consequently, according to Hoggart, "we might conjure up a pretty picture of the way in which old attitudes, simple but healthy, remain unaffected" (Hoggart 1976,

29). In fact, the archaic worldview, especially in areas where life had not been reached by the industrial revolution and geopolitical upheavals, simplified life and made the persistence of poverty and many survival-related problems less harsh.

From another angle, the narrator's voice speaks of the reputation that Maiella had as a land of poets and seers, thus conferring cultural dignity to a part of Abruzzi that, geographically, was far from both the great cities of central Italy and the Adriatic coast. However, as Carl Van Doren recalled in 1924 when presenting *Son of Italy* to American readers, D'Angelo came from that area of Abruzzi where Ovid, one of the greatest poets of the classical world, was born. Therefore, it was not surprising that, before being a laborer, the author of the autobiography was a poet – an authentic poet with his own voice, theme, and precise tone:

> And *A Son of Italy* unquestionably belongs with the precious documents of the literature of Pascal D'Angelo's adopted country. This literature excels all others in the type of which his book is an example. But whereas most of the autobiographies of immigrants are content to tell how this or that new-comer fought his way up to the level of a competence and perhaps of some public post, *A Son of Italy* adds a new note. The uplands of Abruzzi sent to America not another laborer, not another contractor, not another politician, but another son of that Ovid whose fame is still the glory of Sulmona. No American hereafter, watching a gang of brown Italians busy in a ditch, can help asking himself whether there is not some Pascal D'Angelo among them… (Van Doren 1924, xi-xii)

Therefore, Van Doren confers on D'Angelo a dignity that exalts his value as a poet by inscribing his name in a tradition that, while objectively founding its linguistic bases in English literature, found its historical justification in the classical world, in that Latin culture that had been – and partly continued to be – the fundamental reference point of all Western literary traditions. In this sense, the fact that the narrator proudly claims his origins, emphasizing the historical importance of a people who could boast a past marked by heroism, courage, and enterprise, assumes a great value in terms of identity:

> The hamlet where I was born on January 20, 1894, is comprised of a small group of stone houses near Introdacqua, and not very far from the old walled city of Sulmona. Introdacqua nestles at the head of a beautiful valley whose soft green is walled by the great blue barrens of Majella. The mother mountain looms to the east of us and receives the full splendor of the dawn. *We are proud to call ourselves the sons of the majestic Majella.* And our race, the ancient Samnites, is said to have sprung from those sunny altitudes and spread their power over all Italy, making even Rome tremble. (17, my italics)

Regarding his origins, the image that D'Angelo intends to communicate is that of a world where the signs of the past still persist in the present, not only in the pride and dignity of the valley communities but also in the awareness of the value of Maiella as a central element of that reality, a sort of visible representation of the strength and persistence of past greatness (*We are proud...*). Far from being a stepmother and hostile to the valley dwellers, Maiella is the mother who protects her people and never abandons them, even when they are far away, perhaps on another continent. In short, the mountain stands as the epicentre from which that positive energy seems to radiate, an energy that the mature narrator retains in himself after having left his land for over twenty years.

The child Pascal who lived in Cauze, a small group of houses not far from Introdacqua, seems to suggest words to the poet Pascal who, as we read in the first chapters of *Son of Italy*, retains a clear memory of that reality. Introdacqua itself, observed from a distance, stands out in the protagonist's mind almost as a unique example of landscape beauty: "Introdacqua is a beautiful town, and nature appears to have squandered beauty on the surrounding vistas. The people are very quiet and extremely peaceful" (20). These are the phrases of a writer who seeks to make his way through the mists of the past. In this gesture of intense recollection, the town is invested with a process of idealization that, to use Gabriele d'Annunzio's words from "La pioggia nel pineto," evokes the "beautiful fable" that the narrating voice intends to tell not only to American readers but also to himself. Pascal's euphoric drive connotes maternal Maiella as well as his real mother who, never seen again after arriving in America, becomes a living part of a memory imbued with light.[3]

2. The story of Pascal D'Angelo's problematic relationship with education begins at a tender age. The Italian language understood as the language taught in schools and spoken by the entire nation was a gradual and difficult cultural acquisition for him. The passion for knowledge and linguistic culture that manifested in him when he still did not attend school was frustrated by a family context that, in some way, opposed the child's education. Indeed, on the one hand, he had a strong desire to learn and prepare to become what he dreamed of becoming, on the other hand, his sense of responsibility was even stronger, leading him to do what his father asked him to do to make ends meet. Thus, in the second chapter, the reader is informed of the unfavorable family situation for his education. For Pascal, a regular education was a remote possibility, if not a mere mirage:

> I was sent to school at the age of seven. It was a small place kept by a gentle voiced lady. My attendance was irregular, for I was the first boy of the family big enough to help my parents. My father had five or six sheep and four goats and I had to watch them – not because he wanted to prevent my going to school, but because he could not afford to hire an older boy. In spite of my frequent absences, however, I was much ahead of the average and not far behind the best. And their advantage grew from the fact that their fathers and mothers knew how to read and write while mine did not. (22-23)

Although the situation is extremely difficult in terms of schooling, the narrator evokes the events of little Pascal without assuming the melodramatic and sensational tone typical of someone who wants to highlight the heroism and virtues of the experiencing self. Everything is told succinctly and without rhetoric. The cited passage offers an example of the style adopted by the narrator who is persuaded of having the truth

---

[3] On the relationship between Pascal D'Angelo and his mother, Domenica Santomaggio Diraviam observes: "The maternal security and innocent qualities of youth abounded in the author's poetic recollections of the area. [...] The reader witnesses. the catalyst of D'Angelo's physical translation from naïve youth to exploited immigrant in a glace he exchanged with his mother" (Santomaggio Diraviam 2021,28).

on his side simply because every sentence is built on personal experience. Indeed, he does not like to assume the attitude of the highly gifted student who is a victim of a social environment incapable of understanding his intelligence. The reader, however, basing his conjectures on the realistic descriptions, understands that little Pascal is an exceptional schoolboy, even though he is forced to herd sheep and goats: his desire to learn everything that can be learned from the teacher's mouth, his keen sensitivity, his spirit of observation already highlight the traits of a mind that, day after day, broadens its cognitive horizon.

One of the characteristics of the structure and style of *Son of Italy* is its intratextuality. The autobiographical text, in fact, includes a series of poems by D'Angelo himself, published in American magazines or elsewhere, not so much to reiterate their publication but to enrich the autobiography with meaning and poetic intensity. After all, he understands that "things are only potentially poetic, and it is up to language to translate this potential into action. Reality, as soon as it is translated into words, entrusts its aesthetic destiny to language".[4]

The first lyric, cited in the second chapter, is titled "Midday":

The road is like a little child running ahead of me and then
    hiding behind a curve –
Perhaps to surprise me when I reach there.
The sun has built a nest of light under the eaves of noon;
A lark drops down from the cloudless sky
Like a singing arrow, wet with blue, sped from the
    bow of space.
But my eyes pierce the soft azure, far, far beyond,
To where roam eternal lovers
Along the broad blue ways
Of silence. (22)

Before quoting his poem in full, D'Angelo writes a sentence that can be considered a key to understanding not only the dreams of his adolescence but also the meaning to be attributed to the autobiography: "Still

[4] Translation is mine. This is the original text: "[...] les choses ne sont poétiques qu'en puissance et que c'est au langage qu'il appartient de faire passer cette puissance à l'acte. La réalité, sitôt qu'elle est parlée, remet son destin esthétique entre les mains du langage" (Cohen 1966, 38).

there were dreams for me. A poem of mine which was printed long afterwards may perhaps give an idea of that region and light surrounding me" (22). These words reveal how the autobiographical text is ultimately functional to becoming the author of a lyric like "Midday". *Son of Italy*, therefore, presents itself as a narrative aimed at defining the stages of his poetic sensitivity, which was already apparent before his emigration to America. In particular, the poem marks the encounter between the horizontal axis (*The road is like a little child*) and the vertical axis, suggested by the sequence formed by the elements of the natural landscape (*the sun, the cloudless sky*), in an attempt to find a point of mediation between the dreaming child and the pragmatic vision of existence, as a consequence of the precarious social condition. As explicitly stated in the last four lines, in the end, over any practical consideration, the dreamer will prevail, that is, D'Angelo the poet who, as *Son of Italy* intends to demonstrate in every chapter, will never stop listening to his vocation, even paying a high price until the last of his days.

Undoubtedly the autobiography is a narrative about the making of the poet and primarily about the making of his compositions. This is confirmed at the end of the second chapter, where D'Angelo includes another poem that, like the previous one, fits into a context in which the visionary tension of the present evokes scenes from the past. More precisely, the scenes of the landscape of a childhood that is always recalled is an essential element of his imagination, not only in geographical term but also as a cultural stimulus imbued with nostalgia and inspirational force. Indeed, the narrator's voice observes: "The inspiration of Mount Maiella above me, I later sought to express in a poem, which after many vicissitudes was finally printed in *The Nation*" (26). Significantly, in addition to telling the story of his American acculturation, D'Angelo also tells the story of his poetic works that experience the same "vicissitudes" as their author.

Here is the text of the composition ("Mount Maiella") which, in this case, is quoted as the closing of the chapter, albeit without the title:

> The mountain in a prayer of questioning heights
> gazes upward at the dumb heavens,
> And its inner anger is forever bursting forth

In twisting torrents,
Like little drops of dew trickling along the crevices
Of the giant questioner
I and my goats were returning towards the town below.
But my thoughts were of a little glen where wild roses grow
And cool springs bubble up into blue pools.
And the mountain was insisting for an answer from
the still heaven. (26)

What emerges from these lines is the personality of a child who, with a sensitive and restless soul, questions the meaning to give to his life, which unfolds in a rich natural environment that, ironically, contrasts with the material and cultural poverty of the people of those valleys. Referring precisely to this poem, William Boelhower writes: "Here the mountain explicitly acts as a medium for the persona to reach a spiritual peace beyond the world of the town and is an externalization of his own communion with the upper world" (Boelhower 2021, 97). As already mentioned, the upward gaze is symptomatic of a spiritual tension that, while dialoguing with the romantic tradition (primarily with Shelley and Keats), expresses the vocation of a poet who aspires to conquer a space capable of uniting heaven and earth. This tension may be equated to the lark of the homonymous Shelleyan composition, which, albeit indirectly, serves as an intertext in the lyric "Midday," cited above, present at the end of the first chapter (*A lark drops down from the cloudless sky...*).

Considering the textual segments, one wonders what kind of intertextual path led to the creative process of a poet who, indeed, moved between two languages, that is, the language of the culture of origin and the language of the culture of arrival. Is it possible to hypothesize that D'Angelo wrote directly in English, perhaps with the simultaneous help of a bilingual dictionary? Or, given his linguistic limitations, did he start from the Italian language to subsequently, gradually, carry out a process of transcoding that, in practical terms, involved repeated revision of the initial text until the desired phono-prosodic effect was achieved? Unfortunately, in the absence of philologically relevant documents (notebooks, scattered sheets, drafts, letters, and other material), it is not possible to establish the poet's method, nor can we arrive at a clear definition of D'Angelo's creative moment whose English textualization, as is obvious, had to deal with the interference of Italian which, in its dialectal variants (Abruzzese, but also Calabrese, Sicilian, etc.), was the language used throughout the working day, at least in the years when he was part of the gang of laborers coming from the Sulmona area.

3. From the point of view of Pascal's language learning, his true story begins when, together with his father and other Italian emigrants, he arrives in America after a difficult passage aboard the transatlantic *Cedric*. Indeed, it is from his landing in another world that a new scene opens up marking the second and decisive phase of his life and his poetic vocation. After all, compared with his previous experience, America was far from the reality he had left behind. Even at the linguistic level, the American scene presented itself as a challenge to an adolescent who, until that moment, had not had the opportunity to read many books and, above all, to study that foreign language in view of emigration. Full of hopes and euphoric visions, the first image of the New World immediately arouses positive sensations in the protagonist, despite the fog and the onset of night. Delusively, all the Italians share a moment of intense happiness at the thought that the crossing was over and that, finally, they would set foot on that land of a thousand promises:

> It was a foggy day when we *finally* approached New York Harbor, too late to enter. For hours out we had seen small boats with white sails, and *finally* we beheld a twilight strip of shore, which *gradually vanished* under a curtain of mist and darkness. Still it was land – *it was America!* The terrors which the boundless mid-ocean had waked in us soon *vanished* and left us in easeful relief. We strolled happily along the deck. Some of those who had been here before were unsuccessful in trying to point Coney Island to us.
>
> Below all was confusion and noise. Everyone was talking at once. *Gradually*, however, a silence came over us. [...]
>
> Anyhow, on the 20th of April 1910, I and my father with a crowd of our fellow townsmen were allowed *to land in America*! (58, my italics)

In light of the theorization around the intralinguistic mind (that is, around the mechanisms that operate in literary writing on the unconscious level), we cannot fail to notice the double repetition of the past participle *vanished*, which, although applied here to the landscape and its action on the emigrants, already seems to indicate that along with the darkness and fog, that American dream evoked by the narrator in two phrases – *it was America!* and *to land in America!* – where the exclamation mark measures the hopes nurtured by the entire Abruzzese group, will also vanish. Moreover, it cannot escape notice how the pair of adverbs *finally/gradually*, repeated twice, defines a semantic isotopy of waiting and the consequent frenzy at the idea of reaching the land where, for months and months, everyone had placed many hopes and projected their dreams of well-being and happiness. Additionally, the precise indication of the date – therefore, when Pascal D'Angelo was just over sixteen years old – aims to represent the event in its uniqueness, at least in the memory of the emigrants who, from this moment on, will associate that date not so much with the beginning of a phase of social growth, but with the onset of an experience that, almost entirely, will mean disappointment and frustration never separated from the deeply ingrained idea of failure.

However, for Pascal, life turns into an adventure right after having had a first contact with American society. The sixth chapter opens with significant words: "And this is America, I thought. During our way over on the ship I had seen golden heaps of clouds and rainbow vistas toward which we sped, and I had come to believe that they were perhaps the portals of America" (61). Here, the opening phrase seems to summarize all the expectations, all the euphoric and romantically ideal imagination projected onto that vast space full of promises. The initial conjunction of the segment "*And* this is America" indirectly alludes to everything that has led up to that precise point, namely, to everything that is hoped to be conquered, in the illusory vision of a world where the achievement of a condition of wealth is an easy goal for everyone. What does the first representation of America highlight if not the *a priori* mythologization of those lands and that nation, ignoring that the hard life left behind will be replaced not at all by that happy life that the emigrants' imagination suggests? In addition, the chiastic construction of the first paragraph

(*America / golden heaps of cloud / the portals / America*) suggests the work of a mind that has intensely thought about that particular moment; the flow of thoughts is connected – as already mentioned – to the conjunction *And* that establishes the psychological circularity with which Pascal D'Angelo prepares to become a young Italian migrant in New York.

In the following diegetic segments, the characters who will be part of the protagonist's formative journey are shown – each character is characterized with a few strokes, but always very incisive. If we observe the story from the ethnic and social point of view, we can easily conclude that Pascal experiences America without undergoing a major trauma, as all the workers come from the same area of Abruzzi, thus recreating the context of origin, even on the linguistic level, naturally. This is an advantage on the human level, but also a disadvantage on the linguistic and socio-economic level. If in the small community of immigrants, they continue to speak the dialect of origin, it is clear that none of them dreams of studying American. However, Pascal stands out from the others because, despite being young and lacking authority, he fully feels the limits of the native language and begins to reflect on the meaning to give to his life. In any case, in the first phase of his work experience – hard and devoid of solidarity outside the gang of his fellow countrymen – he struggles to consider American as his language, or as the language with which he will soon have to deal, both in the workplace and in society:

> None of us, including myself, ever thought of a movement to broaden our knowledge of the English language. We soon learned a few words about the job, that was the preliminary creed; then came "bread," "shirt," "gloves" (not kid gloves), "milk". And that is all. We formed our little world – one of many in this country. And the other people around us who spoke in strange languages might have been phantoms for all the influence that they had upon us or for all we cared about them. (68)

Only a few terms convey to the reader that fact that their miserable social condition is matched by a very poor linguistic and cultural baggage. In the small circle of people, the knowledge of the language is not even considered, apart from the few words, two of which concern their miserable diet: *bread* and *milk*. Tellingly, in the sixth chapter, the narrative voice well suggests the rough and primitive atmosphere that was breathed in the various shacks of the laborers where each ethnic group formed a world apart. And it was a closure that also derived from the distance constituted by the respective languages and dialects of origin. The linguistic and cultural diversity that separated the various groups represented, as D'Angelo writes, an insurmountable barrier, so that each ethnic group ignored the life of all the others. In a context where the knowledge of English is practically zero degree, the narrator dedicates a couple of pages to recount, on the level of personal experience, the practical effects of his linguistic ignorance.

Thus, it happens that one day the foreman of the laborers' gang asked Pascal to go to the local store to buy twelve eggs, giving him the necessary tips regarding the word to pronounce: "The foreman repeated the word 'aches' several times to me so that I could memorize it. And I hurried down to the road repeating the word to myself, so as not to forget it" (68). Unfortunately, in front of the shopkeeper, an old Pole, his wrong pronunciation made the owner understand "axe" so, after a while, he showed up with twelve axes, causing Pascal's astonishment. Only after insistent gesturing did Pascal manage to make it clear that he only wanted twelve eggs. But before this happened, a lot of time passed, because even the involvement of the old man's wife did not solve the problem: "Then his wife came out into the dim store. she was fat, greasy and ugly, and understood less than her husband. [...] Then I made the sign of an oval with my fingers, at which the understood and brought out the eggs" (69). Therefore, not through words, but only with mimicry, the two shopkeepers managed to solve the mystery.

Although all this produces a repeated comic effect in the reader, his detailed account of the episode provides the measure of the level of linguistic ignorance in which the Pascal of the first phase lived, marked by many similar moments: "Another little catastrophe happened during these early months when I was learning and misusing a few words of English" (69). In fact, the main problem with the new language was his inability to memorize sounds that he felt were completely foreign, sounds that were so different from those of his own language that any process of immediate appropriation was actually impossible. The consequence of all this was that a simple expression like "fall down" ended up being pronounced as "you damn," creating misunderstanding and hilarity on the part of those who knew the English language, aware of Pascal's pronunciation error: "And all around the place I went repeating my sad tale of 'You damn'. When finally one man made me understand what I had been saying, I was so ashamed that I hurried straight home" (71). Narrating the small catastrophes of his relationship with the language spoken in the States, the narrator intends to shed light on the personal drama of a young man who, day after day, realizes that language is something more than a simple tool for understanding each other at work and in community life.

From this point of view, the literary value of *Son of Italy* is expressed by the realism with which D'Angelo dramatizes his gradual transition to a different approach to the language problem, until he conquers – through immense sacrifice – a competence through which he can express his talent as a poet in English. The second part of the novel outlines precisely this journey towards defining himself as an Italian who has become a master of a language that, until a few years earlier, seemed abstruse and foreign, totally disconnected from his own cultural tradition and linguistic corpus.

4. Before a clear and definitive awareness of the socio-economic mechanisms that presided over the American way of life, the protagonist will go through a series of painful trials that, finally, in the twelfth chapter, will lead him to a different relationship with society, language, and himself. It is, in truth, an ontological turning point that will imply the end of the myth of America as a land of plenty. And this process of gradual disintegration of the myth begins precisely in New York, the city of a thousand lights which, however, for Pascal and his companions will mean suffering and darkness. In this sense, in the autobiographical narrative, the image of the melting pot is anything but euphoric:

> Dressed in our best, and rather handsome, in our estimation, we left the noisy house and climbed carefully down the face of the precipice on a narrow coiling footpath that leads into Gorge Road.

> Gorge Road comes pouring like a stream from the cliffs and joins River Road. Dirty shacks and hovels everywhere at the foot of the Palisades. On tiny terraces are barn-like houses clinging to the bare, stony slope, one above the other, filled hive-like with people talking, people arguing, people smoking and eating, singing and strumming guitars.
>
> [...] Men and women, dirty, speaking a mixed jargon of Italian, Polish, Hungarian, English, were hurrying all bout. Two husky laborers were appearing from the gloom of a factory door. One old Italian with golden rings in his ears was prodding some goats upward toward the terraced shacks. Children played everywhere. (75)

This is the New York where Pascal, his father, and the other townsmen find themselves, all now in the grip of deep nostalgia for their land and their people. The detailed description of the shantytown population corresponds to the first decisive deconstruction of the myth; like a Brazilian favela, the peripheral area of New York presents a humanity abandoned and forced to live in conditions that are an insult to dignity. In a few paragraphs, D'Angelo describes the chaotic image of a world where separation and distance between individuals predominate. Despite the presence of different ethnicities and different linguistic cultures, the narrative voice shows that New York was far from representing the ideal of a happy dialogue between the individual groups of immigrants. Divergence dominates over convergence.

On the morphosyntactic level, it cannot escape notice how the portrait of a sort of human hive is constructed through the repetition of a series of gerunds that, in addition to showing the senseless circularity of those existences, also determines an effect of obsessive overcrowding equal to the density of the rickety shacks built one above the other:

clinging
people talking
people arguing
people smoking
eating
singing
strumming.

What does New York mean for the team of Italian workers, all lost, dirty and poor? It does not mean a world of beauty and astonished observation of an extraordinary urban landscape in its wonders. On the contrary, it means confronting the hovels of a metropolis dominated by social contrasts – nothing worthy of humanity in the repeated images where widespread filth, social indifference, and abandonment are the rule. In short, in the area of New York, full of miserable villages, the young Pascal – who still does not want to give up his dream – breathes an atmosphere of total decay: "Town of filthy hovels, towns of congested quarters and unhealthy conditions, all of them, little miniature East Sides and Mulberry Bends, scattered among the green stretches and broad open spaces of America" (76). In his movement from the most squalid periphery, Pascal's discovery of Manhattan means for him above all the discovery of a face very different from the inhuman hives where the Abruzzese laborers have found shelter.

In the seventh chapter, we are given to read some intense pages dedicated to the "magic vista" of Manhattan (79). While revealing something indescribable, something magical to Pascal's eyes, however, after the first approach, he cannot help but notice the large number of people running and bustling in the impressive streets of the center. This restless human presence seems to be the expression of a sad and gray world that does not know the pleasure of life: "Where did they all come from? And why their silence? How pale they all were, I thought. Weakly pale they all seemed, like sprouts of seeds washed up by the rain. Cars clanged and rumbled past, filled with rows of statue-like people who sat within, motionless, ignoring one another" (79). Therefore, even the contact with one of the most celebrated cities in the world appears not at all in line with the myth of America. On the contrary, it confirms its falsehood, highlighting at the same time the dehumanizing force of its extraordinary manifestation of opulence and architectural exaggeration.

Yet, what the narrator expresses at the end of the seventh chapter is an ambivalent sentiment that, at least in part, anticipates his decision to achieve fame precisely in that city: "And we three walked on, wandered in a magic show of forbidden splendor and beauty. And I thought of how lovely and yet how repulsive this enchanted city was"

(80). While wandering around the center with two other laborers, Saverio and Federico, with whom he has formed a friendship, the twenty-year-old Pascal realizes that New York is a monstrous city that frightens and repels. At the same time, almost relying on his prophetic instinct, he cannot hate that view of buildings that seem to challenge the sky, of enormous and seemingly endless streets teeming with people. And this is because his mind, unlike his companions, is still thirsty for life and knowledge experienced in the New World. Here, the double repetition of the conjunction – "And we three walked... And I thought" – cannot escape notice, which, on the level of rhetorical strategies, contrasts the protagonist's solitude with respect to the friends who are with him. His thoughts remain with him, who seems to have already decided that he will never leave that nation.

The following chapters can be interpreted as the narration of the end. The work that the gang manages to find in West Virginia, instead of being the solution to all their anxieties and sufferings, turns out to be another moment of social and material descent. Leaving behind the desolate and miserable shantytown on the outskirts of the metropolis, the Abruzzese workers delude themselves that, in that region south of New York, they will find "the land of sunshine and warmth" (97), that is, a land ready to embrace them and grant what they had longed for at the time of departure for America. But soon the new dream of well-being and wealth also dissolves, and the new state proves to be no less dark than the long path of repeated disappointments traveled so far: "On reaching the West Virginia side we again plunged into the hilly darkness. After we had trudged on for heaven knows how long, we saw the faint glimmer of a lamplight through a small shanty window" (100). In the new workplace, even the last remnant of dignity is erased, forced as they were to live at a level that only animals could endure: "We were pigs in our sty" (103). Extreme exploitation soon turns into tragedy; in that new context, everything seems to fall under the domain of death: a fatal accident causes the death of two of the group's dearest friends: "There was a howl of pain, blood-curdling and piercing. We turned our startled eye. Two men were pinned under the derrick. One of them was Teofilo, the other the huge Andrea" (106). The event shakes the spirits and marks the tragic epilogue of a journey into a dark nightmare, increasingly resembling a scene of death: "Within a few days of the fatal accident the gang broke up. We had lost all heart; work in that place was oppressive; we felt enslaved. And finally, discouraged and saddened by our loss, we decided to quit. Sadly we returned to New York" (106).

With the abandonment of work in West Virginia, the gang ends the great American adventure. Nostalgia and suffering prevail over the remaining margins of hope. The struggle against adversity finally reaches the point where everything suggests abandoning that scene. And so, the disheartened father announces to his son that he has decided to return home with the other fellow townsmen: "One night shortly after our return my father announced to me that he was thinking of leaving for Italy. 'We are not better off than when we started,' he said, and asked me if I wished to go back with him" (106). With the great astonishment of everyone and the father's reaction filled with painful sadness ("a broken-hearted man," 107), young Pascal declares that he does not want to leave America. Not only does he not want to abandon his dreams, but, distinguishing himself from the others and their now deep-rooted distrust, the protagonist still desires to believe in that new life: "Again I shook my head. There was a lingering suspicion that somewhere in this vast country an opening existed, that somewhere I would strike the light. I could not remain in the darkness perpetually" (107). It is no coincidence that the tenth chapter closes with the poem "Accident in the coal dump" (109). In fact, writing became for the poet his cure against all adversity. Probably written many years later, he wanted to dedicate those verses of suffering to the tragedy that had struck the Italian gang, almost as if to definitively overcome the personal trauma derived from that episode. Instead, young Pascal, still unable to write in English, now in total solitude, enters a new phase of his life. In many ways, it is as if he had decided that his new beginning would find nourishment in something different, something that went beyond poverty and a miserable life. Thus, in him, unexpectedly, in this renewed season of hope, the literary vocation was making its way.

5. The protagonist of the autobiography, in his solitary life, begins a journey that alludes to a vision of reality that possesses a cosmic breath.

Before mastering the vocabulary and grammar of the new language that will allow him to express himself correctly, a kind of metamorphosis of the soul occurs in him. This transformation, in essence, anticipates the portrait of the poet he will become, while revealing the spiritual strength and sensitivity that the grim life of the laborer had somehow stifled in him:

> I looked around. *I felt* a kinship with *the beautiful earth*. She was like some lovely hardhearted lady in velvets and gaudy silks – one whom we could gaze at in admiration, but never dare approach. *I felt* a power that was forcing me to cry out to this world that was so fair, so soft and oblivious of our pains and petty sorrows. Then I had to laugh to myself. "After all," I thought, "what are my tiny woes to *the eternal beauty* of those stars, of these trees and even this short-lived grass? (126, my italics)

The passage establishes a connection between the beauty of the earth and personal feelings, between the breadth of vision and the solitary personality of Pascal who confronts his daily sufferings, perceiving their insignificance compared to a universe whose existence went far beyond the brief and ephemeral passage of every single human being on earth. Along with the romantic communion with the miracle of nature, a literary vocation gradually emerges in him, step by step. In light of this nascent impulse, trusting in his self-taught ability and, even more, in his stubborn will to master the language, the protagonist embarks on another journey: it is a linguistic journey. This personal itinerary, although uphill, he absolutely does not want to abandon: "I began to learn some Spanish from these two Mexicans. [...] Somehow, I found English more to my liking than Spanish. And about once a week even bought an English newspaper to look at. [. . .]" (129). In the unfolding of the last part, chapter by chapter, the autobiography shows how, starting from a single word, Pascal manages to create a linguistically stimulating environment, transforming the railway car where he lives into a sort of blackboard in permanent transformation. The vocabulary becomes like a painting on the wall. Words must be studied and at the same time admired: "When I did learn a word and had discovered its meaning I would write it in big letters on the mouldy walls of the box car. And soon I had my first lesson in English all around me continually before my eyes" (129). Finally, the transition from learning the lexicon to writing, albeit simple if not rudimentary, takes place:

> I went home and tried to write something after work. I began it in Italian, but unable to manage the language, on a sudden thought I decided to attempt it in English. After a few Sundays of hard work I had about *three closely written pages of the most impossible English one could imagine*. In triumph, I showed it to a couple of brakemen. They laughed long and loud. There was some doubt whether it was the jokes or the manhandled English which caused their hilarity. However, I gave myself the benefit of doubt, and *agreed with myself that I could write English*. (130, my italics)

Before moving forward, it may be useful to see what Philippe Lejeune observes about the style that unmistakably characterizes Jean-Jacques Rousseau's *Confessions* (1782-1789): "Rousseau explains how style is part of history, and how it will manage to doubly describe his state of mind: without overlapping two chronologically and effectively separate states, the doubling can only be understood as a conduct of repetition" (Lejeune 1982, 57). Precisely in the second part of *Son of Italy*, in the autobiographical search for total transparency, he does not omit to lay bare his psychological oscillations. And he does so also through style. In this way, we witness a transition from the "we," characteristic of Pascal's life together with other Abruzzesi, to the first-person singular "I," which becomes the grammatical and psychological sign of a growing personality. The protagonist increasingly recognizes himself in a permanent struggle, not only against the resistances of society and power but also due to the necessity of overcoming the linguistic obstacle; for this reason, Pascal never stops feeling at odds with the target language, that is, with the English spoken in America.

In his imagination, such linguistic appropriation is configured as an unequal challenge and for this reason all the more stimulating and alive. In the passage cited above, we may notice how, in a few dense lines, the subject "I" recurs with a frequency that is symptomatic of his pressing need for self-assertion:

I went home
I began it in Italian,
I decided
I had about
I showed it
I gave myself
I could write English

Exactly as Rousseau observed regarding his autobiography, here style is indeed part of the story: it recounts its essential stages and outlines, on an ontological level, the transition from a confused and almost indistinct disposition concerning the polyphony of voices to a well-defined personality. This image of himself arises from the moment the experiencing self sets a precise goal: to speak English at a level such that this knowledge can be transformed into the linguistic basis with which to manifest the fruits of his literary talent. The transition is very clearly expressed in the method adopted by the narrator of the autobiography: *I began it in Italian* → *I could write English*. On the level of the language used, the beginning finds no correspondence with the end: the circularity of the sentence, supported by the iteration of "I," expresses an element of discontinuity precisely in the transition from the original language to the language of the nation where the protagonist has decided to remain forever, thus making it his second homeland.

At this point, it is worth noting how Pascal D'Angelo's literary ambition passes through a process of linguistic experimentation that, in fact, transforms the people close to him – simple and not at all cultured people – into the testing ground on which to verify his degree of linguistic appropriation and control that goes beyond simple communication, given that what he writes aims to have a comic effect on those who are called to read his pieces in English:

> So I began to write jokes in 'English,' most of them of my own invention or paraphrased from some paper. My jokes became known around the yard as great curiosities and things to laugh at. [...]
> Later, when I had learned to manage the English language a little better and could write with some degree of clarity, I put a prize of

five cents on some good jokes. That is, if they could keep a straight face while reading a little collection of jokes that I presented them I would give them a nickel. (131)

The comic effects of Pascal D'Angelo's jokes confirm his possession of an intralinguistic mind ready to bend the language to a series of puns capable of arousing hilarity. From a formative point of view, the purchase of the reduced version of Webster's dictionary by the young aspiring author, which he was fortunate to buy at a low price due to the poor condition of the volume, assumes the value of a decisive turning point. With the dictionary, a new world opens up before the twenty-five-year-old Pascal, stimulating him beyond simple linguistic knowledge. In the working environment, his fame as a great connoisseur of English words spreads, so, like a true lexicographer, he declares himself available to accept any challenge in terms of vocabulary. Challengers – among workers and employees in the area – are never lacking in a kind of endless game around the use of English:

> One day they brought me before the whole crowd just to have me ridiculed, perhaps because they were high school lads. They gave me five words to define and I only knew the meaning of three. Throwing up their hands they began to proclaim themselves victorious.
>
> But I calmly gave them two words that they had never heard of. Then I bet them ten words and two more for good measure none of which they could understand.
>
> *I began, "Troglodyte," "sebaceous," "wen," "helot," "indeciduity," "murine," "bantling," "ubiquity," "clithrophobia," "nadir," and instead of adding two for good measure I added seven to make their debacle more horrible.* (134-135, my italics)

As much as it may seem like a fun game, this defeat inflicted on a group of Americans means a lot to the young "lexicographer". After this manifestation of linguistic knowledge, albeit reduced to the simple knowledge of rarely used terms, he more convincingly desires to constitute a literary baggage that will serve as a springboard for his vocation. It is a true awakening full of commitment and characterized by a euphoric immersion in the project that animates him:

During the summer of 1919 I began to hear much about *Aïda*, but I did not know exactly what it was. [...]

About the same time I happened to glance over an Italian newspaper and saw an advertisement that this opera was to be represented in the open air at the Sheepshead Bay race track. I decided to go and hear it. [. . .]

And all at once I felt myself driven toward a goal. For there was revealed to me beauty, which I had been instinctively following, in spite of my grotesque jokes and farces. The quality of beauty that is in *Aïda* I have found only in the best Shelley and perhaps Keats. (137)

As regards the narratological strategies of *Son of Italy*, one of the words we most often encounter in the final chapters is *beauty*, which functions as a hypogram[5] of both the autobiography and the inserted poetic texts. The narrative voice does not cite Keats' famous words – "a thing of beauty" – but it is as if it did, as his formation is predominantly based on the romantic tradition of the second generation, primarily Keats and Shelley. It is no coincidence that Pascal D'Angelo confesses: "[...] I had been thrilled by a new discovery – my senses were all atremble – I had found Shelley" (145). Nor is the inclusion of the poem "Song of Light" at the end of the thirteenth chapter coincidental, given the evident romantic influence that characterizes its diction and theme.

What significance does poetry assume in the protagonist's sensitivity? In short, we can say that poetry is the reason why he preferred to stay in the United States while his father and others returned to the protective embrace of Maiella. Partly by instinct, partly by cold reasoning, at the time of the others' departure, Pascal realized that among the mountains of Abruzzo reigned closure, a sort of spiritual imprisonment, while in the States reigned openness, that is, the possibility of always discovering new paths, new goals, and therefore new challenges, especially for someone like him who was not born to limit his action within coordinates of provincialism and superstition.

5 For a definition of this term see Riffaterre: "The significance is shaped like a doughnut, the hole being either the matrix of the hypogram or the hypogram as matrix" (Riffaterre 1984, 13).

6. "It was hard for me to put my words and thought in order. Grammar gave me plenty of trouble. Rhyme stumped me. Avidly I read all kinds of poetry, during my spare time, and discovered that rhyme was not absolutely essential to poetic utterance. [...] *I was slowly but surely deciding upon a literary career!*" (145, my italics). The last phase of the autobiography, therefore, is placed under the poetic emblem, as his recurring thought is the conquest of literary heights that, as he himself admits, becomes the mania of his existence: "In a rose flush of awakened hopes I dreamed of my poetry. I thought of my ambition to write – always to write. It must have been a mania with me" (146). In short, with tireless study and constant application, Pascal begins to believe in himself in the role of a poet in the English language. Yet, from the initial enthusiasm following the discovery of his literary vocation, the step leading to the first disappointments is very short. His attempts to establish a relationship with the publishing world only lead to the rejections of literary magazine editors. And, with the first rejections, he also begins to understand the mechanisms that, in the States, regulated the literary system and the book market. In any case, when he receives the first response from an editor, upon seeing the letter, even before opening it and reading its content, he believes it is his first victory with a pecuniary reward obtained thanks to his poems:

> [...] I began to search the letter for money or for an invitation to call at the editor's office. Instead I found my poems and a printed slip. It was elaborate and diplomatic, courteously thanking me for my kindness in allowing the editorial staff to consider my poems. I was flattered. I was pleased to think that the editor of a large and opulent magazine should thank me. (150)

Although it is a negative reply, the same sugar-coated words of the letter convince him that he should not be discouraged, that nothing is lost. Indeed, Pascal draws the energy to send the group of poems already submitted to the judgment of the first editor to other magazines. Not long after, however, the bitter discovery: the rejection letters had the same phrasing, the same formulas with words of praise to make the rejection less painful: "Gradually I became skeptical about the honeyed phrases. I strongly suspected that there was some telepathic communication among the magazine editors to drive me and my poems from the thresholds of their temples" (151). Underlying these words is a profound disappointment that evokes biblical language precisely to give the measure of the kind of closure he finds himself dealing with. In his mind, the States remained the land of a thousand roads, a thousand opportunities, but at this juncture in his journey, he understands that the idea of openness and welcome that had led him to the decision to stay takes a hard hit. Paradoxically, the more painful the process of disillusionment becomes for him, the more he strengthens his conviction that, one way or another, he will manage to make some door open.

Extreme poverty, the accumulation of letters with the usual phrases of rejection, the loneliness that becomes harder day by day, and the hunger that forces him to barely eat do not definitively block his literary mission. The idea that he is one of many people at the threshold of the temple of literature somehow gives him the strength to persist in his search for a magazine that will publish him:

> And now I realized that I was merely a small drop in the sad whirlpool of literary aspirants. In my cold stoveless, dingy room or in the Library, I was alone in my struggle to acquire a new language and a new world. But outside of that I was one, only one of the millions of literary beggars who clog the halls of literature, who stand like a sluggish crowd in the way of anyone wishing to forge ahead. (151)

Despite having more than one reason not to believe in the American myth anymore, the Pascal who wants to become a poet still believes in that world. His faith in America persists, even when his degree of indigence pushes him, so to speak, to the most abandoned and lonely periphery of New York. The pursuit of the literary ideal manages to counterbalance all the misadventures of his miserable life. The poet nurtures an unshakable faith in the New World no less than the faith he has in himself: "I had faith in myself. Without realizing it, I had learned the great lesson of America: I had learned to have faith in the future. No matter how bad things were, a turn would inevitably come – as long as

I did not give up. I was sure of it. But how much I had to suffer until the change came! What a thorny, heartbreaking road it was!" (156). Not surprisingly, even in the condition of total degradation, the narrative shows how the literary illusion is never set aside: "When I went home at night, there was nothing to cheer me in the freezing, stoveless room, save the encouraging thought that I had not yet visited all the editorial offices in New York" (162).

With this spirit, the poet decides to make another attempt by sending his poems to one of the most important magazines, *The Nation*. In this case, long weeks of waiting pass without receiving any response – a nerve-wracking wait that suggests adopting an extreme remedy: "I knew that recognition was practically impossible. It was a new year of sorrow and suffering. As a sort of despairing gesture I sent a letter to the editor" (164). By now, Pascal D'Angelo, poor and hungry, closed in his solitude, tries his last card: the autobiography reports in the following pages the long, intense, and moving letter that is, like the inserted poems, a text within the text: four pages that produce an effect of authenticity in the reader because the poet also tells his story as an Italian immigrant, thus offering a sort of synthesis of the autobiography itself. The editor of *The Nation*, who was indeed Carl Van Doren (who is never explicitly named), instead of discarding the long epistle, reads it and does not hesitate to convince himself that the author of those words deserves the first poetry prize and the publication of his poems. The long-awaited turning point happens, America is truly the land of miracles, and Pascal D'Angelo can close his autobiographical journey in the way he had always hoped:

> The miracle happened. All at once I found myself known and talked about. Almost immediately my plea found a sympathetic response and the two editors of the two influential weekly publications in America became interested in my work. Henry Seidel Canby, editor of *The Literary Review* of the *New York Evening Post*, was one of them. Poems of mine were published. Other magazines followed. Soon the newspaper began to print my story and word about me appeared in Europe and throughout America. (167-168)

The narrative concludes with the poet's success, as he suddenly lives his season of glory. It is a happy ending precisely because it culminates in the recognition by the publishing world of the poet Pascal D'Angelo. The autobiography stops in 1919, the *annus mirabilis* shows the victory of a man who believed in himself and his vocation to the point of sacrificing everything, even his health. The diegesis, as already mentioned, does not go beyond and it is good that it does not. In the following years, D'Angelo's star lost its luster until it disappeared altogether. The miracle had happened, but unlike the miracles narrated in hagiographies, it had a life that was all too brief.

WORKS CITED

Barone, Dennis. 2023. "'A Twilight of Memory': On the Life and Writing of Pascal D'Angelo." *Diasporic Italy: Journal of Italian American Studies Association* 3 (October): 3-16.

Boelhower, William. 2021. *Immigrant Autobiographies in the United States: Five Versions of the Italian American Experience.* New York: Bordighera P.

Cohen, Jean. 1966. *Structure du langage poetique.* Paris: Flammarion.

D'Angelo, Pascal. 2003. *Son of Italy.* 1924. Toronto and Buffalo: Guernica.

Hoggart, Richard. 1976. *The Uses of Literacy.* 1957. Harmondsworth: Penguin in Association with Chatto & Windus.

Lejeune, Philippe. 1986. *Il patto autobiografico.* Trans. Franca Santini. Bologna: il Mulino.

Riffaterre, Michel. 1984. *Semiotics of Poetry.* 1978. Bloomington, IN, Indiana UP.

Santomaggio Diraviam, Domenica. 2021. "Translation and Transmutation. Examining the Repatriated *Son of Italy.*" *Via: Voices in Italian Americana* 32 (1): 27-40.

Sasso, Giampaolo. 1993. *La mente intralinguistica.* Genova: Marietti.

Van Doren, Carl. 1924. "Introduction." Pascal D'Angelo, *Son of Italy.* New York: Macmillan Company.

Religious Syncretism and Conversion in Pietro di Donato's Christ in Concrete (1939)

Francesca Caraceni
UNIVERSITÀ CATTOLICA DEL SACRO CUORE

Abstract: This article explores the literarization of Southern Italian religious culture in Pietro di Donato's *Christ in Concrete.* Such a framework, which critics have singled out as a form of "cultural Catholicism" given its mingling of pagan, magical and religious forms of ritual and performance, will be reevaluated as a faithful depiction of a peculiar Southern Italian type of religious sensibility, aptly framed by Ernesto de Martino as "Southern Catholicism" in his seminal work *Sud e Magia* (1959). After briefly outlining how Southern Catholicism and Southern Italian identity and ethnicity are represented in the novel, the argumentation will move to weigh the dynamic that these cultural markers play out with American work ethic and capitalism, symbolized in the book in the ruthlessly pagan features of "great God Job". Job, an almost supernatural entity demanding workers to sacrifice themselves to it continuously, acts as de Martino's notion of *negativo,* which the characters try to oppose by employing archaic beliefs, prayers and practices steeped in Catholicity. Finally, Paul's conversion to Job and his lapse from Southern Catholicism will be assessed as a trope that signals an abandonment of his Italian identity to embrace the pursuit of the American Dream fully.

The more that word is diminished, the more it's not real
Kendrick Lamar

This essay explores the literarization of Southern Catholic religious culture in Pietro di Donato's *Christ in Concrete.* Set in the Italian-American community of bricklayers in the aftermath of the 1929 financial crash, the novel chronicles the formation of Paul, a 12-year-old boy who, following the tragic death of his father Geremio at work, finds himself leaving school and taking his father's place on the construction site. The author meticulously crafts the narrative, arranging it around a limited number of chronotopic references. The sole date that can be ascertained with any degree of certainty is precisely 1929, while the spatial framework within which the narrative unfolds, devoid of any explicit geographical determination, is delineated by precise semantic coordinates along the home/work axis (Tenement/Job). Italy's geographical setting is evoked in the memories and words of the first-generation immigrants surrounding Paul and their tales from the homeland, recounted in nostalgic and dreamlike tones. These tales constitute an additional mental and interior space that the author proposes to the reader through streams of consciousness, which give voice to various characters in the moments before sleep, in pre-death states, or during prayer. This literary technique serves to portray Paul's assimilation process within a narrative setting characterized by a dichotomy between the stark realism of everyday life, encompassing the domains of home and work, and the ethereal, unbound by the constraints of space and time, encompassing the realms of dreams, memory, prayer and the words that convey them.

This dichotomy is also naturally reflected in the discourse and stylistic strategies employed by the author. di Donato's prose, clearly immersed in the modernist dominants, oscillates between a naturalistic or realist register when it deals with the representation of mundane facts while veering sharply toward classic modernist syntactic and morphological deconstruction when it aims to theatricalize the ineffability and imaginative power of thought and feeling during the states of semi-consciousness in which the various characters find themselves. The handling of diegetical modulations of voices by di Donato goes in the same aesthetic and formal direction. The author creates a peculiar idiolect to characterize the Italian community by translating word for word from the Abruzzi dialect into English while letting the narrating voice have a more neutral, naturalistic register and tone.[1] This estranging discrepancy in tone – what Robert Viscusi defined as a "dance of Italian and English" (Viscusi 1981, 37), while a means to represent the Italian immigrant identity "through the disfigurement of traditional sign systems and eventual reconstruction of his peculiar sign system" (Tamburri 2003, 12), also effectively conveys the main conceptual opposition underlying the narrative structure, that between the values and ethics found at home (Tenement) and those found at work (Job). More specifically, this linguistic "disfigurement" of English signifies the painful process of Paul's assimilation to the American work ethic and values, his loss of identity as an Italian and the regaining of a new,

[1] Cf. Mulas 1991, 315: "I have always thought in Italian and still think in Italian, and then I express myself. My English words are a re-coniage from my Abruzzese-Vasto Italian, because I have never been influenced by the English language. I have always found it inadequate and never, never comparable to or as rewarding as the Italian language, the language of my people".

dashed self as an Italian-American. Thus, linguistic deconstruction, becoming more evident in the expression of the altered states of consciousness just described, reflects the loss or fragmentation of identity consequential to the loss, or forgetting, of the community's cultural markers tied to their homeland.

Therefore, as I will argue in this contribution, di Donato's linguistic reworkings of English embody, in discourse, a deeper structure in the narrative, which primarily tackles the demise of southern Italian religious culture after coming in contact with the US work ethic. I argue that such is the conceptual center of the book, which di Donato develops as a tale of religious conversion where religion constitutes an organic narrative element rather than a descriptive one. As Fred Gardaphe aptly puts it, assimilation for Italians has come at a high cost, namely the loss of "the language of their ancestors" and the subsequent detachment from their history but, more importantly, that of "subscribing to the cultural values [...] of whiteness" by which "ancestral traditions become ancillary side shows that we can foster only in our spare time" (Gardaphé 2002, 187). This contribution aims to highlight the narrative dynamics that signify Paul's conversion, starting from these premises, while also reassessing the religio-cultural markers in the novel through a methodology derived from Ernesto de Martino's anthropological method. Indeed, if Paul's story in *Christ in Concrete* is a prime metaphor for the trade of "ancestral traditions" to acquire a glimpse of the American dream, such a trade is represented in di Donato's book by assessing it as a loss of what de Martino defined as *presenza*. According to de Martino, *presenza* refers man's *ethos* of being present in history by means of rituals and practices aimed at giving a tangible form to loss and suffering: "Esserci nella storia [...] dare orizzonte formale al patire, oggettivarlo in una forma particolare di coerenza culturale [...] ciò definisce insieme la presenza come *ethos* fondamentale dell'uomo e la perdita della presenza come rischio radicale a cui l'uomo – e soltanto l'uomo – è esposto" (de Martino 1975, 15). *Presenza* is thus a form of agency defined by its contrary: absence, loss, or actual death, which in *Christ in Concrete* is the conceptual and narrative catalyst that triggers Paul's detachment from his Italian identity.

The narrative is punctuated by various deaths and rituals to counter it practiced in Tenement, which appears to be the place where Annunziata functions as a preserver of such regional religious rituals. Annunziata is thus the pivot on which the events of Tenement revolve, as well as the symbolic-literary expression of that specific magical-religious and Southern sensibility imported to the United States by the first generation of immigrants. In the story of di Donato, such a religious sensibility is symbolically overwhelmed and drained by the adaptive and affirming aspects of the US work ethic. In this sense, Job constitutes a complete denial of the values of the motherland and a new type of religion to which Paul finally converts. The depiction of Job as a quasi-supernatural entity and the author's insistence on characterizing Job through religious imagery and Christian references allows us to read Paul's existential trajectory as a conversion *per se*, where the protagonist undergoes a radical paradigm shift akin to the "fragmentation of the innermost self" (Leone 2003, 4) with which converts often engage, rather than as a lapse or an apostasy. In other words, while it is undoubtedly true that Paul undergoes a "spiritual disintegration" (De Angelis 2005, 142), the overarching religious dimension in the novel indicates that Paul's is, in fact, the story of a conversion in which, after enduring immense trauma and suffering, he fully embraces Job's profit-driven culture and values by rejecting Christianity. Therefore, Paul's identity crisis and renovation, which Bachtin identified as "metamorphosis" (Bachtin 2001, 278), cannot be separated from the complex of religiocultural norms that he finally rejects.

To advance the religious imagery and symbolism in the novel, the "pre-Christian, matriarchal roots of Catholicism" should be re-assessed as, in fact, quite a stark portrayal of the type of religion practised by southern Italians at the turn of the twentieth century. What di Donato narrates, therefore, is not so much a "revisitation" (De Angelis 2005, 143) of some ancestral quasi-pagan practices but a hyperrealistic painting of authentic southern Italian culture and its peculiar syncretism between its pagan origin and the Roman Catholic Ritual – as di Donato himself put it, "I'm a sensualist, and I respond to the sensuality of the Roman Catholic Church... We Italians are essentially pagans and realists" (Von Huene-Greenberg 1987, 36). As already noted, the religious isotopy in the novel weaves around an axiological dimension between concrete reality (Job) and its spiritual counterpart (Tenement), which are punctually signified in the paratext. The title of the novel plays on a semantic ambiguity that refers to Geremio's atrocious death, suffocated on Good Friday by a pour of concrete after falling in a crevice between the scaffolds in a pose reminiscent of crucifixion, thus signaling Geremio as the "Christ in concrete", or "carpenter Christ" as Jesus is referenced in the novel.[2] However, the title universalizes the underlying Christology of the narrative by indicating that the novel is also concerned with finding "Christ in concrete," that is, concretely, in physical reality, which indeed seems to be Paul's mission – or, rather, his failure. The crucifixion/sacrifice of Geremio is the reason for Paul's estrangement from his childhood and the traumatic impetus for his own painful and immediate maturation, which will find fulfilment in an angry, conflicted, and violent rejection of the Tenement's values. But Paul's conversion is a final reaction to the various tragic and physical deaths that he has to deal with: first, his blood father and, second, his spiritual father, or *padrino*, Nazone. If these deaths signify the crisis of the *presenza* of the cultural complex imported from the motherland, Annunziata's final passing and Paul's complete loss of parent figures stand, symbolically, for the termination of the *presenza* of authentic Italian culture on US soil:

> "Mama! What are you praying for!"
> In votive lamp's lume she turned.
> His words strangled her.
> "Our Dio?"
> "Oh what Dio and Dio!" [...]
> "Mama", he pleaded, "do not kiss the plaster man and wooden cross!"
> "Save save save save..."
> She proffered the cross in supplicating tears. [...]
> He pulled the crucifix from her and crushed it in his hands.
> (di Donato 1993, 256-258)

[2] On the Christological imagery in Italian-American literature, see Gardaphé 2014, 410 *et passim*.

Significantly, closing the work are the prayers uttered by Annunziata on her deathbed: "Né... né... né... How beautiful he little Paul my own whose Jesu self glorified our home... Nadi... nadi... nadi... Gifted to me by the Madonna was he... And of this son shall rise a topless lighted column!" (266).

In contrast to Paul, who knows and frequents both poles of the Job/Tenement axiom and who is therefore exposed to the dynamics of the signification of both places, Annunziata inhabits almost uniquely the space of Tenement and inhabits it by ritualizing much of her existence around a religious practice that seamlessly synthesizes pagan, magical, and more specifically Catholic elements. This kind of religious sensibility has been noted and interpreted by critics. In his study, Michele Fazio (2007, 133) notes how the Catholic symbolism in *Christ in Concrete* is tightly entwined with representations of food, suggesting an "inextricable relationship" defining both the Italians' cultural identity and their "resistance to assimilation". Along with this interplay recreating "the sacred in the secular" (117), Fazio also acknowledges Paul's character as a stylization of class conflict, representing "the second generation's struggle to negotiate the conflicting values of Italian and American cultures" (121). For Kvidera (2010, 157), the Catholicism of *Christ in Concrete* is a "cultural articulation, but also a performance by which they simultaneously retain tradition and create new standards for coping with tragedy and disappointment". While it is undoubtedly true that the religious expression found in the novel can be defined as "positional" because it "changes and develops according to individual histories, individual economic and social situations, and individual religious affiliations" (157), in the broad pluricultural context of the early twentieth-century United States, it is an equally valid statement that this positionality and these individualistic developments of the profession of faith find their original matrix in a highly collectivized cultural pool, described in great detail by Ernesto de Martino in *Sud e Magia* (1959).

According to de Martino (2015, 78), the persistence of faith in the magical and the resulting syncretism with Catholicism are due to precise socioeconomic conditions that apply in postwar southern Italy but can also apply to the situation in which Paul's family finds itself after

Geremio's death. This extends to the first generation of southern immigrants to the United States. de Martino writes: "la precarietà dei beni elementari [...], l'incertezza delle prospettive concernenti il futuro, la pressione esercitata sugli individui da forze naturali e sociali non controllabili, la carenza di forme di assistenza sociale [...] costituiscono [...] condizioni che favoriscono il mantenersi delle pratiche magiche".[3] The magical practice, coordinated "con le forme egemoniche di vita culturale a cominciare da quella forma egemonica religiosa che è il cattolicesimo,"[4] is used, according to de Martino, in the form of averts and other practices syncretically superimposed on the prayers of the official ritual. These syncretic practices serve to limit the power and grip of *negativo*, that is, tragic events and extreme difficulties of material existence, adding to the unfavorable living conditions mentioned above. The entire story of Paul and Annunziata revolves precisely around the ways in which the characters deal with *negativo*, which when approaching them involves the death of Geremio and Paul's subsequent employment with Job as a child worker.

The circumstances surrounding Geremio's death, in particular, suggest that the demise of the *paterfamilias* might have been influenced by what de Martino defines as *fascinazione*. According to de Martino, a *fascinazione* needs an agent and a victim. When the agent has a "human form", the *fascinazione* qualifies as *malocchio*, *jettatura* or evil eye. de Martino defines *malocchio* as a malign influence that proceeds from an envious glance, so much so that *malocchio* is also commonly referred to as *invidia* (envy). Malocchio can be involuntary or deliberate, involving the performance of specific rites (*fattura*) that can also result in the death of the victim (*fattura a morte*). De Martino (2015, 9) also goes through various remedies to *malocchio*, that is, specific rituals to be performed by specialised magicians that involve ritual repetitions of formulae that invoke, for example, "Father, Son and the Holy Spirit", and the use of salt, olive oil, and water. The *fascinazion*e that supposedly victimised

[3] "the precariousness of elementary goods [...], the uncertainty of prospects concerning the future, the pressure exerted on individuals by uncontrollable natural and social forces, and the lack of forms of social assistance [...] constitute [...] conditions that favor the maintenance of magical practices". All translations from Italian are by the Author.

[4] "With the hegemonic forms of cultural life beginning with the hegemonic religious form that is Catholicism", de Martino 2015, 80.

Geremio might have been an involuntary evil eye cast upon him by his coworkers when he shared with them the joy of being on the verge of buying himself and his family a new house, along with his hopes that his son Paul would never have to lay bricks for a living but profit from a proper education:

> "Are some of us to be laid off? Easter is upon us and communion dresses are needed and…"
> That, while Geremio was dreaming of the new house and the joys he could almost taste. Said he, "Worry not […]". It then all came out. He regaled them with his wonderful joy of the new house. […] They listened respectfully and returned him well wishes and blessings. […] "I tell you, son of Geremio shall never lay bricks! Paulie mine will study from books – he will be the great builder!"
> (di Donato 1993, 15)

Interestingly, the co-workers themselves, possibly knowing that their well wishes and blessings were tinged with envy, warn Geremio to protect himself from the evil eye through rituals they had known were practised in the motherland, involving Christian imagery, salt, and holy water.

> "Master Geremio, in my province it is told that for good luck in a new home, one is to sprinkle well with salt… especially the corners, and on moving day sweep with a new broom the center and pick all up – but do not sweep it out over the threshold!"
> "That may be, Pietro. But, Master Geremio, it would be better in my mind that holy water should bless. And also, a holy picture of Saint Joseph guarding the door" (15).[5]

That Geremio might indeed be the victim of the evil eye is signalled in the subsequent passages, where he "marvelled at the strange feeling

---

[5] See de Martino 2015, 84: "Il fatto che il 'malocchio' sia chiamato anche 'invidia' è in rapporto ovvio con la frequenza di sentimenti invidiosi in un ambiente caratterizzato dalla precarietà dei beni elementari della vita. D'altra parte, la credenza che l'invidia […] può essere involontaria ha la sua base nella angustia e nella fragilità della presenza individuale […]. In questo senso alla malignità segreta che circola nell'aria […] sente talora bisogno di difendersi non soltanto l'invidiato ma anche l'invidioso, recitando formule rassicuratrice ed esorcizzatrici."

which permitted him to sense the familiarity of life. And yet – all appeared unreal, a dream pungent and nostalgic. Life, dream, reality, unreality, spiraling ever about each other. 'Ha,' he chuckled, "how and from where do these thoughts come?' " (17). Geremio no longer has a grasp on himself and his own thoughts and, much like any victim of evil eye, as de Martino (2015, 9) tells us, is experiencing symptoms of an overall loss of agency on himself, "una condizione psichica di impedimento e di inibizione, e al tempo stesso un senso di dominazione, di essere agito da una forza altrettanto potente quanto occulta, che lascia senza margine l'autonomia di una persona, la sua capacità di decisione e di scelta".[6] De Martino calls this domineering, occult and powerful force *negativo* (negative), "una oscura forza fascinatrice, che lascia la presenza individuale senza margine di autonomia" (17).[7] In other words, in popular Southern Italian credence, human agents can voluntarily or involuntarily harness the power of the *negativo*, but in and of itself, the *negativo* works as an occult force that is potentially able to deprive human beings of their agency or *presenza*, especially in cultural terms: "[il] negativo [...] mette in luce il rischio che la stessa presenza individuale si smarrisca come centro di decisione e di scelta e naufraghi in una negazione che colpisce la stessa possibilità di un qualsiasi comportamento culturale" (62).[8]

In di Donato's book, Job undoubtedly represents such a force. Indeed, a few moments before finding his demise, Geremio mulls precisely over the "dominating" grip Job has over his life: "Something within asked, 'Is it not possible to breathe God's air without fear dominating with the pall of unemployment? And the terror of production for Boss, Boss and Job? To rebel is to lose all of the very little. To be obedient is to choke. O dear Lord, guide my path" (di Donato 1993, 18). Just like the *negativo*, Job has a stronghold over man, and if rebelling against it only results in more hardship to follow, the only way to counter it is to embrace it and convert to it – which is what Paul will do. A conversion

---

[6] "a psychic condition of impediment and inhibition, and at the same time a sense of domination, of being acted upon by a force as powerful as it is occult, hindering a person's autonomy, capacity for decision and choice".

[7] "an obscure fascinatory force, which leaves the individual presence with no room for autonomy".

[8] "[the] negative [...] highlights the risk that individual presence itself is lost as a centre of decision and choice, shipwrecking in a denial that affects the very possibility of any cultural behaviour".

to Job, moreover, implies a transubstantiation of sorts, where flesh and soul become one with the entity: "This is the fresh stink of Job, this is the eight houred daily duel, this is the sense of red and grey, and our bodies are no longer meat and bone of our parents, but substance of Job" (159). That Job is some immaterial force rather than a place steeped in the sensible world is signified by it being a biblically-based *double entendre*, characterized in the narrative as a supernatural, cruel and ruthless power that requires constant human sacrifices, including that of Geremio, to sustain its uncontrolled superfetation. It is, indeed, "the great God Job" (13), a "noisier expanding organism" (159) represented in the novel as the giver of freedom ("Job that day would never be forgotten: the day when Job gave its first communion of freedom" [96]; "Job is freedom… for us" [157]), and as the giver of sustainment, "a familiar being through aches and hours, […] a new sense which brought the excitement of men and steel and stone […] it was men's siege against a hunger that travelled swiftly, against an enemy inherited" (97). Job is also the ruler of the night, requiring its adepts to work for it: "Before the grace of morning properly rises over the earth, before Christians can gather their senses and stretch upward to God's heaven in the joy of living, they are bent and twisted into unfeeling reds and greys of Job" (159). Job's equivalence with organized religion transforms its tools into Faith, or some sort of garments ("Brick in left hand and trowel in right, he had cherished them as Saint to Faith" [184]), and the total devotion to Job allows its practitioners to transcend and find holiness, as in "building possessed his mind, but gave Divinity" (191).

After the death of the *pater*, the narrative provides other clear instances of ritual practices variously documented by de Martino, all set out to counteract the power of the *negativo*. Annunziata and the characters revolving around Tenement, in particular, are the prime expression of the syncretism between magic and Catholicism that de Martino reported in *Sud e Magia*. A significant scene in this respect is the characterization of Dame Katarina in the segment where Annunziata is about to give birth. Katarina enters the scene as "a huge wizened creature, high priestess of ceremonials from cradle to grave" (40), with a sack full of "herbs, evil eye amulets, love mixtures and dirty linen" (40) to help with Annunziata's delivery. Katarina is, in fact, a personification of the *fattucchiera*, usually an older woman able to perform magic rites to counteract *malocchio* but also functioning as a midwife in rural communities.

Furthermore, di Donato's allusion to Katarina as a 'high priestess' of ceremonials that encompass birth and death suggests that she also represents those female figures who, in Southern rural communities, would perform what de Martino defined as *pianto rituale* (ritual crying). This ancient euro-Mediterranean tradition survived in those communities until the early 20th century. Echoes of this practice are found in the funeral scene at Geremio's home, where a polyphony of primarily female voices is represented, commenting on Annunziata's pain and Geremio's untimely and horrible death. Luigi's speech near the casket, in particular, is very reminiscent of a type of lamentation directed at the dead, where the living person interrogates the corpse to see if it can come back to life and give them answers.[9] Thus, along with the other characters in the novel, Katarina works as the mouthpiece for the Southern religious sensibility expressed by her generation of immigrants in the US. Her role is highly apparent in her speech when she defends Paul after the child is denied help by the priest. In her words, a further religio-cultural axiological dichotomy is set up: the irreconcilable distance between the "poor Christians" and the greedy hypocrisy of the institution: "Man of God? Man of God? Bursting gut and sausage in mouth!" (di Donato 1993, 69). Such criticism towards the Church as an institution is also reinforced in this line from the carpenter Lucy, uttered shortly after the church scene: "What cock of Christians are you to let this child watch you eat?" (76). While there would be room to reflect on the interethnic dynamics between the power of an Irish vicar and the destitute Italian, and the scene as symbolic of the transformation of the Catholic institution when in contact with the same cultural soil as Job, for the scope of the present work it will suffice to point out that this dichotomy between the Church as a power

[9] Compare Luigi's invocation to Geremio "Speak. I am your big Luigi, your Gigi, who carried you on his shoulder in Abruzzi and gave you sweet things to eat. Ah, Ger, Ger, will you not tell me how it was?" to the Amatrice octave, reported in de Martino 1975, 59: "Vienci dumane, vienci a cunsulare, ca la risposta ti la voglio dare!"

structure and the peculiar sentiment of popular syncretic rites in Southern Italy are evident in the 'Fiesta' segment, which is loaded with imagery and scenes that speak of this religious syncretism, merging religious symbolism with aspects of pagan rituality. The excess of the banquet is naturally reminiscent of pagan festivities, such as *Saturnalia* in ancient Rome, where social norms were subverted for a limited time. The segment of Nazone's 'crucifixion' speaks to this paradigm of subversion by integrating Christian imagery into it while also flipping it on its head by letting a woman, Fausta, perform an exorcism of sorts on Nazone: "Fausta dipped biscuit in wine and painted circles on him. He yelled unintelligibly until he gulped and vomited gushes of sour wine and lunch into Fausta's face" (181).

Furthermore, Annunziata performs counteractive practices to diminish the power and reach of the *negativo*, mainly by invocations towards 'Jesu'. Now, it should be underlined that Jesus, in Southern Catholicism, is inscribed in an "orizzonte mitico Cristiano" where he is taken as 'esorcista esemplare', but also as the embodied analogy of various manifestations of the *negativo* that needs to be dissipated from the victim. This analogical framework is reminiscent of magic invocations and rituals; for example, the invocation of Jesus's blood elicits healing from blood diseases such as jaundice (Cf. de Martino 2015, 81). Similarly, Annunziata constantly calls for 'Jesu' or prays when facing adverse events. For example, Paul would hear her "praying intensely at the votive light in soft Italian" while stuck in bed and sick from fatigue. In that same situation, Paul is presented with a crucifix to kiss to speed up his recovery as Annunziata invokes "Jesu" to "save me from him", asserting that "it is the Jesu who keeps us living and not their gold" but at the same time invoking "young Jesu" to "cast from him the power of wealth" (di Donato 1993, 109).

Another system that Annunziata puts in place to gain solace from her loss is seeking contact with Geremio through spiritistic practice, twice going to a psychic, The Cripple, who becomes the bearer of messages from beyond. These messages, which bring solace and temporary relief, are brought back into the institutional religion through Catholic prayers but hint at some private sanctification of the *pater* compatible with the syncretic matrix of Southern Catholicism: "Annunziata and

Paul clasped their hands and closed their eyes. They prayed to God. They forgot themselves and their trouble. They prayed to God: O God, our wish is for the peace and happiness of him who is in Paradise, our Geremio, our father and husband who is in Heaven" (129). However, the second visit that Annunziata and Paul pay to the Cripple reveals as detrimental in the sense that it seems to foreshadow – or influence as a *jettatura*, the tragic death of Nazone, which is the catalyst to Paul's complete conversion to Job. Indeed, Nazone's death closely follows the second visit Annunziata and Paul make to Cripple. The psychic offers her clients an even more comforting reading on that occasion. Geremio appears in the almost angelic guise of a protector who, she says, will provide from beyond to relieve the family of all kinds of financial difficulties. When one relates the psychic's words and Nazone's fatal fall from the scaffolding, or when one considers that Geremio dies shortly after revealing that he was in the process of buying a house, one cannot help but think of what de Martino writes about *jettatura* as "effluvi o emanazioni che si staccherebbero dai corpi dei fascinatori [...] prodotto di ' immagini' che con il loro carico di invidia e di malignità si dipartirebbero dall'occhio e dallo sguardo, onde poi dall'azione di tali [...] immagini [...] deriverebbero per la vittima funeste alterazioni nel corpo e nell'anima" (de Martino 2015, 89)[10]. Furthermore, The Cripple, whose character is defined by physical deformity, is perfectly compatible with the characterisation of the *jettatore* as someone who bears on his body the outward signs of an evil nature, showing in their "viso anche i vizi dell'anima" (100).[11] What is of interest here is that the narrative seems to suggest that the malign influence of the Cripple could get hold of Annunziata and Paul because the medium woman was American – therefore, practicing a ritual and speaking a language that was only partly comprehensible by Annunziata and Paul, who are culturally wired in a different way than her.

Bringing these data back into a broader narratological framework, one can recognize how the events traceable to the semantics of the

[10] "emanations that would come off the bodies of the fascinators [...] product of 'images' that with their load of envy and malignity would depart from the eye and the gaze, so that from the action of such [...] images [...] would result for the victim fatal alterations in body and soul".
[11] "face the vices of the soul".

negativo in the de Martinian sense find their matrix in the antagonist Job, who, as mentioned, is placed in the axiological dimension that holds the novel together in opposition to the Tenement, the house. From the point of view of specifically religious cultural markers, if the Tenement is the realm of Annunziata, and thus a house/temple where a type of Catholic religion firmly rooted in southern folklore and archaic substratum is professed, Job constitutes a Moloch under construction, a divine but almost demonic entity, a kind of Chronos in Concrete who devours his worshippers, left with no other way out than to vow themselves entirely to him. And once the conversion is accomplished, Job's follower can no longer decipher the rituals and meanings of the old faith, so much so that he manifests a physical malaise, again traceable to *fascinazione*:

> Never back to Job, my son! We will starve, we will wander the streets and crowd ourselves in holes and corners, we will walk on our hands and knees, we will humble ourselves low, low, rather than you go back to Job. […]". To Job he went. […] As he approached Saint Prisca, he felt a dread. His head began to ache. He became acutely alive to the strangeness of the ceremony, the candles and press of Christian faces, the faces and wings of the statues, the temple architecture, the convolutions of mass, the torment of incantations, the ultimate decision of Father John, and nausea assaulted his bowels, breast and brain. (di Donato 1993, 255)

In this context, Job's semiological significance is deeply rooted in the southern religious syncretism described by de Martino. It serves as a narrative representation of the dynamics involved in defending against the power of *negativo*. This framework positions di Donato's text as a novel of formation that centers on a dominant religio-cultural isotopy, transforming Paul's journey into a conversion to Job's materialistic and almost archaic pagan beliefs. Job's demand for continuous human sacrifices and the ineffectiveness of practices tied to Southern Catholicism, such as consulting psychics, made Paul gradually distance himself from the Tenement. While Geremio's death physically removes Paul from home, it still leaves him connected to the religious and cultural values of his upbringing. On the contrary, Nazone's death catalyses Paul's complete and final abandonment of the Tenement faith. In this sense, Annunziata's passing works as a symbolic marker of Paul's ethnic transformation from Italian to Italian-American. Embracing the 'religious' work ethic personified in Job, Paul trades a substantial part of his identity to ensure his family's survival and the full realization of the American dream, making *Christ in Concrete* a conversion novel and a textbook depiction of a *crisi della presenza* moment according to de Martino's anthropological method. More precisely, Paul's conversion to Job's materialistic work ethic concludes a desperate struggle to regain cultural agency/*presenza* when such agency is systematically challenged by loss, death, and other manifestations of the *negativo*. When bringing back di Donato's depiction of Italian immigrants to their historically, culturally and, more importantly, religiously determined cultural roots, the narrative pristinely reflects the image of assimilation as a process that works by subtraction, a painful and forceful subtraction of language and religious, cultural, moral, and ethical values.

WORKS CITED

Bachtin, Michail. *Estetica e Romanzo*. Torino: Einaudi, 2001.

De Angelis, Rose. "The American Nightmare: Reading and Teaching Pietro di Donato's Ethnographic Novel *Christ in Concrete*." *Forum Italicum* 39, no. 1 (2005): 137-156.

De Martino, Ernesto. *Morte e Pianto Rituale*. Torino: Bollati Boringhieri, 1975.

_______. *Sud e Magia*. Roma: Donzelli, 1994.

di Donato, Pietro. *Christ in Concrete*. Berkeley: 1993. Kindle.

Gardaphé, Fred. "We Weren't Always White: Race and Ethnicity in Italian American Literature." *LIT: Literature Interpretation Theory* 13 (3) (2002): 185-199.

_______. "Italian-American Literature and Working Class Culture." *Annali d'Italianistica* 32 (2014): 409-428.

Leone, Massimo. *Religious Conversion and Identity: The Semiotic Analysis of Texts*. London: Routledge, 2003.

Mulas, Franco. "The Ethnic Language of Pietro Di Donato's *Christ in Concrete*." In *From the Margin: Writings in Italian Americana*, edited by Anthony Julian Tamburri, Paolo A. Giordano, and Fred L. Gardaphé, 307-15. West Lafayette, IN: Purdue UP, 1991.

Tamburri, Anthony Julian. "Pietro di Donato's *Christ in Concrete*: An Italian American Novel Not Set in Stone." *LIT: Literature Interpretation Theory* 14 (1) (2003): 3-16.

Viscusi, Robert. "*De Vulgari Eloquentia*: An Approach to the Language of Italian American Fiction." *Yale Italian Studies* 1 (Winter 1981): 21-38.

Von Huene-Greenberg, Dorothèe. "Interview: Pietro di Donato." *MELUS* 14 (no. 3-4) (1987): 33-52.

Tony Vaccaro: Postcards from Italy: People and Places, Images of the Soul of Italy and Its Future

Piernicola Maria Di Iorio
UNIVERSITÀ DEGLI STUDI DEL MOLISE

Abstract: This essay explores the journey of Tony Vaccaro, an Italian-American photographer born in Pennsylvania in 1922 but raised in Molise, whose identity was forged between two continents. A protagonist of "reverse migration," Vaccaro experienced what he termed "twin nostalgia" - a perpetual emotional back and forth between Italy and America. In particular, this paper analyzes his return to Italy in 1946, which he documented with his Rolleiflex 6x6, showing a wounded but resilient country. His visual poetics, which are characterized by extraordinary expressive lightness grasping the persistence of life beyond historical contingencies, can be summarized by the expression "Life goes on." From his experience as a war photographer to his evolution into a master of portraiture, Vaccaro created a style that transcends mere documentation, making a significant contribution to the history of contemporary photography

If, for some existential contingency, Tony Vaccaro's parents had not taken him to Molise at the age of just three, the entire biographical trajectory of the future photographer would likely have unfolded within the reassuring confines of his native Pennsylvania. With the typically American determination to engage in intense work aimed at accumulating financial wealth, he might have pursued a career as a barber, a mechanic, or perhaps a travelling salesman, selling insurance policies through the streets of Greensburg, the town of his birth. Such a path may well have included marriage to a charming American woman, the birth of pleasant offspring and satisfaction deriving from a long and comfortable life spent in some idyllic location in Florida or amid the exotic scenery of the Caribbean islands, following that model of personal fulfillment deeply rooted in the American collective imagination.

However, a family trip to the Italian town of Bonefro, and the sudden premature death of both his parents, led to the unexpected rooting of the young man in Molise. This was a circumstance that would radically subvert the pre-ordained American script that seemed destined to characterize his existence. In the Italy of this particular historical period, the existential experience of the young child underwent a rapid metamorphosis: it was reconfigured into a daily battle for survival, conducted almost at a primordial level, following the elementary dynamics of the animal kingdom that distinguish the relationship between prey and predator. With his original family unit, the young boy had not had the opportunity to learn about reproach, of physical beating or corporal punishment; until that moment he had been familiar only with the manifestations of parental affection. However, this condition of privileged innocence would quickly give way to a brutal reeducation.

The day after his father's death, Vaccaro was subjected to beatings and physical humiliations. This treatment would continue for the following fourteen years, the period he spent under the protection of his paternal uncle. His condition as a 'foreigner' was not limited to the domestic sphere, but extended into public, social spaces: from the city streets and to the boy's school. Here he would acutely perceive his own otherness, experiencing daily the stigma normally reserved for the figure of the emigrant. This was despite his own unusual circumstance as an American having moved to Italy, representing a sort of 'reverse migration' when compared to the usual migration flows of the time.

The first time the term "emigrant" was used in reference to him occurred during his schooling, where the young boy was the only member of his class without the *Balilla* uniform – an outfit he was later forced to wear in order to comply with the Fascist regime's regulations. His teacher, after administering punishment with a disciplinary "rod," publicly subjected the child to collective ridicule, calling him "the dumb American emigrant not dressed as a *Balilla*" – an episode emblematic of the nationalist indoctrination that characterized education during the Fascist era. The escalation of events leading up to the Second World War hastened the young boy's repatriation to the United States, which took place in November 1939. During the ocean crossing, the adolescent's heart was filled with joyful anticipation for the return to his homeland, finally free from the daily humiliations he had endured in Italy. His providential arrival coincided precisely with the celebration of Thanksgiving, a holiday embodying the essence of American warmth, gastronomic abundance, and conviviality – a circumstance that seemed to foreshadow a happy reintegration into his original social fabric.

However, the young boy soon realized that even in the American context, feelings of foreignness and alienation would prevail. The entire local community, including the descendants of Italian immigrants, now perfectly integrated, ostracized the newcomer, considering him a common Italian emigrant, without taking into account his birth or his American citizenship. Only with the gradual passage of time – after a considerable number of years – when the young man achieved recognition on the sports field as a runner and professional status as a photographer, did he begin to establish genuine friendly relationships. Nevertheless, even this apparent integration would ultimately prove to be illusory.

Unbeknown to the photographer, what was taking root within his psyche, is what he would come term "twin nostalgia," an existential state that placed him in a perpetual inner turmoil comparable to a metaphorical "tug of war." Periodically, the irresistible nostalgia pushed him to return to his beloved Molise, an impulse he felt that ultimately, he could not resist. However, after a stay in his Italian ancestral village of San Vito, the opposing nostalgic polarity would invariably emerge, calling him back to his equally beloved America. This determined an existence characterized by this cyclical emotional and geographical 'oscillation', an existential swing that the photographer continued to experience, and likely characterized his life until his last breath, or to quote the great Dylan Thomas, until "...that good night." The latter, a poetic appropriation, alluding to the inevitable conclusion of the human experience, a moment in which all inner turmoil finally finds peace.[1]

Migrations, Style and Lightness of A Photographic Master

Into a complex historical-cultural panorama of transatlantic exchanges, appropriations and transformations, entered the paradigmatic figure of Tony Vaccaro. He was born in Pennsylvania in 1922 to Italian emigrant parents. His personal and professional biography followed the emblematic path of physical and cultural migrations reflecting the social dynamics of the twentieth century. Leaving the new continent to return to the old during childhood, thus passing his formative period of adolescence in Italy, he then returned to the promised land – the "America,

[1] Interview published in *Il Ponte*, anno XI, no. 1, February – March 1999

America, America..." mythologized by the European collective imagination – in the crucial year of 1939, when Europe was about to be overwhelmed by the catastrophe of war. This biographic trajectory was significantly intertwined with that of numerous other American photographers of European heritage – many of whom remained in the shadows like the "unknown, silent Vivian Maier" (Newhall 2009) who traveled the streets of New York at the same time – who came overseas for economic need or to escape racial and political persecution. Simultaneously, they contributed to the creation of a fundamental chapter of world photographic history, which saw an extraordinary convergence of sensibilities and different cultural backgrounds. Their work merged and interacted with that of other more established American photographers such as Stieglitz, Steichen, Strand and Evans, in an interweaving of influences and contaminations that constitutes the unique richness of US photography (Trachtenberg 1989).

Tony Vaccaro embarked on his artistic journey with a fresh and unbiased gaze, using the technical and expressive modernity of the photographic medium to capture the people he encountered in everyday life. He later documented them in his epic and dramatic war reportage, in which he became a privileged witness of the events in Normandy and in the Italy of 1943-45. He managed to reveal aspects of life and poverty previously overlooked by official narratives. His distinct, sensitive approach ran parallel to that of Robert Capa who simultaneously documented the advance of Allied troops up the Italian peninsula from Sicily. Vaccaro's work captured human and social landscapes that were politically disregarded until the emergence of postwar neorealism in cinema and photography – a cultural movement that would become one of the most significant expressions of Italy's reckoning with the tragedy of war and the difficult return to democratic normality. What made Vaccaro's approach distinct was the fact that he never settled for being just a reporter, a mere technical operator serving the demands of passing news coverage; rather, he established himself as an authentic photographer driven by talent and a conscious artistic vocation. He was constantly striving to imprint a personal and recognizable style onto his images through his own aesthetic and emotional sensibility. Deliberately distancing himself from the purely journalistic urgency of news reporting – too often influenced by predetermined political alignments – he pursued a visual authenticity that photography, by its very nature, should be able to guarantee. His work maintained a delicate balance between objective testimony and subjective interpretation, between the immediacy of observation and the formal construction of an image.

Following his intense and traumatic experiences as a war photographer during the Normandy landings and his subsequent reports from the front, Vaccaro deliberately sought a significant shift in his artistic and professional work, turning to portraiture and fashion photography. He moved toward a realm that was increasingly free from documentary constraints and more "private" in both subject selection and stylistic approach. This evolution allowed him to progressively build an extensive and nuanced catalogue of significant cultural figures of his time, all unified by the common thread of his photographic vision and his unmistakable authorial style. His images were never merely flattering or celebratory; rather, they were driven by an instinctive aesthetic and structural need, evident in the composition of the frame and the masterful use of chiaroscuro. These technical and formal elements blended harmoniously to capture that *sublime moment* in which the subject's expression reveals their inner truth – a magical balance between chance and control that constitutes one of the most fascinating aspects of photographic art.

Back to the Origins: A Journey through the Memories of Post-War Italy

During the tumultuous period of the world war, the photographer's psyche was repeatedly pervaded by a deep sense of nostalgia for his Italian homeland, particularly Molise and the town of Bonefro – the ancestral home of his family and the fundamental backdrop to his teenage years. This longing gradually crystalized into a firm determination to embark on a journey back to those places so intimately connected to his personal identity and the cherished memories of his youth.

Carefully setting aside three hundred dollars – by diligently saving the proceeds of his professional work in photography – Vaccaro was able to purchase a decommissioned military vehicle. Together with his close friend Nick Baccari, who also had Molisan heritage, he finally made his long-cherished dream a reality: to set foot on Italian soil after years of forced separation due to the war. The conflict had not only devastated Europe but had also reshaped the geographic and cultural boundaries of the old continent (Vaccaro 2005).

Leaving Munich on September 22, 1946 – a date left etched forever in the photographer's memory as the symbolic beginning of his personal reconciliation with his roots – the journey quickly led him to the Italian border, reaching the northern city of Bolzano the very next day. Thus began a journey through a peninsula still deeply scarred by the recent war, yet through the artist's eyes – filtered through the veil of emotion and affectionate memory – Italy retained its intrinsic beauty. This beauty revealed itself in the crystal-clear waters of Lake Garda, the architectural elegance of Verona, the contemplative serenity of Padua, the enchanting lagoon of Venice, the Renaissance refinement of Mantua and finally, in the learned capital of Emilia, Bologna. Here, the two travelers stopped for a night, finding accommodation in a modest guesthouse tucked away in a corner of the grand Piazza Maggiore, the beating heart of the city.

The artist's photographic activity intensified significantly during his stay in Bologna with remarkable sensitivity; a period during which his lens captured both the urban landscape and the people who brought it to life. In 1946, the city had become a paradigmatic symbol of Italy's reconstruction. This is reflected in Vaccaro's images of the city's inhabitants walking through Piazza Maggiore and Via Rizzoli and even in the mythological Sirens sculpted in the Giambologna fountain. These elements collectively embodied an irrepressible aspiration for national rebirth after the dark years of dictatorship and war, forming an extraordinary visual synthesis of historical testimony and a poetic interpretation of the surrounding reality.

At the foot of the historic Garisenda Tower, the photographer's lens immortalized his friend Nick Baccari in an emblematic shot that transcended mere documentation. It became a symbol of their shared return to their Italian homeland, and ultimately Molise – a journey that, for both, marked a first opportunity to reconnect with their origins after the traumatic experience of the war. This voyage took on the nature of an existential pilgrimage laden with emotional resonance and identity-driven significance, resonating both on a personal level and within the broader collective memory of history and culture (Vaccaro 2005).

The biography of Nicola Baccari (who was later known as Nick) was deeply intertwined with that of Vaccaro. It was marked by a series of parallels and divergences that reflected the complexity of the Italian migratory experience during the first half of the twentieth century. Born in Bonefro (Molise) in 1921, Baccari shared his formative childhood years with the future photographer – who as we have seen, arrived in Italy from America with his parents in 1925 at the age of three. Between 1926 and 1932, their respective farms, located in close proximity in the San Vito district, became the focal points of a shared daily life that would leave an indelible mark on their imaginations, despite their later separations and differing life paths.

The destiny of Baccari took a significant turn in 1932 when his father, who had emigrated years earlier and found work at Ford in Detroit, called him to America. This marked the beginning of his journey toward education and Americanization, symbolized by the transformation of his name from Nicola to Nick. His path culminated in a degree in pedagogy at Fordham University in New York, with a specialization in Shakespearean literature that would form the foundation of his subsequent teaching career in Detroit. Eventually, he secured a prestigious managerial position at a High School in Lansing, Michigan, eloquent testimony to the social mobility that the New World offered to talented and determined children of Italian immigrants.

The bond between the two friends was revived in 1939, when Vaccaro also returned to the United States after his formative years in Italy. Their friendship grew even stronger with the outbreak of the Second World War, which saw them enlist at the same time, though in different branches of the armed forces: Baccari in the Air Force and Vaccaro in the Infantry. Miraculously surviving the atrocities of war that had claimed countless members of their generation, they were united again on their return journey to Bonefro, the place that represented for both, the origin of their identity and the repository of foundational memories that shaped their adult selves.

Baccari's life ended in 1998, when he suffered a heart attack. He left behind a daughter, Angela, who had married an investigator from

Butler, Pennsylvania, and a twelve-year-old granddaughter named Nicole. She was named in honor of her paternal grandfather, following the Italian-American tradition in which the continuity of names across generations serves as a crucial element in preserving cultural identity, even as families gradually integrated into American society. A passionate golf lover, Nick Baccari was likely the most significant friend in Vaccaro's life – a privileged witness to an existence that spanned two continents and two cultures, embodying the Italian diasporic experience of the twentieth century (Vaccaro 2005).

The day after their stay in Bologna, the two travelers resumed their journey towards the Adriatic coast. As they passed Pescara and headed toward Termoli, in Molise, the landscape starkly revealed the devastating consequences of the bombing that had ravaged the coastline during the war. For the photographer's keen eye, the scene of destruction contrasted painfully with the natural beauty of the land and the memory of the once-pristine coastal landscape – a tangible testament to the wounds inflicted on Italian territory by the recent world war.

The arrival in Molise providentially coincided with the celebrations of the San Celestino fair, an event that enriched the experience of returning with a particularly significant anthropological and ritual dimension. This allowed the photographer to immediately immerse himself in the intricate fabric of popular traditions and cultural expressions that formed the very essence of Molisan identity – an identity all the more precious for having endured despite the traumas of war and the early signs of modernization that would gradually transform Italian rural society in the decades to come (Titone 2021).

During this crucial period of his artistic development, Vaccaro used a Rolleiflex 6x6 camera, a tool that accompanied him during an intense phase of experimentation with various subjects. His constant goal was to refine a personal expressive language that could transcend the limits of mere documentation, striving for a genuinely artistic and interpretative representation of reality. This pursuit stemmed from his deep dissatisfaction with the results of his early work, during which his greatest technical shortcoming was his limited speed of execution. This limitation unintentionally allowed subjects enough time to adopt studied, artificial expressions, compromising the authenticity of the image and its ability to convey the emotional and psychological 'truth' of the moment captured. His technical and expressive research was part of a broader paradigm shift in the role of photography within the informational ecosystem, a transformation succinctly analyzed by Herbert Schiller, who observed,

> "The camera's ability to represent reality, seemingly without human intervention, became a standard of credibility [...] The scientific aura surrounding the medium even rendered objective the field in which it was used: that of journalism." (Shiller 1981)

This insight sheds light on the process by which the camera's apparent mechanical neutrality endowed photographic images with an unprecedented testimonial authority. By extension, this conferred an aura of objectivity upon journalism as a whole, creating a system of mutual legitimization between technology and information that profoundly shaped the collective perceptions of the veracity of the media throughout the twentieth century. Within this cultural context, the photographer's pursuit of immediacy and authenticity took on a significance beyond aesthetics – it became an epistemological endeavor, questioning the very nature of truth in visual representation.

The methodology developed to overcome this fundamental limitation involved meticulously pre-setting all technical parameters – focus, shutter speed, aperture, and preliminary composition – so that, at the crucial moment of encountering the subject, the act of photography could be reduced to the essential gesture of framing and shooting simultaneously. This approach allowed him to capture the genuine emotional essence of people immersed in the concerns of everyday life, before their awareness of being photographed could prompt them to adopt studied poses that would inevitably distort the truth of the moment. This technical and philosophical approach to photography would later become one of the defining elements of the artist's style and one of his most significant contributions to the evolution of a new documentary photographic language – one that seamlessly combined the rigor of observation with the depth of interpretation. Moreover, it joined technical precision with emotional intensity, in an expressive synthesis of extraordinary communicative power (Grisenda 2021).

Vaccaro's remarkable artistic sensitivity is exemplified in a comment he made about one of his most famous photographs, taken in 1947 during his return to his family's homeland. The image portrays an elderly man in Bonefro. Of it, Vaccaro wrote: "I saw him leaning against the town's stone wall, smiling, 'absorbing the sun,' happy in his poverty. Life goes on…" This seemingly simple reflection encapsulates the photographer's unique worldview. In a Europe still deeply scarred by the material and psychological consequences of the Second World War, Vaccaro's vision transcended the mere depiction of wartime tragedy. He elevated the image of an anonymous elderly man from the provinces to represent a symbol of resilience and the continuity of life – an aesthetic operation that moved beyond contingency to reach a universal dimension of the human condition.

In the immediate post-war period, when Italy still lay literally under the physical and moral rubble of conflict and dictatorship, Vaccaro's photographic gaze stood out for what critic Tommaso Evangelista aptly described as "a different perception of History and Time, a lightness that only great artists possess." This quality directly recalls the concept systematically developed by the renowned intellectual Italo Calvino in his celebrated American lectures, where the English term "lightness" was masterfully explored in multiple and complementary semantic nuances: formal grace, conceptual levity, clarity of expression, visual brilliance, creative intuition, temporal suspension, and even subtle irony – an intricate interplay of meanings that resonates perfectly in Vaccaro's photographic approach. This creates a unique tension between the weight of the subjects he portrays and the lightness with which he interprets them. (Evangelista 2019, 108).

The seemingly simple yet powerful phrase "Life goes on" takes on profound philosophical significance in the artist's visual poetics. It subtly alludes to an existential flow that transcends mere historical and political contingencies, continuously reshaping characters and settings according to biological and cultural forces that endure beyond any man-made catastrophe. These traces of resilience remain as delicate and intangible as photographic films – briefly capturing the ceaseless movement of life itself. This distinctive interpretative sensitivity was already strikingly evident in Vaccaro's early Berlin works, where he persistently sought glimpses of "indefinite vitality" amid the ruins of the destroyed German capital. This pursuit was masterfully crystallized in his paradigmatic work *Walking the Dog*, where the presence of a simple, familiar element – a dog on a leash – becomes a poignant symbol of a normality stubbornly pursued even in the most adverse circumstances.

Distinguishing himself clearly from the approach of Frank Monaco – whose photographic series *Women of Molise* (1950)[2], mainly explored the archaic, ancestral, and primitive aspects of his Italian homeland almost as if wanting to document a pre-modern world destined for disappearance – Vaccaro always looked at the reality in Molise with intrinsically contemporary eyes. He was certainly disillusioned by the tragedies he experienced but he was always open to the wonder and marvel that daily life can offer, even in the most difficult of circumstances. Moreover, his extraordinary photographs of Germany during post-war reconstruction, taken in that crucial moment of cultural transition in which the symbols of American consumerism were rapidly replacing those of the defeated Nazi regime and young Germans were abandoning rifles for sports equipment, reveal significant spiritual and formal affinities with the shots taken in his native Bonefro. Here, despite having suffered comparatively minor material damage compared to larger European towns and cities, Bonefro nevertheless bore the indelible psychological signs of the conflict in the expressions and gestures of its inhabitants.

Vaccaro's photographic investigation systematically privileges faces and human expressions, configuring itself as a sort of contemplative and reflective pause after the atrocities of war, which he directly experienced during his time as a military photographer. While the physical consequences of the war emerge only occasionally in the ruins that serve as the backdrop to some of his compositions, the extraordinary vitality of "life in peace" stands out with greater expressive evidence. Here we see traditional, daily activities inevitably marked by en-

[2] See Monaco 2019.

ergetic tensions that are both graphic and conceptual. This is exemplified in a paradigmatic way in the visual and sociological contrast between works such as *Famiglia Ruccolo* – an image of static peasant dignity – and *Tutta Bonefro al cinema! – a* representation of a community that collectively embraces new forms of entertainment and sociality offered by the cultural modernity of the postwar period.

Paradigmatic works such as *Ragazzo al Campo Sportivo* reveal the distinctive stylistic characteristics of Vaccaro's mature language: a static solidity of the central figure, both in the geometric composition of the framing, and in the calibrated lighting that shapes the elements of the picture. This is despite the deliberate precariousness of the posture that introduces a degree of dynamic tension in the formal structure of the image. This compositional and interpretative approach differs significantly from the contemporary practice of Robert Capa who, in emblematic works such as *Diletta, Girl with Suitcase,* distinctly favors accentuated chromatic divisions and more markedly dramatic tendencies. This is emphasized further by the representation of the physical and existential uncertainty of the subjects portrayed and by the bold inclination of the lens that deliberately breaks the classical equilibrium of the composition, visually suggesting the uprooting and instability of the post-war condition (Bauret 2022).

The most profoundly distinctive quality of the entire work of Tony Vaccaro, particularly evident in the works dedicated to the Molisan microcosm that constitutes the location of his soul and cultural identity, consists precisely in the explicit abandonment of representational insecurity and transience in favor of an interpretative lightness that is never superficiality or escapism. Rather it is an ability to grasp the persistence of life beyond historical contingencies. Within his intrinsically philological photography, existence endures, moving forward thus becomes a complete expression of a continuity of meaning in the slow and difficult return to normality and hope in post-war Italy. This testifies to that process of material, but above all moral and cultural reconstruction that characterized the second post-war period in Italy and Europe, allowing, through the intensity of the photographic gaze, the reaffirmation of those fundamental human values that not even the catastrophe of war can definitively erase. This confirms the *American Italian American* migrant Tony Vaccaro, as one of the most authentic and significant protagonists of the contemporary history of world photography.

WORKS CITED

Bauret, Gabriel. 2022. *Robert Capa. L'opera 1932–1954*. Cinisello Balsamo: Silvana Editoriale.

Evangelista, Tommaso. 2019. "La vita continua." In *Fotografie di una vita – Shots of a Life*, a cura di Andrea Morelli, 108. Padova: ALDE Edizioni.

Grisenda. 2021. *La mia vita con Giampaolo Pansa*. Milano: Fabbri Libri.

Interview published in *Il Ponte*. 1999. *Il Ponte* 11(1), febbraio–marzo.

Monaco, Frank. 2001. *The Women of Molise: An Italian Village*. New York: St. Martin's Press.

Newhall, Beaumont. 2009. *The History of Photography: From 1839 to the Present*. New York: The Museum of Modern Art.

Schiller, Herbert I. 1981. *Who Knows: Information in the Age of the Fortune 500*. Norwood, NJ: Ablex Publishing.

Titone, Junio V. 2021. *Pagine di Novecento molisano e del Mezzogiorno d'Italia: Massoni, briganti e ribelli*, a cura di Fabrizio Nocera. Isernia: Volturnia Edizioni.

Trachtenberg, Alan. 1989. *Reading American Photographs: Images as History, Mathew Brady to Walker Evans*. New York: Hill and Wang.

Vaccaro, Tony. 2005. *La mia Italia – Fotografie, 1945–1955*. Padova: Associazione Culturale Balbino del Nunzio.

Pascal D'Angelo's Literary Itinerary: Poetry and Poetic Models in Son of Italy

Francesca Crisante
UNIVERSITÀ DEGLI STUDI DI MESSINA

Abstract: From a strictly biographical point of view, the element that emerges from the novel is Pascal D'Angelo's conviction of being primarily a poet who narrates his story as a making of himself as a poet in the English language. In this sense, this article intends to demonstrate the importance of the British romantic tradition in the formation of Pascal D'Angelo. In particular, his poetic production is greatly inspired by the poets of the second generation of English Romanticism who most struck his sensitivity, namely, P.B. Shelley (especially "Prometheus Unbound") and John Keats whose *Endymion* he greatly admired. Indeed, from the poetical works of Shelley and Keats, D'Angelo drew the diction that he adopted to express his personal experience first as an Italian emigrant and then as the author of *Son of Italy*.

1. From a strictly biographical point of view, and also based on literary references, the element that emerges from the autobiography *Son of Italy* concerns Pascal D'Angelo's conviction of being primarily a poet who narrates his story as a construction of himself as an American poet. In his opinion, his poems are the expression of a genuine feeling that, in the translation into a language that is not his mother tongue, acquires full expressive force. In a sense, American English becomes a language beyond his own language, an artistic metalanguage on which to build his literary identity. Moreover, if we consider that, as the semiologist Jurij M. Lotman writes, "art literature" (and therefore also poetic language) "is expressed in a particular language that is built upon the natural language as a secondary system" (Lotman 1980, 28), we can well understand the degree of elaboration achieved by D'Angelo, who, in fact, does not find his natural language in English. This results in the strong control exercised by Pascal D'Angelo over his poetic texts – a control that implies full awareness of an expressive medium that requires verification at various isotopic levels – from the lexical level to the grammatical one, up to the semantic-structural level understood as artistic elaboration of the contents.

The journey from a barely literate young man from a remote village in Mount Maiella to a recognized poet in the American literary scene undoubtedly has something exceptional that cannot be explained by the simple will to assert his self against the adversities of daily existence in the American territory. The combination that I believe is right to evoke here concerns sensitivity and imagination: Pascal D'Angelo shows an incredible responsiveness to the sounds of the English language and, at the same time, grafts this responsiveness onto a literary imagination that is the interface of his natural talent that always acts and thinks poetically, never setting aside the urgency of a writing that wants to be truth – artistic truth, truth as an integral part of the text and not as truth reductively considered in opposition to falsehood.

2. If we now move on to a quick analysis of the models adopted by the poet, we cannot avoid considering the centrality of romantic poetry and, specifically, of Percy Bysshe Shelley (1792-1822). In fact, Chapter XIII opens with a series of crucial considerations from a cultural point of view. In 1919, the protagonist is 25 years old and permanently lives with the anxiety of acquiring a musical culture to complement his literary one:

> During the summer of 1919, I began to hear much about Aïda, but I did not know exactly what it was. [...] About the same time, I happened to glance over an Italian newspaper and saw an advertisement that this opera was to be represented in the open air at the Sheepshead Bay race track. I decided to go and hear it. [...] And all at once, I felt myself driven toward a goal. [...] The quality of beauty of this Aïda I have found only in the best Shelley and perhaps Keats. (D'Angelo 2003, 17)

What is narrated by the voice is the gradual, euphoric, and confused formation of a vocation. Starting from a cultural background close to nothing, Pascal D'Angelo begins to build a space all for himself dominated by a deeply ingrained literary awareness. And, even among epiphanic naiveties and simplistic representations of the art and literature scene, the protagonist feels he is among the privileged who know how to understand the spiritual and salvific value of beauty. Thus, one of the words that most often appears in the final chapters is "beauty". D'Angelo never refers to the well-known opening line of John Keats (1795-1821) that we can read in the poem *Endymion* (1818):

"A thing of beauty is a joy for ever" (Keats 1982, 107). He does not quote this line, but it is as if he did.

From an angle that considers the poetic genealogy, it is evident that the romantic tradition constitutes the basis from which D'Angelo drew those elements that, appropriately filtered and revisited, form his sensitivity and turn his gaze towards external reality in a positive, if not exalted, manner. More than Keats, it is Shelley who influences him decisively, providing him not only with themes and suggestions but also what is commonly called *diction*, that is, the choice of tone to give to his verse. Among the readings of this period, D'Angelo shows a clear preference for the verse drama *Prometheus Unbound* (1820) in which Shelley presents a Prometheus who, as an interpreter of the beginnings of humanity, becomes a symbol of romantic rebellion and the rejection of any limitation of individual freedoms. Significantly, in *The Library of Greek Mythology*, Apollodorus writes:

> Prometheus, after forming men from water and earth, gave them fire, which he had hidden in a stalk of giant fennel to escape the notice of Zeus. When Zeus found out, he ordered Hephaestus to rivet the body of Prometheus to Mount Caucasus, a Scythian mountain, where he was kept fastened and bound for many years. Each day an eagle would fly to him and munch on the lobes of his liver, which would then grow back at night (Apollodorus 1975, 12).

Thus, everything begins with an act of insubordination and thus of rebellion against Zeus. If in the Greek mythological tradition the conflict between Zeus and Prometheus ends with an act of reconciliation, in Shelley's interpretation the conflict remains open and the tyrant, as such, is ousted to the advantage of humanity. Inspired by the eponymous tragedy of Aeschylus (of which only a few fragments remain), Shelley's verses attracted D'Angelo's attention for the – so to speak – democratic dimension, for the revolt against any form of conditioning by the despotic god, as well as for the yearning for social justice that means liberation of the body and soul.

In Chapter XIV, the encounter with Shelley's poetry marks the turning point: the young Abruzzese laborer feels the deep dissatisfaction of living in a reality that does not correspond to the world of his readings:

> Men were hired; some merry old fellows came to live in the boxcar. Life had taken on a lively aspect. Yet I was dissatisfied for I had been thrilled by a new discovery – my senses were all atremble – I had found Shelley.
> I had already learned that there was a public library nearby in Edgewater. Going there, I was kindly received despite my broken English and the ragged appearance of my working clothes. And it was there that, while browsing among books, I finally wandered upon "Prometheus Unbound" (D'Angelo 2003, 144).

D'Angelo fully grasps the political message of the romantic poet, but his response cannot be limited to the contents alone. As Angela Leighton has observed, "while the political message of Prometheus Unbound is the inevitable fall of tyranny and the liberation of the race, the dramatic interest of the works centers on how those events may be imaginatively motivated and apprehended" (Leighton 1984, 74). It is no coincidence that D'Angelo realizes that having ideas is not enough to write poetry – for a poet, the how matters more than the what. In this sense, reading and reflecting on Shelley's work constitutes a crucial stage of his apprenticeship.

3. At a certain point in his complex and painful wandering through the roads of America in search of work, D'Angelo discovers the existence of libraries – which means for him the possibility of acquiring a culture, despite living in the most unbearable state of misery and social isolation. The miracle of such a discovery materializes with the encounter with the authors who, one after another, will shape his consciousness both as a poet and as a man. Probably, in the library, D'Angelo also read the works not only of Shelley but also of other romantic poets. Before deciding to become a representative of American letters, the protagonist possessed very few tools to base his ambitions on any certainty. The narrative voice does not hide his total ignorance of Italian literature.

In fact, in Chapter XI, when the narrator is 22 years old, the episode of the encounter with Michele, an old Abruzzese laborer, highlights the zero degree of his literary knowledge: "[Michele] had worked on our gang for a week and often mentioned Dante whom I thought was an ancient king" (121, my italics). The admission of his ignorance further emphasizes the audacity of his journey, which will culminate in publication, despite having started his literary "pilgrimage" from a cultural level that can be equated to zero – indeed he started from an absolute cultural desert. Yet, despite a thousand disadvantages and a thousand obstacles of linguistic, social, and economic origin, the young protagonist did not want to stop. And, again, starting from scratch, he decided that he would learn to speak the language of the country where he had decided to live. In the heroization of himself, Pascal tells himself that he will not only learn the language but will be an author on par with the most established American poets and novelists.

After discovering his objective limits in terms of literary knowledge, the protagonist decides that it is time to acquire a culture that is not limited to the linguistic level but moves almost exclusively in the domain of *belles lettres*. In short, a vocation takes root in him – a vocation that transforms him into an assiduous reader who makes the library his main resource for that qualitative leap towards which he strives with all his might. If we read *Son of Italy* from an autobiographical angle, it can easily be concluded that the relationship between the young reader and the library constitutes a diegetic gap. To be clearer: we know that Pascal frequents the library, and we also know of his preference for Shelley and Keats, but we know nothing else. From the point of view of his readings and preferences, the protagonist narrator seems to stop at the threshold of the building. The reader is told nothing about the books he reads and his reactions, his reading method, and the criteria on which he bases his choices.

We do not know if the authors of American Romanticism strike him in the same way he was illuminated, indeed, struck by the author of *Prometheus Unbound*. Probably, he had the opportunity to read the poems of the most important exponent of transcendentalism, Ralph Waldo Emerson (1803-1882), who, partly following the European romantic culture, celebrated the return to nature by adopting Rousseau's lesson, rejecting the obligations of community life, and emphasizing the affirmation of the self. In many ways, we can imagine that Pascal

D'Angelo's readings were heterogeneous, without excluding figures like Walt Whitman and Edgar Allan Poe. We can only imagine the segments that constituted Pascal's *Bildung* as a real person, while as for the implicit author of *Son of Italy*, we must adhere to the text. After all, if the narrative voice had focused its attention on individual readings, the narrative economy would have suffered – a novel that is very enjoyable precisely because of the rhythm and tone that characterize it.

At this point, it is necessary to say that, in light of the nascent creative-vocational impulse, D'Angelo experiences the transition from reader to writer. In fact, he begins to write some pieces in English, relying on his self-taught ability and, even more, on his stubborn will to become someone in the field of American letters:

> I began to learn some Spanish from these two Mexicans. [...] I had gotten to think of a newspaper as something to start a fire with or to wrap objects in. But now I began to read again – very little at first, I must confess. Somehow, I found English more to my liking than Spanish. And about once a week even bought an English newspaper to look at. [...]. When I did learn a word and had discovered its meaning I would write it in big letters on the moldy walls of the boxcar. And soon I had my first lesson in English all around me continually before my eyes. (D'Angelo 2003, 129)

It is possible to understand the nature of the enterprise accomplished by the protagonist only if we take into account the distance that separates this Pascal D'Angelo who begins the linguistic climb of the English language and the emigrant poet who is able to appreciate that pinnacle of romantic poetry that is Shelley's *Prometheus Unbound*.[1] Yet the semi-literate young man manages to bridge the gap that seems unbridgeable, manages to express what until a few years earlier belonged to a sensitivity that had no words to convey his feelings. And he does so by fully embracing that perception of the universe and nature that, based on the romantic lesson, contrasts the great breath of

[1] Undoubtedly, it would be interesting to precisely reconstruct the formative years and, even more, his relationship with the English Romantic poets. For example, D'Angelo never mentions Wordsworth in his autobiography, but certain aspects of his poetic sensibility seem to suggest those poems of Wordsworth in which humanity is celebrated in terms of innocence, wonder, and euphoric adherence to nature.

the cosmos with the insignificant segments of suffering of the individual condition:

> That night I lingered a long time outside the shanty, thinking. And the darkness made the vast solitudes of heaven populous with stars.
>
> I looked around. I felt kinship with the beautiful earth. [...]. I felt a power that was forcing me to cry out to this world that was so fair, so soft and oblivious of our pains and petty sorrow. Then I had to laugh to myself, "After all", I thought, "what are my tiny woes to the eternal beauty of those stars, of these trees and even this short-lived grass?" (D'Angelo 2003, 196)

The beginning of Chapter XII shows the nocturnal restlessness of a young man who does not want to surrender to a destiny that wants to recruit him among the losers: "I was a poor laborer – a dago, a wop or some such creature – in the eyes of America. Well, what could I do?" (D'Angelo 2003, 126). Against all this, the protagonist reacts with all his might – and in this reaction, the dominant force is constituted by literature which, more and more, as Pascal becomes aware of himself, assumes the profile of a mission that admits no alternative or fallback. Literature and nothing else – this seems to be the motto of the young Abruzzese emigrant.

4. Finally, I believe it is important to remember that *Son of Italy* includes exactly ten poems. Of course, these are not compositions that Pascal D'Angelo inserts as a form of embellishment of the text or for the simple vanity of quoting himself by inserting, perhaps out of context, his favorite lyrics. On the contrary, each text is an integral part of the creative process, so we can say that, in its economy, the narrative text closely dialogues with the poetic text and, together, they constitute a coherent and never discontinuous autobiographical journey that, at the same time, stands as lived experience and fiction. Definitely we can regard *Son of Italy* as a lived experience because every word written by the author has real referents with their precise definition; fiction because the narrator tells only what he intends to convey to the reader in

order to make the text dense with meaning according to a strategic line based on coherence.

However, the fictional principle remains because there are too many *lacunae*, too many silences, too many empty spaces to be able to say that this is the life of the emigrant Pascal D'Angelo. We know nothing about the real reasons that cause father and son to part ways; we know nothing about the hero's private life, who apparently lives in a world without women; nor are we informed in detail about how he managed to acquire a culture, his possible encounters in the library, his specific readings, or the presence of possible mentors.

Ultimately, Pascal D'Angelo was interested in creating the context in which the poet is formed, briefly outlining the transition from Italy to America and highlighting the stages of his life. His way of approaching the creative act made me think of the words that Rainer Maria Rilke sends as advice to a young poet: "[...] to go into yourself and test the deeps in which your life takes rise; at its source you will find the answer to the question whether you must create. Accept it, just as it sounds, without inquiring into it. Perhaps it will turn out that you are called to be an artist. Then take that destiny upon yourself" (Rilke 1962, 20). It seems to me that these words can apply, without any forcing, also and above all to Pascal D'Angelo who took destiny upon himself and, without letting himself be discouraged by the adversities of a grim and squalid life, wanted to follow to the end what the source of his inspiration suggested to him.

WORKS CITED

Apollodorus. 1975. *The Library of Greek Mythology*. Transl. Keith Aldrich. Lawrence, KS: Coronado Press.

Keats, John. 1982. *The Complete Poems*. Ed. John Barnard. Harmondsworth and New York: Penguin.

Leighton, Angela. 1984. *Shelley and the Sublime: An Interpretation of the Major Poems*. Cambridge: Cambridge UP.

Lotman, Jurij M. 1980. *La struttura del testo poetico*. 1970. Transl. Eridano Bazzarelli, Erika Klein and Gabriella Schiaffino. Milano: Mursia.

Rilke, Rainer Maria. 1962. *Letter to a Young Poet*. Transl. M. D. Herter Norton. New York: W. W. Norton & Company.

Permanent Alternations, Provisional Identities. The Literary Lens of Reportage and The Italian-American Concept

Arianna Mazzola
UNIVERSITÀ DEGLI STUDI DEL MOLISE

Abstract: This proposal investigates the concept of alterity and identity in travel literature concerning Italian migration to America over a wide chronological arc, from the 1930s to the present day. The aim is to highlight the hermeneutic impact that the genre of reportage has had in the construction of the concept of Italo-Americanity. In fact, the Italians who moved abroad are sketched by the pens of writers traveling to America, on the one hand they tend to preserve the traditions of their regions of origin, customs that crystallize over time; on the other hand, they often merge customs belonging to different regions, giving rise to a foreign identity that does not coincide with the country of origin, Italy, and often does not integrate with the country of arrival, the United States. Here, then, the concept of *ostranenie* proper to the best literature, is able to return as much the polysemy of the literary, as a problematic definition, and that can be called only provisional, of Italian-Americanity. Therefore, starting from the works of Odeporica, we would like to propose a theorization of Italian-American that from the literary disorientation comes to a broader framing of the concept, since the best texts are those that allow a gnoseological survey both considering the plane of forms and style, either not isolating the contradictions that inhabit the world of every time and latitude. That, on the contrary, is the level that accommodates the complexity of reality between pages.

The Issue of Literary Gender. Reportage As a Form of Interpretation of the Real Through Literariness

Can a literary form become a cognitive probe of reality? It is from this question that the premises of this essay move. In fact, questioning a concept and proposing a theory would seem to be the task of philosophical speculations, rather than literary criticism. Yet, if the idea to be defined is the concept of Italian-Americanity, the theory of literature - and in particular the theory of literary genres - cannot be said to be foreign to the question. The genre of reportage is uncertain by its status, since it establishes a dialogue with the existing, that is to say, with the real and the places, as well as with the literary, or with the forms and style, as well as with the themes addressed. The text of the journey moves, in short, on several levels, considering that the truth of the surroundings and the verisimilitude narrated both find citizenship in the pages. The short circuit between accurate, plausible, and deliberately invented could be possible. It is true, however, that in this hybridization one should not see a limit but, on the contrary, a hermeneutic resource to be investigated. In fact, only if we stop at a superficial level can the report be considered a faithful account of what the writer-traveler saw during his stay in another place, more or less distant from the place of origin. It often happens, however, that those who travel add to the notes and annotations recorded in the time of the move a reworking which constitutes, in effect, a second trip. It is the journey made by the author together with notes, thoughts and rework made by writing that integrates memories, rewrites the temporality of events, orders in narrative form an experience otherwise difficult to communicate.

At this point, it is appropriate to highlight a distinction in terms of method and content between the different forms that reportage can take. For the purposes of our analysis, journalistic reports will be excluded. In contrast, the narrative reports by Mario Soldati and Italo Calvino and the novelized report by Alberto Arbasino on America will be taken into account. Thus, in a broad chronological arc, encompassing the 1930s, the 1960s and the 2000s, three-time stages are set around which critical reflection takes place (Cf. Arbasino 2011; Calvino 2015; Soldati 1959).

The journalist-reporter experiences the impulse of immediacy: he has a rapacious view on things and intends to communicate in real time an absolutely unpublished news or, at least, proposed as such. The aim of a journalistic report is, in short, to take a snapshot and then to hurry up to develop it in the shortest possible time. The shorter the time between travel and publication, the more successful the journalist's task can be said to have been. The writer of narrative reports, instead, at the speed of the news story, replaces the patience of reflection; it follows that the meeting between reliable description and narration becomes possible within the work. Sometimes the experience of travel is separated from the publication of a report for years, because the mediation between notes and descriptive-literary writing requires more diluted time than the spasm of the elzeviro. Finally, the author of a report labeled as "fictionalized" is the writer who adds the imaginative component, or invention, to the description and narration. The temporality, the order of events, the facts that happened, and others only imagined find equal dignity within the report. It is an experimental form, the boundaries between true, false and fiction are undefined (Bottiglieri 2001).

In the famous essay on *Goethe's Elective Affinities*, Walter Benjamin distinguishes two ways of approaching literary works: criticism and comment, stating unequivocally that "the critic seeks the content of truth of a work of art, the commentary its real content" (Benjamin 2011; Lukács 1957, 269-323). The comment precedes the criticism and the metaphor used by the author is particularly powerful to better under-stand the difference: "one can compare the critic to the paleographer before a parchment whose faded text is covered by the signs of a stronger writing that refers to it. As the paleographer must begin by reading the latter, so the first act of the critic has to be the comment" (Lukács 1980).[1] The real content is the initial moment of a broader cognitive task for the critic, who seeks to see the metaphorical text fade, what you do not see, or the truth content of the work, thereby enhancing their diopters in the eidetic capacity of vision and penetration. The other significant image worth taking is that of the chemist and alchemist. So Benjamin: "if one wants to conceive, with a metaphor, the work in development in history as a burning, the commentator stands before him like the chemist, the critic like the alchemist. If for the first wood and ashes are the only objects of its analysis, for the other only the flame keeps a secret, that of life. Thus, the critic seeks the truth whose living flame continues to burn on the heavy stumps of the past and on the light ashes of the lived" (Benjamin 1982, 179). Only in appearance does the resumption of the two metaphors proposed by Benjamin represent a digression. In fact, as the commentator is interested in the visible text, so the reporter-journalist outlines the physical contours of the geographical region visited: as if the objective was precisely to draw its obvious boundaries. The writer of narrative reports and fictionalized reports, on the other hand, like the critic, is interested in seeing what is not seen but exists: the content of truth of a place, not the map, but the history behind the places, the different forms of Americanity emerging from lost or invented regions. Therefore, the pure description of the direct and relia-ble eyewitness, typical posture of the reporter of news outlets, is ir-relevant to our

[1] See p. 53: "A good report is based on a comprehensive and exhaustive study, embraces a vast and well-organized set of events and presents its examples clearly"; See also Baudrillard 1986, 78-79; Ginzuburg 2023; Mackey 2010; Marchese 2014; Marchese 2019.

theorization. Because of its complexity, it requires com-parisons, reconstructions, reflections that find in the structuring and selection the tools of a critic of places as is the writer of narrative and novelized reports. The set of rhetorical elements that constitute the so-called literalism, then, in their organization in narrative forms reality, do not abstract generalizing, but follow the way "of intensive deepening" (179).

In this way, we trace the shift from specific forms and style to universal thought, thus raising the work to the level of the idea. In other words, in our case, analyzing the collection of selected works is a preliminary step before theorizing the idea we are exploring (Zuccarino 2000, 24).

The Concept of Italo-Americanity

The concept of Italian-Americanity concerns not only reportage, but also fiction and poetry. In this sense, masterful are the works of Tamburri, among others, *Una semiotica dell'etnicità. Nuove segnalature per la scrittura italiano/americana*. As regards an autobiographical and, at the same time, narrative Italian-American condition, two contemporary classics are represented by *Unto the Sons* by Gay Talese and *Ask the Dust* by John Fante. About the latter, as D'Alfonso (2013, 12) notes, "the balances between the elements are always variable, never fixed, even if there is a circularity [...] in which the reaction [of Fante] is to reposition his restless personality on the margins of the scene".

We intend to dwell on the concept of Italian-American, as well as on the construction of the idea of alterity and identity in Italian migrants overseas.

It would seem an impossible challenge, considering that the issue concerns not only writers but also millions of migrants heading for America. But it becomes a viable approach because the lens of observation for the phenomenon is singular; without metaphor, it was chosen to focus on a single literary genre: the report. In particular, to map the phenomenon, three authors were identified: Mario Soldati, Italo Calvino, and Alberto Arbasino. The intention was to return a broad diachronic that could capture in an extended chronological arc the aspects that are intended to be deepened. The corpus of works, therefore, is represented by *America primo amore*, *Un ottimista in America* and *America amore*.

How do you express nostalgia and dream within a complex and hybrid concept like the idea of Italian-Americanity? And what is the cognitive significance of reportage in the construction of the concept itself? Let's think of a two-arm scale and use the image to clarify the theoretical hypothesis between Italianity and Americanity or shift in favor of one or the other arm. It is a question of weights, or rather taxonomies. To be tested by the test: the instrument can mark a balance condition.

In fact, by trying to reason on the concept, three situations can be identified: In the first one, the component of Italianity is more important, since it constitutes one of the two parts of the idea of Italo-American. Sometimes, the distance from their mother country and the nostalgia that follows, for immigrants represents an almost paradoxical experience of *nostos* in the crystallization of traditions, beliefs, linguistic islands that prevent a full integration into the American fabric. We are faced with a past that is always present, in which, to say it with Roberto Esposito, a deep actuality of the ancient is rooted.

In the reports of Soldati and Calvino, the question is deepened by detecting a common key criterion, that is crystallization. Invited to a Sunday lunch by an Italian couple in New York, Soldati enters the neighborhood with the highest density of Italians, the infamous Bronx. In the report, alongside the recordings of descriptions and impressions, there are also some highly saggistic fragments. Thus the author of *America primo amore*: the Italians, "emigrated between the 800 and the 900, they kept unchanged the image of life that then left in the Kingdom" and "they have reproduced, crystallized, between the Hudson and Long Island, the mentality and the Italian society as they were at the time of their emigration" (Soldati 1959, 41). There is no lack of more explicit reflections about the fossilization of the characteristics of the Italian province, and the archaic variants of the dialect. Continue Soldati, it is

> Possible to recognize the provincial and bourgeois society of Avellino, or of L'Aquila, Benevento, Potenza, etc. before the war. A

serious historian of the Umbertine era, should live for a year in Brooklyn or the Bronx. Like some glottists, to study the spoken French of the '600, they go to Canada where the French emigrated in that century. (41)

Among the pages of *Un ottimista in America*, the *facies* of the Italianity preponderant in the concept of Italian-American assumes macro-regional contours, coinciding, in fact, with the post-unitary South, loaded with agro-pastoral culture and dialect of small rural centers:

> Largely detached from a pre-national Italy, from the countries of the South for a few decades annexed to the Italian state, arrived here without any other experience of civilization if not semi-Chattolic and semi-pagan that agricultural-pastoral, another means of expression than the dialect, culture than folklore. (Calvino 2015, 20)

The first reaction of Italian migrants arriving in the US is that of disorientation. It is often the case that "each of the ethnic groups which make up the American cauldron has lost, in the hard years of struggle for life, some of its characteristics and has invigorated and engrossed others. The ones who suffered most and for the longest time from this dis-orientation are the Italians", because "as if they had come out of the womb of biological nature, they were suddenly thrown in the middle of the impetuous growth of industrial society and urbanism" (20). The low level of schooling among the poor is also to be considered. It was precisely a precariousness of means that pushed the southern migrants to cross the ocean in the direction of the American dream. The tight working rhythms of the American factories did not give the possibility to free themselves culturally from their initial condition, so that the Italian immigrants "They never knew how to bond with a layer of intellectuals, such as could be the one constituted by political exiles compatriots, before and during fascism, and therefore had no other leaders and other ideals than those of the small business politics. But they are not alone in being so: there is no ethnic group that has come out unscathed from the trauma that cost everyone the insertion into the new world" (20). So, if on the one hand, even after years remains a state of things unchanged from the time of arrival, on the other hand the Italian-American we could call of adaptation leads to unite more local realities in an idea of Italy - peripheral region of the world, yet able to create old and new myths. An important example is the spread of espresso-*places,* or meeting places whose fundamental feature, in addition to the possibility of drinking an espresso and not an American coffee is represented by the experience of reasoning on the idea of Italy conveyed abroad. Calvino notes that "the espresso-*places are* often run by newcomers, Italians born in Italy, not by the usual Italo-Brooklynese" (Calvino 2015, 24), so not by second gener-ation families, but by migrants who have recently moved to America. However, the owners of these cafes manage to erase all memory of what Italy really is, "invent an unreal Italy, which corresponds exactly to what Americans expect it to be. Or maybe, they also believe it, perhaps they think that the concept "Italy" can be thought only in these allegorical terms, the Roman busts, the romances of Tosca, and everything else is empty, nothing, fog formless and unmemorable" (21). In the process of crystallization of traditions and dialectal variants, the origin of regions not coinciding with our own, for Italian immigrants, first causes alienation towards the country of arrival.

In a second moment, however, in the defense of that last expanded regionality, prejudices and clichés do not stop acting as much in the expectations of Americans as in the lived experience of migrants. So far, the progress of prose Calvino e Soldati has not spared essay tones, precisely because these are two pens that, in their reports on American trips, have not been limited to the description of what they saw. But it is with Alberto Arbasino that the reportage becomes, in all respects, a work of fiction. In fact, the narrative of the present foregrounds episodes from various journeys undertaken by the author, attempting to absorb the world overseas and insert it into the page of invention, i.e., an American love. The same story of a moment lived while walking through the popular streets of Boston takes its cue from a simple question but is incisive in capturing the reader between the plots of the real experience narrated in the report, and leads him to a broader reflection. So Arbasino asks: "but what is a slum? How is this kind of social plague that devours the heart of cities formed, as a test of decadence and vitality together, and is one of the biggest problems that the nation must solve today?" (Arbasino 2011, 268). And it goes on:

> A first walk through Boston, which was once the noblest of the American cities, can already begin to teach something. The central districts, built by the more traditional aristocracy, [...] are now deserted in large part. [...] The floral palazzos of Back Bay, the whims of billionaires who filled them with Benedictine cloisters, Pompeian mosaics, Tiziani and Raffaelli [...], are slowly going into ruin: closed, [...] or even divided among numerous families of immigrants. These are mostly Italian and Irish, and they practically have the city in their hands: there are more pizzerias than bars if you browse through the telephone directory that looks like the one from Naples stuck in the one of Dublin. (268)

The degradation of the slums has been for more than fifty years one of the social and housing plagues of American cities. But, if Arbasino tries an urban archeology of Boston, to map the condition of Italian migrants living in America are mainly Soldati and Calvino. The reaction of Italian-Americans to the American life recorded by the two authors is twofold, since, on one hand, migrants do not give up their origin, until they self-marginalize, or, vice versa, they come to deny their origins.

Therefore, the second situation is offset in favor of that Americanity which constitutes the other side of the concept. The American dream is the protagonist and Italian migrants, even accepting humble and poorly paid jobs, hope for a better future, invent it and sometimes manage to realize it. The focus on tomorrow and self-renewal as American citizens defines this further point of the hypothesis. In *America primo amore* and in *Un ottimista in America* the author trend recorded by Soldati and Calvino is very similar, although the final tones belong more to the first than to the second. Calvino, all in all, does not fail to see in the gestures a nostalgia almost unaware of its origins. Thus, the Ligurian author:

> The important thing, just arrived in a place, is to feel a past behind the back, maybe all questionable, anecdotal and legendary, but still a past. Coming to America means leaving behind the European history, which is no longer valid here, and European historicism, which is not known here; and in return, this desire to save is immediately acquired - in the midst of a reality that changes from year to

> year, where the landscape, the houses, [...] the people's class, everything is labile - of the remnants of memories handed down, a pathos of gracili memories, a suggestion of local spirit. (Calvino 2015, 17)

Instead, much more radical are the tones of Soldati, when he notes:

> I met many Italian-Americans. [...] More or less rich, more or less educated, the bottom was always that. [...] over these differences and characters, [...] as a humiliating pact that limits and atrophies their lives, is the stubborn and mystical sense of America. How many times, late at night, in the desert subway, I happened to observe two men, two inhabitants of New York, who sat face-to-face, unknown to each other, staring at each other in silent conversation. They came from far away, most likely. Far from America and far from each other. [...] Yet they had left the old house, and lived a new age, with the same hope and the same doubt. "This is our homeland", the poor swinging heads seemed to say with the train's jolts. We don't want that this shore and this life. "America America I am a Citizen I am an American Citizen". Magic words. [...] The Red Passport, the Statue of Liberty, the Stars and Stripes, the Dollars, the Skyscrapers, this roaring Subway: they believed, the two citizens still believed in the eldorado that they had dreamed, for poverty and youth, from across the Ocean. Obstinate people claimed the way to paradise. And in face of catastrophe, martyrs of spatrio, they would swear that they had not been deceived. (Soldati 1959, 47-48)

Americanity in the reportage of Soldati is characterized by concrete objects, and the concept is captured in materiality and presented through an enumeration with strongly descriptive traits: being American (the passport), belonging to a land of freedom (the statue), the flag, a synthesis of the states that make up a nation, the currency, the object of well-being, the vertical tension upwards, the skyscrapers, and the heap of the subsoil that moves perpetually, the subway.

Finally, the third case brings both the first part, the Italianity, and the second, the Americanity, into a state of provisional equilibrium. However, this is the true hybrid identity in which the two components combine with each other giving rise to a happy multiplication of so much of the essence of one who lives in a permanent transition, which, however, represents an oxymoron only in appearance and, it is a way of being and of existing. In the tension between nostalgia and dream, between past and future, we draw destinies, lives and identities of millions of Italian-Americans and the authors of reports manage to grasp the nature of this aspect as well as the other. It is a status identity and make it not only documentary testimony, but also, and above all, work of literature tout court.

The author of reportage is interested in seeing what you can't see, but it exists: the truth content of a place, not the map, but the history behind the places, the different forms of Italo-Americanity. As we have seen, the excesses represent the norm, or rather, we have caught the two extremes of a polarization between Italianity and Americanity, on the one hand, the ghettoization in the degraded neighborhoods with high crime rate, on the other hand, a forced integration and manner, In this last case study, on the other hand, synthesis is a rare and happy interpenetration of the initial cultural substrate which finds expression in forms of integration into the American social fabric such as to be said to have been successful. This is what Calvino says about the Italian-American population that has settled in California. In fact, it is not clear that living and dwelling in the places coincides with a cancellation of local regional realities. In San Francisco, for example, "the Italians are Piedmontese, Ligurian, Tuscan, have well-defined professions (it is only here in California that agriculture is in considerable part in Italian hands, with the famous wineries)" (Calvino 2015, 84-85). Moreover, the linguistic knowledge is still maintained, considering that "many of them understand and speak Italian", the identity is manifest from the registry office, in fact many "have recognizable surnames" and in the physio-gnomy "resemble the Italians of today" (85). The period quoted is in fact interspersed with a comparison which takes place between parentheses, in the sense that, literally, if the reasoning about the Italians in San Fran cisco constitutes the main discourse, between incidental and parenthesic Calvino compares the happy state of things in California to the problematic situation in New York. The knowledge of Italian by mi-grants who settled in California is clearly higher than those "Italians who landed and stayed in New York [who] did not know Italian when they arrived nor learned English, and for a couple of generations they remained completely unarticulate" (85). Moreover, different for the onomastic melting-pot, "the strange Italian-New Yorker surnames belong to an Italy that has never faced history", and, peculiar in appear-ance, "the Italian-New Yorkers only resemble themselves" (85). There-fore, even in this last case, the writer does not spare an acute and punc-tual analysis of a comprehensive look.

In our case, interpreting reality and investigating a concept can also mean questioning the works, starting from the assumption that, in literature, "the elaboration in the form of language gives concreteness and effectiveness to the meaning, to the content that wants to be expressed" (Gadamer 1986, 201). The literary field has a content of truth that it is up to the critic to bring to light, and in "mediation, operated by thought, with present life" the idea of Odeporic hermeneutics of Italo-Americanity is situated. The cognitive and aesthetic strength of a text, especially in modernity, is represented by the questions that are asked, not by the reassuring answers that might emerge. The richness of literature is inexhaustible, then, ambivalence and imbalance, not order and end, and this is especially true in travel texts, where the encounter with the different is at the basis of the very existence of the work. More generally, with regard to the concept of alienation, Šklovskij (1968, 86-87) defines literary writing as "strong in a capacity for disorientation that allows it to perceive the extraordinary that is hidden in everyday life", capable "to escape the automatism of recognition and wander into unknown sensory universes" and that "finds in the journey the ideal territory to develop fully its foreign path" (207).

Reportage writers' eyes observe anomalies and comprehend the complexity of the constant redefinition of two essential concepts, yet from the unstable boundaries of identity and alterity. The constant and always provisional reformulation of the relationship between identity and alterity is in dialogue with the Lacanian idea, taken from a famous phrase taken from a letter by Rimbaud, according to which "myself is another" (Lacan 2002; Lacan 2006), and with the thesis proposed by Francesco Orlando, that we understand better "the other who is in us" (Orlando 1996) through contact with what is alien to us. As we have seen, identity is not a compact and definitive thing, but it is always at play in an interaction with the other that can be repelling or welcoming.

It is undoubtedly a complex cultural and anthropological problem, but perhaps reupdating the ability of literature to deliberately violate the principle of non-contradiction could be the key to conceptualize the presence of the other that lives in us, besides the possibility of better understanding as individual and collective identity in comparison with what is foreign and disturbs the certainty of arrival, as happened to Italian migrants in America more than a century ago (Eriksen 1992; Geertz 1988; Geertz 1990). As it always happens when you leave your country of origin, you take with you a life expectancy to unknown lands, all to discover, live, and know.

Works Cited

Arbasino, Alberto. 2011. *America amore.* Milan: Adelphi.

Baudrillard, Jean. 1986. *L'America.* Milan: Feltrinelli.

Benjamin, Walter. 1982. "*Le affinità elettive* di Goethe." In *Il concetto di critica nel romanticismo tedesco. Scritti 1919–1922*, 179. Turin: Einaudi.

Benjamin, Walter. 2011. *Il narratore. Considerazioni sull'opera di Nikolaj Leskov.* Turin: Einaudi.

Bottiglieri, Nicola. 2001. "L'esperienza del viaggio nell'epoca della sua riproducibilità narrativa." In *Camminare scrivendo. Il reportage narrativo e dintorni. Atti di Convegno, Cassino, 9–10 dicembre 1999*, edited by Nicola Bottiglieri, 5–48. Cassino: Cassino UP.

Calvino, Italo. 2015. *Un ottimista in America (1959–1960).* Milan: Mondadori.

D'Alfonso, Francesca. 2013. *Nel mondo di John Fante. Autobiografismo e furore letterario.* Rome: Aracne.

Eriksen, Thomas Hylland. 1992. *Us and Them in Modern Societies: Ethnicity and Nationalism in Mauritius, Trinidad and Beyond.* Oxford: Oxford UP.

Gadamer, Hans Georg. 1986. *Verità e metodo.* Milan: Bompiani.

Geertz, Clifford. 1988. *Interpretazione di culture.* Bologna: Il Mulino.

_______. 1990. *Opere e vite.* Bologna: Il Mulino.

Ginzburg, Carlo. 2023. *Il filo e le tracce. Vero, falso, finto.* Macerata: Quodlibet.

Lacan, Jacques. 2002. *Lo stadio dello specchio come formatore delle funzioni dell'io.* Turin: Einaudi.

_______. 2006. *Il seminario (Libro II). L'io nella teoria di Freud e nella tecnica della psicanalisi (1954–1955).* Turin: Einaudi.

Lukács, György. 1957. "Narrare o descrivere?" In *Il marxismo e la critica letteraria*, 269–323. Turin: Einaudi.

———. 1980. *Essays on Realism*. London: Lawrence and Wishart.

MacKey, Robert. 2010. "Fact, Fiction and Kapuściński." *The Lede*, March 8, 2010. https://archive.nytimes.com/thelede.blogs.nytimes.com/2010/03/08/fact-fiction-and-kapuscinski/

Marchese, Lorenzo. 2014. *L'io possibile. L'autofiction come paradosso del romanzo contemporaneo*. Massa: Transeuropa.

_______. 2019. *Storiografie parallele. Cos'è la non fiction?* Macerata: Quodlibet Studio.

Orlando, Francesco. 1996. *L'altro che è in noi. Arte e nazionalità*. Turin: Bollati Boringhieri.

Šklovskij, Viktor. 1968. "L'arte come procedimento." In *I formalisti russi. Teoria della letteratura e metodo critico*, edited by Tzvetan Todorov, 86–87. Turin: Einaudi.

Soldati, Mario. 1959. *America primo amore*. Turin: Einaudi.

Tamburri, Anthony Julian. 2010. *Una semiotica dell'etnicità. Nuove segnalature per la scrittura italiano/americana*. Firenze: Franco Cesati Editore.

Zuccarino, Giuseppe. 2000. *Critica e commento: Benjamin, Foucault, Derrida*. Genova: Graphos Edizioni.

Index of Names

Diaspora

As "diaspora" is the dispersion or spread of people from their original home-land, this book series takes its name in the intellectual spirit of willful dispersion of subject matter and thought. It is dedicated to publishing those studies and creative works that in various and sundry ways speak to or offer new methods of analysis and/or articulations of the Italian diaspora.

Carmelo Fucarino. *Two Italian Geniuses in New York: Broken American Dreams.* ISBN 978-1-955995-05-4. 2023

Anthony Julian Tamburri, ed. *Re-Thinking* The Godfather *50 Years Later.* ISBN 978-1-955995-06-1. 2024

Anthony Socci. *United We Stand. Pre WW II-Chronicles of the Italian Colony of Stamford.* ISBN 978-1-955995-07-8. 2024

Antonio D'Alfonso. *I Could Have Been a Contender. (On Five Films).* ISBN 978-1-955995-09-2. 2024

Antonio Vitti and Anthony Julian Tamburri, eds. *Studi mediterranei: bellezze e misteri. Mediterranean Studies: Beauty and Mystery.* ISBN 978-1-955995-10-8. 2024

Luigi Fontanella. *Bertgang. Fanatasia onirica.* Translation by Michael Palma. ISBN 978-1-955995-11-05. 2025. Poetry

Mark Saba. *The Shoemaker.* ISBN 978-1-955995-12-2. 2025. Fiction

Anthony Julian Tamburri, ed. *Living Biculturalism, Writing Transculturalism: Essays in Honor of Luigi Fontanella.* ISBN 978-1-955995-13-9. 2025

Antonio Vitti and Anthony Julian Tamburri, eds. *Studi mediterranei: bellezze e misteri. Cultura mediterranea: variazioni su un tema.* ISBN 978-1-955995-15-3. 2025

Paolo A. Giordano. BETWEEN TWO WORLDS *Navigating "Italian" Studies in the United States.* Edited and with an Introduction by Anthony Julian Tamburri. Afterword by Fred L. Gardaphé. ISBN 978-1-955995-14-6

Theresa Lombardi Magistro. *Antonetta. An Immigrant's Story.* ISBN 978-1-955995-18-4

www.ingramcontent.com/pod-product-compliance
Lightning Source LLC
LaVergne TN
LVHW010546110826
845149LV00003B/573

* 9 7 8 1 9 5 5 9 9 5 1 9 1 *